THE GUITTON JOURNALS 1952-1955

Jean Guitton

THE GUITTON

JOURNALS

1952-1955

TRANSLATED BY FRANCES FORREST

Harvill Press LONDON

Printed in Great Britain
by Collins Clear-Type Press
London and Glasgow
for the publishers
HARVILL PRESS LIMITED
23 Lower Belgrave Street
London, s.w.1

First published in 1959 by Librairie Plon
under the title 'Journal: Études et Rencontres'

To Marie-Louise

Contents

Foreword

One evening in the month of September 1915, on returning from a country walk, I wrote a few lines on a blank sheet to remind me of certain things and of myself. Since this casual gesture, I have practically never stopped keeping what one calls a Journal—being unwilling to let what is fleeting in life slip away. To give myself patience and courage I wrote at the beginning of the first notebook the following verses which I have always loved to reread:

> *Et d'abord, sois fidèle à la chambre d'étude;*
> *Prends-y pour chaque jour d'une stricte habitude*
> *Un temps pour la pensée et pour la solitude.*

> *N'ouvre qu'à peu d'amis ton cœur et ta maison:*
> *Car ils sont rares ceux qui, sans autre raison,*
> *Te cherchent pour toi-même et dans toute saison.*

> *Quant aux muets amis les livres, fais la somme*
> *De tous ceux qu'en un jour pour un jour on renomme*
> *Et sois encore ici de ton temps économe.*

I would have wished, like Montaigne or Marcel Proust, to leave only a single work, beginning it after I was forty, at the time of one's second and true beginning; amplifying it in the margins from edition to edition, and returning continually to the same subjects with heightened insight. Existence is an indivisible whole. And time, though made up of separate moments, is a vast tract, which we must try to see at one glance. What an author calls 'my books' are simply pieces cut from this large whole. Necessity compels him to isolate a fragment of the whole and give it an exaggerated unity. This then becomes a work of the mind, a 'book' as it is called. But the true form would be to bring together all forms, and to talk as lengthily, meanderingly, and uninterruptedly as life itself.

I myself have never thought of my books except as accidents—precipitates from that grave dream which must never be detached from my life. And I think that in spite of their variety, they resemble each other. If I have made them seem different it is only so that, in the eyes of those who understand, they should converge the more.

Sometimes I see my books like puddles at night after a storm, each reflecting my whole heaven, with my constellations. I have a very keen sense of the characteristic which each thing, event, and person has—that of being an epitome and a mirror. It has always seemed to me that if one could experience a single thing to its very depths, one could experience by and through it everything: in the same way that all things are revealed to the lover through a chosen being.

Journal? It would be better to say 'Extracts from a Journal' made by its author. I have left out a great number of pages which had no meaning except for myself. I have kept in what is relevant to the unity of my spirit at its final point of convergence. These are my plots of land, the soil of the tree of thought, my tilth, my seed bed; fertile earth made up of reflections, of memories, and also of discussions with people I admire. I find nothing so boring as those Journals which don't spare you anything. To write is to select and to pass on. In a Journal, as in a poem, one can allow oneself long silences, brusque interruptions. One is spared transitions, introductions, and that connecting material which takes so long to prepare and to shape.

Joubert said that one should write as the angels think, in harmony, but 'so that things follow on each other in order, easily at due intervals, without touching each other or becoming confused—yet not without sequence, concord and selection '. He also said that it is best to write 'after one's spirit has had a long rest, and as one who remembers '.

The reader will easily see that I am guided by a quest for wisdom—for an art of life. How much I like Nietzsche's saying: 'My task is to let the fruit of my existence grow in sweetness and maturity, without allowing anything acid or bitter to mix with it.'

The way of life which is here suggested is that of a return to the beginning, to the kernel, the germ. And although I may have made a resolution not to speak of philosophy, the core of this Journal is a meditation on Being. It seems to me that the things most endangered in our time are the links which in time past bound the spirit to matter, man to nature, son to mother, citizen to motherland, the workings of the mind to life. Everyday love, everyday existence, orderly, sombre and splendid; country, land, religion—lived out in time. In fact 'Incarnation' in all its varieties and forms. Everything that is a refuge, a womb (encircling cavity), aid, shelter, forest, woodland, earth, is tending to disappear. We have no more peace, only a sequence of excesses, which cancel each other out. Mothers have disappeared, and so in a general way have reverence, the sense of decency and moderation.

This Journal will be shocking in a quite inexcusable way: that of still believing in the simplicity of being.

At what point should we plunge into the past? I think that to be remembered usefully, correctly, and tranquilly, the past should not be too remote. But if the past is still recent, if its links with the present are too vivid, a Journal will be like a scar. Five years make a good distance. But I have allowed myself to leaf through some older notebooks, and to celebrate some anniversaries. Everything is always present.

In an *édition de luxe* of this Journal there will be sketches in the margins. For, ever since childhood, I have loved drawing. For me, writing itself has never been separated from a kind of drawing. To write a Journal is to reproduce a seismographic curve—the gentle tremor of one's life. Oh! the dire necessity of cold print, of seeing these intimations of body and soul vanish under uniform type! In days to come some new technique will preserve the quiver of a voice.

The era of printing is in fact recent enough; that of alphabetic writing is far older. In his day Plato criticized it because it swallowed up words, accents, and the individual utterance.

I

The Incommunicable

Often when we have lost a friend and realize that communication is no longer possible, we reproach ourselves for having let him depart without having confided our troubles, our wishes, some secret, or even our love for him—that love which we had concealed during his life through shyness or because of the sameness of days. And now he is dead—rigid, ironic, noble and asleep. And we never knew how to speak to him! Does he know at last what we have been unable to say, or dared not say? Will he be unaware of it for ever? One seldom expresses such griefs, felt after partings; yet who in the shy and sensitive part of his nature does not feel them?

But can one, should one, even during life say everything? Are there, in life, calm and splendid moments when one mind may open itself to another, so that no part remains in shadow, and there is a sense of deliverance? I do not think so. I have noticed that when one's mind or heart is heavy, and one has a chance to confide, one comes away feeling that the essential has been left unsaid.

I have given many lectures during my career, and always I have been left with the impression of having circled for a long time, like an aircraft waiting to land, around what I wanted to teach. I have questioned those who receive confidences, and they have told me that it is perilous to dig down to the roots.

Is this kind of sincerity on which our age prides itself really possible? Can one ever be sure that one has said everything or even that what one feels is true? If love is in question, who can make me believe that great love can express itself in a letter, or even in hundreds of letters? In a word, or even in thousands of words? If the letters of lovers and prayers too have the relentless monotony of the sea, it is because they cannot say everything, so they begin over again.

This border of the inexpressible which encircles our innermost thoughts is a result of their depth. I think that one should not wish to remove it, but rather accept it, as a necessary haze, like the *sfumata* which Leonardo da Vinci used instead of outline, and which was, he said, his last and most exacting work.

Rest in peace, my beloved dead! From now on you know all that I cannot say. If I seemed inattentive, if I left some of your questions unanswered, if indeed I hid a part of myself from you (not through ill-will but through impotence), be content to see me now without intervention: such as I am, and unknown to myself.

In misunderstandings between friends, should one 'have it out' as they say? Yes, if the explanation is given in good faith and based on facts unknown to the other person, which have caused the misunderstanding. Certainly not, if the explanation arouses resentment, dark moods and hateful accusations between friend and friend, between husband and once loved wife, between father and son. In this case to explain oneself implies the right to express one's lower depths; but lower depths are never the whole truth. I submit that in bad things as in good ones, one should not force the incommunicable.

The rules of politeness are apposite here. They advise one to express only what one might call moderate feelings, and to keep quiet about one's moods. It is the same thing with prayer. The 'unutterable groanings' of the Spirit are not suitable to gatherings of the faithful. Liturgical forms substitute set and rhythmic prayers in which one believer may join with another. The incommunicable part of us is the pasture of God. It must be left to him. Let us often be content to express our thoughts (as children and the dying do) by our expression only. Expression atones for inadequacy of words.

Solange and happiness: To want and to deserve

I asked Solange how she managed to find a four-leaved clover in the enormous meadow; she had picked the only one there for me with the nonchalance of an angel on holiday. She answered: 'It is hard to explain. The first thing is not to want the clover—just to deserve it . . . Be cheerfully resigned to never finding a four-leaved clover—to being laughed at by everyone for looking for it—to being thought an idiot. And make yourself fit to find it by the renunciation of finding it. Then look at the field; and there'll be a four-leaved clover in front of your nose. Above all, do not think about it; and don't say to yourself that you are going to find the clover; if you did, the field would take its revenge.' 'Solange,' I said, 'I shall never find a four-leaved clover!' 'Ah,' she replied, with a little sigh, 'you *want*, and you don't understand what it is to deserve . . .'

It is true that the thing one wants too much eludes one. The will reaches out and gets entangled in itself. Montaigne observed this in games of chance; the winner is he who plays without trying too hard. Bacon, too, said that in order to succeed we must not aim at the main object, but achieve it as though we were trying for something else. And I have often noticed that the best gains are realized through some secondary indirect desire, by the methods of the saint or the poet, who at the summit of the soul has renounced possession, and whom destiny rewards with a fortuitous joy. This shows that in a difficulty, an undertaking, a battle, an examination (and I would even venture to say in a lottery), the first task is to purge the self, to make it more detachable, to cut adrift. What a difficult attitude of mind this is! Gamblers, dilettanti, adventurers, arrive at it more easily than do the patient, the hard-working and the conscientious. The lily of the field finds no difficulty in being a lily. But how does one become a lily when one has been a pink or a hortensia, accustomed to the greatest care?

How can we bring into our busy lives what the mystics mean by the word detachment? Yet, there is in all this a law of human life which may be explained thus: the excessive wish works in reverse, and often the absence of wish accomplishes more than the wish.

Artists and women know that the art of pleasing lies in stimulating the imagination without ever completely satisfying it, leaving an infinite margin of possibility. They know that beauty should be as fugitive as a ghost. And even in human affairs one should not pursue perfection too far. 'The love of truth,' said Gandhi, 'taught me the value of compromise.' The rough and ready adjustment, the provisional arrangement, is often the only way of securing a present peace. A fragile peace which is a reprieve—an improbable parenthesis. But what if the parenthesis spins itself out, if the improbable lasts until tomorrow? In the past it is such compromises that have often stood firmest, like that famous Constitution which was passed by one vote.

We ought not to wish to finish or complete a work, but suspend it just before the end. Often the secret of a reputation has been knowing how to give up before boredom sets in. Life flows on in these intermissions! He who exhausts a subject exhausts himself! 'You would not have found me had you sought me,' says happiness.

A talk with Paul-Louis Couchoud

WEDNESDAY, 7th JANUARY 1952
1 *rue Henry Jacquier, Vienne*

I enjoy his conversation, always so graceful and so human, and made up of concentrated thoughts which make an effortless impression like those of an Old Testament Sage— Ecclesiastes if you like—disillusioned, yet always mystical. In writing as in speech, he often starts a new paragraph like *Salomon de Tultie* (the pseudonym of Pascal) who used frequent full stops to give his style the rhythms of a real-life conversation.[1] We spoke of Christ, in whom he believed in his own way, which is not that of history. A strange state of mind. 'I believe all the Credo,' he said to me, 'except the interpolated clause *sub Pontio Pilato*.' He thought that outside Christ one could not find God, and that no one has really formed an idea of God apart from Jesus. That those who believe in God are, whether they admit it or not, disciples of Jesus. To convince oneself of this one needs only to see what Plato and Aristotle thought of God. This was not God the Father—the God of whom one always thinks in prayer. It was not the God of Jesus; it was not God. He thought also that one could not believe in Jesus without believing in him as God. That a Jesus who was not God (like Renan's *Jesus*) would mean nothing; that to take his divinity from Jesus would be to take away everything from him. We spoke of the Virgin and of my book on *The Virgin Mary*. He liked this book (although he is an unbeliever) because, he said, I have shown

---

[1] I got to know Dr Couchoud over my books on the Problem of Jesus, in which he also was engrossed. He thought unceasingly about the mystery of Jesus, and talked about it all the time. P.-L. Couchoud died in April 1959.

in it the very natural movement of consciousness towards the Concept of Motherhood. Human intelligence, left to itself, finds only a cosmic god, the bleak and lordly architect of worlds. But the spirit follows its inclination, and at root, it is a Woman-God which it invokes. Nature, considered without male prejudice, steers belief towards a Mother-God. Something inside us, he said again, seeks the Mother, the woman *par excellence*, the sister, the bride, the protecting embrace.

And that is why in the Church of Christ, the Woman, the Virgin Mother, has been so greatly honoured. To such a degree indeed that, to many minds, God and even Christ—these ineffable things which are beyond us, and to which we can only attain with difficulty in the daily routine—are known only through the refracted and lunar light of Mary. Christ himself was human only in what he took from his Mother.

These are the reasons why Dr Couchoud enjoyed this book on the Virgin. He said he preferred it to any other. He is a man without faith; faith which, according to Pascal, 'is not within our power'.

'The story of man's corruption,' he went on, 'and of his redemption is to me no legend, but a very profound truth, vital to man, whom it provides with an explanation of himself. But this revealed history is not drawn from historical fact in the strict sense. It rests on another mode of knowing.'

Sem qui a vu Lamech, qui a vu Adam. I recalled this phrase from Pascal. Pascal seems to have thought that the longevity of the patriarchs would have allowed for the handing down of observed facts. No! Adam is known to us through revealed history. I am in favour of the witnesses to truth and not of the witnesses to fact. There is nothing in the Gospels which is not significant. This is not so with history pure and simple, it is not true, for instance, of the story of Mahomet.

We came back to historicity. Could anyone show him a single line about Jesus by a non-Christian historian? One only? I said that this was to ask the impossible. 'For if an unbeliever testified to Jesus, then he would no longer be an unbeliever, but one of the faithful. You suggest an incompatible condition.' 'Yes,' he said, 'that goes to show that in this instance one needs faith to make history. But does faith use the words: to *see*, to *establish*, to *witness* . . . in the same sense as we do? Observe too how my conception helps faith. The unbeliever strives to destroy faith—to reduce Jesus to a historical being. He makes him vulnerable, by placing him on the stage of history. I, by taking him away from this stage, make him invulnerable.' 'Invulnerable perhaps,' I said, 'but reduced to nothing. What you reject is the basis of Christianity—the mystery of the reality of the Incarnation.' 'Let us overstate nothing. I do not deny. I wait, I am like the publican, a proselyte in Catholicism. Like Bergson or Simone Weil. The catechumenate should be restored. That was Christ's thought in the Parable of the Publican.'

Then he spoke to me about Bergson's lectures; 'of his aspirates, which when he spoke were like exclamation marks in sound'; of his astonished eyebrows, his hollow voice—sunken and metallic—sure of its direction, yet as caressing as that of Madame Récamier. With him there were mystical overtones rather than mysticism, and always great circumspection. He had the rare gift of making himself heard pleasantly for three hours on end, without tiring his hearers, and without anyone ever thinking of taking a note. He was envied for this. But it must be said that such a gift is not without danger, and that he realized the fact. Indeed one is not effective through success but rather on the margins of it. Loisy's audience was negligible. So put what you do into cedarwood caskets. Throw bottles in the sea!

A professor should not be compelled to give lectures. The idea of lecturing is basically a very primitive one; to speak fifty times for an hour in order to say about fifty times what anyone could compress into three hours, or better still write in a book! A year of research can always be concentrated into an hour. Absence always teaches more. Think of Christ . . .

It was Bergson who first introduced Couchoud to Pascal, and his muted, mysterious, insinuating tone. Then he followed Boutroux's lectures on Pascal—in a hut which was open to the winds; that was in '97, when the new Sorbonne (now so enclosed) was being built. Couchoud described to me how Boutroux arrived, cocooned in various layers of silk, mummy-like wrappings, which Madame Boutroux undid with great respect. Pale, thin, austere, as though he were about to fade away . . . A dying voice . . . Then, imperceptibly, he gained strength like the dawn, and finished almost in a blaze. Never any notes. He seemed like Pascal come to life again and explaining himself.

Then we spoke of the future of the human race. 'Human beings,' he said, 'have existed about two million years. But a species can live for twenty-five or thirty million years; that still leaves time. Conceptual language (I do not say articulate language) is fairly recent. Perhaps eight or ten millenniums? An animal can articulate, but it has no concept. A dog who could say "yesterday" or "tomorrow" would be human. Before concept, man had only utterance or gesture.'

On Joan of Arc. 'To Michelet she appeared as a daughter of the people; to Péguy she was a saint. Anatole France wished to approach Joan historically—the method so dear to the nineteenth century, and so mistaken. See what Renan made of Jesus with this famous historical treatment. Anatole France was once a palaeographer. I often saw him when he was writing "Joan of Arc". Jean-Jacques Brousson did research for him.' Anatole France's idea was an interesting one. France thought that, to write this enigmatical story (everyone projects a little of himself into what is most fervent and most pure —which, in parenthesis, makes the beauty of Joan of Arc) and to write it impartially, he ought to consider not the main point which attracts our fine feelings, but to take a secondary, marginal subject, as for instance the story of Chancellor Regnault. There would be scope to see the story of Joan through the story of this Chancellor, who doubtless said to himself—as no doubt Anatole France also said to himself: 'Joan does not know if Orleans is on the right or left bank of the Loire . . . What does it matter? She will be the mascot of the army. Instead of going to Paris, as she might try to do, I can easily suggest to her that she goes to Rheims.' Anatole France thought it would have been better to swoop first on Paris, after the capture of Orleans, as Joan felt instinctively.

'I delight in the story of Joan of Arc,' said Couchoud. 'Her faith in herself was boundless. Joan showed that faith can also be applied to one's country. She demonstrated the power of faith. Joan was helped by the picture of the Blessed Virgin as Queen; it is still in the arms of Holland. The Church must have been very enfeebled to allow her to be burned. But remember that, at that time, there was one Pope too many.'

On war and peace. 'I have inside me a book on war and peace which I shall perhaps never put together. To make a book is, as you well know, a clockwork affair which depends on two wise sayings: compose, cut out. Bring about order (without saying so). In fact, do what Alain taught Maurois. But, at my age, the enthusiasm which is so essential for writing a book cools off. I like the dictum of one of my great friends, a mystic, to whom I confided my difficulties about writing. She said: "Take notes, take notes—until the moment when your notes are shot through with boundless hope." Well, I will tell you what I would like to say in this book, were it written.'

I said: 'Basically all our books are either projects or testaments.'

'That is what a book is,' he replied. 'And I would always like to put as the sub-title of a book: "This is my testament." So would Jesus have done had he written.'

I have the feeling that we are at the crossroads of great adventure. That we are entering an era in which the old terms of peace and war (which will still be used because of the momentum they have acquired) will not have henceforth the same meaning. Ever since neolithic days war has been considered a judgment of God through the fortune of battle.

' "Officers and Gentlemen, the fortune of war has gone against you." I can still hear,' I said, 'this declaration of that German General when we were prisoners in 1940.

'There it is, the old ordeal even in 1940! Sadowa, Sedan, a three-weeks' war, that was the perfect kind of "war". Small wars about stupid disputes, in which the simplest *juges de paix* could have arbitrated: for all reasons for going to war are ridiculous. The plan is to isolate some incident, that it may give a motive for attack or for self-defence.'

Nowadays we have reached quite another phase. From now on, war cannot be limited, and it ends not in peace but, one might say, in war; a war which is more universal, and which holds out no hope of cessation, withdrawal or slackening. The idea of universal war is here. What we saw in Korea and in Indo-China are only sectors of a universal war. Neither side can stop without turning virtual universal war into actual universal war. Hence, armistices which formerly were made to last for a limited time go on for ever. But there is a compensation: universal and interminable war may end in universal peace.

Dr Couchoud explained his ideas for a tribunal of higher arbitration resembling on a world-wide scale what has already come into force within states. The initial character of the state is the capacity to arbitrate and this is based on a police force. Nevertheless war remains a possibility. 'What is discon-

certing is that men like war—the wonderful game in which
one is housed, fed, relieved of everything, and honoured into
the bargain, the risk of death meaning little when it is experienced collectively. War relieves all anxiety—not to mention the passions . . . It seems to me that in case of war
Europe will suffer and particularly France, this closely
watched Power. Russia would not be interested in occupying
countries but in destroying them. The ports, the towns, the
power stations. There would be panic, compared to which
that of 1940 would only be a shadow. The hydrogen bomb
would be like the sun touching the earth at one point . . . One
can picture a country being blotted out.

'The year '53 will be enigmatic, and so no doubt will be all
the years which follow . . . These,' he said, 'are my ideas on
war and peace. I work away at them. But I always feel the
truth of the saying (of du Bos, I think) which you quoted to
me. "The non-compulsory subject is the only blossoming tree
in the garden of the spirit." That is why I shall perhaps never
write this book. My tree will be always in flower.'

'Writing does not consist in filling up pages. Anatole France
said to me: "It is easy to write a page a day, and eighty-five
volumes in a lifetime." Who would read them? What waste!
Look at Pascal whose works I am editing. Périer was very
mistaken in thinking that Pascal took notes to help his
memory. He got hold of large sheets of paper. Then he wrote
his paragraphs, and after that, cut them up with big scissors.
He then made holes in them, and threaded them together,
as was usual in those days, to make packets of them. The
holes he made are not always visible nowadays, because
when the book was bound in 1711 the binder often cut them
off. Pascal suffered from nervous migraine. A sheet of the
Pensées manuscript shows a curving line. Victor Giraud
thought that he saw in this the zigzag of evolution; it was no
such thing. When Pascal had hemianopsia in the right eye,

27

he wrote in a column on the left. But his genius made a wonderful use of these phosphenes, these darknesses and flashes. Dr René Onfsay seems to me to have established this, and it makes Pascal even more human. Pascal often dictated to someone who was near at hand, as did your Pouget; and this person took it down phonetically, not orthographically. Pascal wrote at great speed. And following such outbursts the scissors were as useful to him as a pen. Pascal did away with many passages. He only kept the best. But for that, his thought would have been miraculous. Those which remain have meaning: the others have disappeared. That is the true way to write.

'I would like to grow old in the Far East. In Japan life is pleasant. Volcanoes discharge into the sea from a distance of four thousand metres. Japan enjoys every climate; it takes in every climate from Norway to Morocco, and Tokyo is in the same latitude as Algiers. Its people have a sense of the beautiful. When snow falls things close down so that everyone may enjoy the falling flakes. In the same way people sleep during the day so as to be able to enjoy the light of the full moon. Organized "happiness" (giving a full, convenient and comfortable meaning to the word "happiness", so vague in the West) is far better realized in Japan than it is with us.

'I would like to grow old there; for there an old man is respected, which is not the case in America. In China Christianity is persecuted. But never doubt, it will continue to exist—because of its secrecy and silence—and a kind of sublime obstinacy. Chinese and Japanese are capable of doing without priests for several generations. In Nagasaki, about 1890, I knew families thus preserved. Each year a member of these Christian families, who were without priests, sundered from the visible Church, shut himself up, fasted for a month and then began baptizing.'

My cast of mind

This morning I dived into myself using insight without object, like Montaigne, that insight which one cannot have in youth. This is eventide knowledge, the knowledge of the middle years, when at last one understands the stuff one is made of. I was helped by Joubert's analysis of his character, in which I recognize more than one trait of my own.

'In my opinion,' he says, 'there are in every man two things which must be carefully distinguished; his structure and his "constitution". If man were an automatic machine, I would call the springs of the machine its structure and the substance its "constitution".

'I think my springs are excellent; but the wood of which I am made is soft, frail, and delicate. It often interferes with the play of the machine; and it often prevents the movements towards which it is most drawn, and to which it is most suited. What serves for thought abounds in me, but what serves me for living my life is in short supply. If I try to force my nature, I produce appearances, but not reality. I write or I speak without saying anything. My pen and my tongue may act, but my thoughts and feelings are not expressed. I make only vain attempts, far more likely to displease those who read or listen, than would my inaction or my silence.

'That, ever since my birth, is the cause and only reason for unevenness in my relationships. Some people have thought me lazy. I swear to you in all truth that I am not so, not in the least. Neither am I capricious. On the contrary, I am immutable. But my flesh and blood are capricious for me.

Nothing can control them but some deep and heartfelt motive. If for instance I feel myself to be obviously needed, my machinery begins to work with a strength and constancy which have often surprised me. Only complete exhaustion will make me give up, for this faculty is kept ever alive in me by being rooted in the will.

'On the other hand, it seems obvious to me that I have, by nature, a brain and nervous system which are as finely adjusted as human harmony allows, and that when they are irritated I get out of tune. Everything that provides my brain with more matter than it can normally carry, disquiets it and prevents its functioning; everything that inflames my affections causes the same trouble.

'That is why, as regards the first point, long or too intense concentration makes me sterile and why, as regards the second, it would be well for me to have few attachments and few friends. To function successfully, my mind and sensibility need an impulse that stirs up what is there already, but which adds nothing. It may well be that intellectual pleasure which is so necessary to make me work (and which I condemn as a kind of spiritual vice) is essential to me; this is suggested by the fact that my serious ideas come in profusion when I am at ease, and cease when they have got me fully stretched.'

I am like that. I have a mind which is flexible at its surface, but pretty well fixed in its depths. This division, which is natural to me, makes me live as it were on two levels. And no doubt many minds live in this way, two in one. For we all have two natures (perhaps in the likeness of the God-Man, the ineffable hidden pattern?). I think that we might begin to understand mankind if we started from this hypothesis of the two levels of existence. At all events I wish to state how I feel this ceaseless disunity which I assume and still more how I endure it in myself. It is certainly a constant element of patience and of suffering which is bound to human experience. The surface can be disturbed. The least wind of chance makes me bend and sometimes shiver. This wind is often the breath of imaginary fear, because my imagination is not cheerful. The word 'morose', which I am fond of, well describes it. On any given subject, what first springs to my mind (shining, fervent, seductive, and better shaped, refined and selected than they are in the works of my rivals) are the reasons for doubting the very things to which I am most profoundly attached. My fault is to give too much weight to objections and to concede too much. I must keep watch. The act of reading, comprehending, of listening to another mind, even that of my dearest friend, tires me quickly. I can do nothing by halves or drowsily or by cheerful automatism as many of my fellow-men do so easily, in the course of duty. The slightest attention to someone I am fond of, or to some idea, stirs up in me a sheaf of ideas, feelings, possibilities, fears, calculations, forecasts and echoes. The sheaf wilts, exhausted! If only I could have caught and fixed it at that moment! But all forms of expression (writing, dictation, even conversation) seem to me too slow. People who classify characters would say that I was 'emotive and passive', as Gaston Berger told me, when he used to have time to brood over my character. But I have never believed in these definitions of character. Lavelle told me that he had said to Le Senne who was a classifyer: 'As for character, I have them all.' Anyway, if I am upset, it does not prevent me from remaining at bottom fairly unmoved, fairly unsusceptible to the influence of others, however much I feel it immediately. My mother, whom I resemble in this, told me about the device which M. Rulhières once gave to Madame de Beaumont. An oak tree. And under this oak tree the motto: 'A trifle shakes me and nothing loosens me.' Watching myself in the troubles of life, seeing how I rebound in a lively and improbable way, better than many of my friends who were accounted strong, and who certainly had greater courage than I had, I have often wondered how in my poor nature the sensitive and the insensitive are combined. I have never credited myself with outstanding qualities of intelligence or fortitude. And I have always admired many good friends for pre-eminence in fortitude, and simple courage. I feel weak and lacking in talent. I like to admire, to have models, to find masters for myself. I was created to live beside a genius, to be the Joinville or the Eckermann to some outstanding man. That is what in time past, twenty-five years ago, made me so fond of General Weygand, who had a similar vocation. I need to have someone to admire, even more than someone to love. And I feel the truth of Descartes's idea that admiration is the leading passion, preceding love itself. Sometimes it has led me to admire too hastily. In order to learn I must be taught. I will create masters for myself—if necessary right up to the end. I will go to the extremities of the earth to hear an oracle. Furthermore, I will take notes in order to learn, while listening to one of my students. It seems to me that a small child could teach me a great deal, if I could question him without intimidating him, like Saint Francis talking to the swallows.

Continuity tires me very quickly. I must distract myself. Digression I love to excess. And that is why a Journal, which digresses from digression, suits me so well. It makes one draw up a plan—to disregard it! When I decide on a route, I know I will turn off it, and this idea of possible disobedience delights me. Encounters, hazards, margins, divergencies, are vital to me. I wait in silence for the lifting latch—the angelic visitant. I look out eagerly for the unexpected. The work of supererogation, the gratuitous, the final task, the supplementary, is the one that gives me greatest scope and pleasure. My best things have been with the edges of my mind—done through Grace, and without premeditation. I love the sudden, the improvised.

Sometimes I adopt the peculiar method of 'the supplementary'. 'Over-exertion is the way in which the brain keeps its health,' said Édouard Herriot, or so I have been told. The extra worry saves me from others, in keeping with the rule that one can only have one anxiety at a time. The present anxiety, 'the evil of the day' of which the Gospel speaks—yes indeed—that is sufficient to me.

This is a disposition which I cannot alter, a bad habit of nonconformity which I notice also in my father, who is always so plucky despite his great age. Boring classes from which I have found escape by thinking of something else, helped by the vague droning, have taught me how not to listen—a valuable habit.

While I work I keep a net in which I can harvest the fruit of my distractions and digressions—as does this Journal in my life. R. said to me: 'The plan, the premeditated, the settled thing—that is man more or less falsified. Digression is man taking shape, the real man.' Pupils feel this. And that is why I realize that if I want to speak in public I must reach a state of abstraction, and see the audience only as a landscape of souls or destinies. Then I can really communicate with them, through this elimination of their bodies and my body. When I speak like this I feel an instant rapture, if by chance words or ideas, without merit on my part, without premeditation, I arrive at this dual forgetfulness of others and of myself. Then I no longer hear breathing or coughing, and, looking at the audience on the sly, I see them listening with wide-eyed gaze to one of the thoughts which have sprung to my mind.

I never experience this in a conversation or even with a very small audience. There needs to be a kind of mass, where each person forgets himself, where there are no longer individuals but one multitude, making a single body. That is how I like writing my thoughts, thinking vaguely of this multitude. To be the unknown who arrives, who does not give his name and who goes away after having left on the table exactly 'what they had need of'.

When I was twelve years old I wrote in an old copy of Telemachus this summary of wisdom according to Fénelon: 'Do not make hasty confidences, not knowing in whom you are confiding. (How many times have I erred in this way!) In speaking do not give play to vanity. Beauty, to charm, needs fine simplicity and modest goodness. Trials toughen. The good life is ever youthful. Rashness teaches. (How true this is!) Obedience can be costly, worse luck. Relaxing pleasures are the good ones. Wisdom is as much in youth as in age. (I realized this as a small child.) Understand mankind. Encourage your fellow-men. Unshakable courage in the face of death (who would dare to say it!). Do not desire grandeur overmuch. At all costs do not forsake a good friend.'

All this seems acceptable to me still as advice, and it is certainly what I say to myself. Yet I do not like Fénelon.

I would like to take a look at myself also under the heading of cheerfulness. For I have a melancholic disposition. But at the same time I have an amiable nature, and immediately I talk to somebody I begin to feel happy. My ideal for writing and for speaking would be that of Nietzsche when he said: 'May wisdom and gaiety clasp hands affectionately within me.' This mixture of the serious and the cheerful is at the ultimate quintessence of me. I have never allowed the two notes of anxiety and contentment to become separated. I want a kind of 'wrapping' of joy—even a certain carelessness and nonchalance—around what is most deeply serious. Plato, Montaigne, La Fontaine, show me the way. Nowadays I find models of this kind hard to come by. We have classified types too much. To me gaiety seems like a luminous haze in which we should be able to clothe even heart-breaking

34

things. In Purgatory Dante heard the *Labia mea* sung: *per modo tal che diletto e doglia parturie . . .*[1]

That is why I always feel an affinity with the intermediate stage of Purgatory, where I sense a strange mingling of deep sadness and growing hope. I do not like excess and dithyrambics. I like praise emerging from shadow where light and shade are mingled. I would like to be criticized sympathetically, to be praised with reservation.

2nd FEBRUARY 1952

I am working at present on my second book about Monsieur Pouget, commissioned by Gaëtan Bernoville, and it is making me relive a past stage in my life, that of apprenticeship. M. Pouget's nature was so different from mine, and no doubt that is what attracted me to him so much. He was completely indifferent to art, to form, to what one vaguely describes as the 'beautiful', which I find so essential if I am to understand and to create. M. Pouget was so at one with nature, so strong and energetic, a kind of machine which thought and remembered perpetually; 'universal' like the men of the Renaissance, but indifferent to the art of acquiring, pleasing, and even expounding; utterly different from the Jesuit outlook which always has the idea of converting, conferring, persuading, alluring, so as in every instance to get the maximum out of the other person, just as they try to get the maximum from themselves by way of the Exercises. With Jesuits, amongst whom I have always lived, though detachedly, for two of my father's brothers were in the Company, I felt myself in the realm of art—in the highest sense of the word— strategy, rhetoric and politics. I am not finding fault with the Jesuits on this account, and I am something of a strategist myself. I like pondering on ways of getting things. I like the

[1] *Purgatorio* 23, 11-12.

35

characteristically American expression: 'I've thought of a better way.' M. Pouget was a stranger to this universe. He was nature, not art, a wild wind, a listener to strange hearts, an oak filled with birds, and also as little prone to give counsel as is possible—to such a point that his habit of never coming to conclusions or advising began to tire me.

I am different from many of my intellectual contemporaries. From early days I felt a stranger amongst them in an intellectual world which was too clever for me. I have not much room in my skull for receiving or concentrating on obscure ideas. This is a quality much needed nowadays if you are to acquire reputation or attract the young. I like clarity. And depth as well. Depth in transparency, as in calm water. In particular there is a kind of obscurity in the philosophy of today which I cannot assimilate, and I wonder if this is not also the case with others who claim to understand it? Yes, I wonder whether, for many of my contemporaries, the most familiar words, such as to understand, to love, to perceive, or to be, hold the same sense as they do for me. To *think* means, for many notable intellects of these days, to enjoy (in the world of language) a kind of dense obscurity; to hover gently in the mist and to make it thicker, led by a vague idea of a possible solution, in itself obscure. For such minds, to seek clarity through depth is to acknowledge in advance one's unfitness.

I think that this distinction derives from a different sensitivity to language. The Germans see their words down to the roots, but they do not give each word a distinct and unique meaning. Every German word is a programme for uneasy, enthralling research. For me a word is a stopping place, a boundary, a halt. It must be crystal-like and have a definite form, yet at the same time hold echoes, but these must die away quickly. Then thought alone remains. I should say that since the time of Plato and Aristotle, this ideal has been swamped; with Plotinus words already have other uses, as they have also in the 'rhetoric' of St Augustine whose sanctity did not purge him of rhetoric—sanctity never does. The fact is that, for language, seventeenth-century France is my spiritual home, more especially the end of the seventeenth or even the eighteenth century when everybody, even women, knew how to talk. All that has gone. But throughout my education there has run a kind of cord, binding me to the age before the great Revolution.

I understand the expression 'to live by faith'. To live does not mean making an effort to obtain. It is breathing through the gills. My faith does not rest on an abyss of uncertainty. It does not require a wager, or call for excess of will. I have never been at home in the world of Bloy, Bernanos or Mauriac. And in the same way I have never thought of liberty as something which rends, but as something which achieves.

There is in my make-up a desire for the whole, which both helps and frustrates me: the horror of a partial view, of attitudes, of parties; the need to reach a viewpoint, which takes in other opinions, a secret aspiration towards the impossible, in brief—the fear of renunciations. This has often unfitted me for action, which needs an almost fierce will to achieve. I remember my meeting with Foch, about 1920, and the advice he gave me to have one plan, one goal, one method (emphasizing *one*), saying that his secret was relentlessness, obstinacy—far more, according to him, than the 'spark after midnight', which Bonaparte extolled, and which Foch called 'the clairvoyance granted to a man'. When I saw Foch, whose genius I so greatly admired, I was torn between the contemplation of his brow, furrowed with thought, though graced with light, and his obstinate, strong chin, shadowed by a fine drooping moustache. There was the rectangle below and above of which Napoleon spoke: the chin and the forehead, symbols of man's two powers. My own chin is very sharp, thin and overshadowed by the height of

37

the face. It is a sign no doubt of the difficulty I have in using the knife—in cutting through the flesh which the cruel word 'decision' implies. If I allowed myself to follow my bent, I would gladly say like Thérèse of the Child Jesus, when she was pressed to choose: 'I choose everything.' He who seeks a particular end with all his power dooms himself to setbacks, to mistakes, to unavoidable hardships. This is startlingly illustrated by military leaders who arrive at their goal with troops who are dirty and worn out and leave behind them thousands of dead. Even in the world of letters the same is true of Balzac, and of Goethe, Claudel or Sartre. Little does it matter to them if there are wasted paragraphs, errors of taste, padding, provided that the shocking, massive Napoleonic effect is produced.

Joubert is the exact opposite of this. The abhorrence of writing an indifferent page condemned him to perfection, and killed him.

'I have associated mostly with priests, pious women, and soldiers. The priests taught me to pray; the women taught me tenderness (without which knowledge is vain); the soldiers taught me comradeship, and that all our fears are exaggerated.'

'I say in fact that youth is the time of illusion; but that is because it sees things as infinitely less lovable, abundant and desirable than they are. Age cures us of this misunderstanding.' (Claudel in *Le Soulier*.)

'*Omnis consummationis vidi finem. Latum mandatum tuum nimis.*' I would happily translate this verse from the Psalms as follows: I have seen the end of every system. Thy commandment is infinitely greater than one can conceive.'

'Remember, my soul, that there are more than a thousand minutes in a day, and that one minute itself is long. Everything in my life comes about through the co-operation of a hidden spirit, and a wandering self. What an immense, cloudy, immeasurable territory is this—self-exploration!'

André Maurois

This was the time at which Grasset published Maurois's little book called *What I believe*. I sent my impressions of it to Louis Chaigne, who passed them on to Maurois. I said amongst other things: What has surprised me in this booklet, *De Fide Mea*, is the absence, not of faith, but of the problem presented by faith. It is remarkable that after middle life, after so much testing, so much human experience, so many confidences received, so many Catholic friends (I am thinking particularly of Charles du Bos), so much travelling in countries both actual and mystical, André Maurois should remain so naturally Christian. Mauriac is a Catholic haunted by an uneasy conscience. Maurois is an atheist inhabited by the *Bona conscientia*. Combining these by alchemy one would perhaps find, to the pleasure of theologians, a tormented atheist and a joyful believer. No one could think that the scanty paragraphs which Maurois gives to the problem of evil and to providence could define his whole thought. One cannot in so few words answer philosophers and believing men of the spirit. And Maurois well knows this. Had he been born an Anglo-Saxon, a way of life as moderate and as modest as is his own would have been able to reconcile itself with the deepest mystical call, even though inarticulate. But for him, born a Frenchman, it seems that moderation excludes the sense of the infinite, of the unknowable, of devotion to the *Deus ignotus*. You have perhaps noticed that in the booklet, it is not a question of the Judaeo-Christian religion, nor of Christ, of whom the author never quotes a word.

All that makes me think that Maurois has not put his

whole thought into this book. He has spoken of his human faith; he has treated his divine faith by preterition; there is something essentially modest in his material, the frail fruit of oversensitivity. Perhaps he also felt it unsuitable to touch on these fundamental questions before the two worlds which comprise his public. (Perhaps also he did not wish to wound good Catholic friends, such as yourself.)

If one pursued the lines of this little work to their logical conclusion (but has one the right to do so?) one would say that faith is a sweet illusion of which those who find comfort in it ought not to be deprived.

I wonder if this is really your friend's last word? Whether you should not ask him to 'reconsider', as one says, this vast question? So many good people, so many young people, in these two worlds have taken Maurois for a sage, that it is impossible for such an upright person not to give a more detailed answer to the queries of so many minds. I was reading Jean Santeuil at that time, and I compared what Maurois tells us of his doubts about eternity with the grave hope expressed by Proust in youth, in what he said about 'the lovely precepts which set us on our way to another state'. It seems to me that Proust has a continual feeling of the preparatory and emblematical character of this world, and of our loves in it, which is the basis of mysticism.

What could the art of living mean if life itself lacked meaning? What would love be, if . . . ? These ideas, which are the substance of our Christian thought, do not seem to come within Maurois's horizon. Perhaps he is one of the people described by Pater in *Marius the Epicurean*, those who need to feel tenderly and passionately loved by souls given to Christ, without, however, themselves being able to have faith, and who are obliged by their uprightness, by their modest and demanding sincerity to affirm their doubts and their passivity. You know that for thirty years I have felt gratitude towards Maurois, who has taught me so much about order in art, taste and the sense of proportion. A disinterested gratitude.

Maurois replied with this delightful letter: 'You know (for we have already spoken of these things) that my religious education was short, very conventional and that it left no deep mark on me. At fifteen I read a great deal of Anatole France; his hedonistic rationalism suited me; his sceptical attitude towards Judaeo-Christian beliefs seemed to me intelligent and wise. Twenty years later I found it again in Paul Valéry, but with more depth and hermetic wisdom. Then came Alain who upset my ideas, for contrary to what perfunctory readers think neither Alain nor I are complete rationalists. We do not believe that discursive logic can explain everything. Alain's last word, like that of Descartes, is Freedom, and that is a mystery. To my mind, Alain puts materialism and determinism in their place as working instruments only. He taught me the religion of the spirit. "The spirit," he said, "is neither within nor without. It is the all in all, one and indivisible." The day I understood that, I glimpsed the sublime and fanatical Jewish religion. But Alain thought, and I think with him, that this religion, if it is to come close to man, must fulfil itself by the incarnation of spirit. This is Christianity, of which Alain always spoke with respect and even with faith. He never tired of explaining its parables and its rites. "The Spirit is meek, righteous and good and its promise is the cross of wood." The only difference between Alain and an orthodox Catholic is that the historical truth of religion was a matter of indifference to him or rather that the very idea shocked him. "What matters," Alain said, "is not that Jesus said a particular thing at a particular time, but that this thing is true." There was his stumbling block, and it is mine also. This does not mean to say that we refuse to believe. Very much to the contrary. It means that to believe we have no need of miracles, nor of witnesses. Our faith goes beyond facts. Reread *Les Dieux*.

'After the spiritual retreat which a year of philosophy provides, life took charge of me, but metaphysics continued to haunt me. I married a Christian wife, and I found great happiness in accompanying her to church, without, however, undergoing conversion. During the war of 1914 I had an intellectual shock—I read Chesterton.

'I read *Orthodoxy* in Flanders to the sound of the guns, during nights when suffering and death were abroad. The book pierced me to the depths. Then I had great griefs, which made me yearn desperately for the consolations of a faith. I opened St Augustine and was struck by an idea he propounded: to invoke, *in vocare*, is to call within oneself. I appealed within myself for something more than myself, and I found it. And the fact that this identical something exists in beings of your calibre, dear friend, and indeed in every man, constitutes a communion of souls in which I believe with all my heart. But though that may be a Christian idea, it is not the whole of Christianity.

'At that time I had near me to help me in the search one of my dearest friends: Charles du Bos. I felt very close to him. "When I say that I believe in God," he wrote at that time, "I mean that I feel God within me and maybe this is simply the same as saying that my best moments belong to the sphere of religion." That was where I stood also. We both had moral preoccupations, and the wish to live a good life. "But, for the true Christian," said du Bos, "it is religion which helps him to live well; with me the very fact of living well opens up my religious potentialities to me." I would like to have signed that phrase.

'A little later, this man with whom I had for some years shared my most intimate thoughts became once again a practising and militant Catholic. He remained my good friend, but I admit that sometimes I ceased to understand him. His vocabulary was no longer mine. I remained a humanist in the sense that though I might identify in man

42

something which went infinitely beyond man, I did not see in the vast surrounding world the traces of a Providence. All the same, in brief moments of rapture I caught, and still catch, a glimpse of the nature of these mystical facts, which you reprove me for ignoring. If I listen to Fauré's *Requiem* with the rapt devotion it demands I perceive beyond it a kingdom which is not of this world. The sublime chapter on Mgr Myriel in *Les Misérables*, Swann's pages on the *petite phrase*, suddenly open up vistas over wide landscapes of the spirit. Then, like Proust, I begin to hope that gazing long and raptly at three church spires or a hawthorn hedge, I will at the finish tear their secret from them. Perhaps some day by sheer devoted interrogation of this seemingly indifferent universe and by a fervent desire to grasp its meaning, I shall see the cloudy barriers which veil the promised land lift and disappear. Then fugitive ecstasy would remain. And that would be Grace.'

When I visited André Maurois whom I had not seen since that first visit, which took place on the day on which Lindbergh crossed the Atlantic, I found no change in him. Modesty, moderation, a *modus vivendi* in a beautiful setting which was no doubt a necessity to him. He does not see himself as a genius, but as a conscientious craftsman. In every context he seems to have wanted to avoid the giddy heights, the extreme position. And that is why the realm of faith (in which one must be affirmative to excess and cut one's moorings) is not natural to him. With him love is hardly distinguished from habit, and faith from a sacred legend; man himself from dream; and, more generally, illusion from reality, or beauty (charm) from truth. I do not reproach him for it. Some flexible spirits would be exhausted by the firm dividing line which I persistently try to draw through everything. Maurois's art of living does not include this art of death. His ultimate thoughts are silent.

His voice is gentle and modulated, irresolute, low-pitched,

welcoming, but nervous. A director of conscience, of wisdom, of method, with an element of irresolution and attachment to the world and as Alain says of 'tenderness'.

'You will be happy,' said my mother to me in days gone by. 'You are vulnerable and you are touching.' It is this kind of human weakness which Alain did not possess. I feel that Maurois, like myself, has much indulgence for the frailty which springs from tenderness. I said so to him. He defended himself by replying that his characters are doomed from within, when they have not kept their integrity as in the first part of *Climats* or in the *Cercle de Famille*. He showed me that the two pivots on which his thought has turned are: first, the search for a way of life and action; the making of the self which Goethe called the *Bildung*. I would call this wisdom. Second, the study of extraordinary lives, in so far as they show the working of destiny. And from this point of view his whole work has great meaning for me.

I tell myself the story backwards, as I love to do in my Game of Inversions: this gives me a better understanding of the transitory element in every life.

'Like Jules Lemaître, he started by writing books about authors, but in the context of literary destinies: Hugo, then G. Sand, then Chateaubriand. Then he turned to history, and towards the novel, or rather towards a mixture of novel and history. Finally, like La Fontaine towards the end of his life, and remembering French Anglomania, he wrote those admirable fables, *The Silences of Colonel Bramble*, in which he sums up the experiences of his life; this is the tranquil work of an old man.'

Lastly we spoke of Valéry and of Alain. About Valéry he thought as I think that the prose writer excels the poet. To prove this he brought up some youthful verses of Hugo, which are so 'Valéryan' that one could be mistaken about their author. Alain respected the thinker in Valéry as a kind of Parmenides or Pindar. For Alain, thought must above all else 'suggest', while maintaining its own dark ambiguous aspect. How little I belong to this type! Does this mean that one cannot suggest through clarity?

A visit to the Louvre

Delacroix. The girl in the cemetery. Staring eyes. *Odalisque. The Prostrate Horse mauled by a Lion.* What a profusion of themes, of research into all genres, all forms, like an army which fights on every front! And to which he gives life in great things and small.

Madame Rose. Nude. Flesh with bluish veins, rose-grey tints, that air of lassitude.

Corot. One feels that he loves structure as in the *Colisée*, that little château in the French style. His landscapes take an architectural form. Corot prefers small canvases, small figures. Reproductions of his works which reduce all sorts of pictures to the same size—how misleading they are, levelling great and small! Corot actually gains by this, for his scale is human and brief.

Another look at the celebrated *Pont de Narvi*, unfinished. One sees it reproduced everywhere nowadays to prove that the sketch was better than the painting completed according to the conventions of that day. In fact, Corot reached fulfilment at an early age—save for his melancholia.

I looked again at *Saint Anne* by Leonardo da Vinci; advanced geometry rather than painting; geometry of curves, spirals, ovals, spaces between forms—which themselves are forms. In one space I imagine a vulture. It accords with Freud's hypothesis—and is quite plausible in the case of this enigmatic painter who loved threefold disguises, ultra-secret significance, whether angelic or depraved. The peculiar gesture of the Virgin can only be justified by learned arguments which are beyond me; one divines hermetic symbolism all over the place.

For Leonardo, *La Joconde* was not so much a picture as an epitome of his thoughts on woman, on nature, on existence; a manner of life and destiny, possibly the search for inner unity. No poem could have the presence of a painting; never rigid, and always capable of modification and improvement. Leonardo kept the *Joconde* beside him. It was a mirror of the unexplored and the impossible in his creative dream. He needed this message in cypher. Every work of every man is that, but the code is secret. What is astonishing about the *Joconde* is that, for the masses, it has kept its magical character. One still halts before it as before a tabernacle, throwing it a glance of timid adoration. To what extent was the *Joconde* (too finished for my taste) completed by Leonardo da Vinci? And what was really the face which he kept beside him at the Château of Amboise?

Winter reading

MARCH 1952
Saint Étienne. Staying with my father

'When a man has come to the end of a long career, when he has overcome the obstacles with which all human life is strewn and has nothing left to do but to die in the radiance of his virtues and the affections of his dear ones—to be compelled to plunge into the performance of a final duty is a trial in which the best succumb.'

I have always relished Lacordaire when he is like an ox at rest or in the ecstatic mood of an orator when he unfurls the banner of a platitude. This saying about the old man in action is prophetic of the fate of many men and above all of one destiny, which remains a deep mystery for France, a mystery on which she keeps silence—perhaps will keep silence for ever. The old age of those who have achieved great things . . . 'The most exalted,' says Lacordaire, 'succumb to the mysterious poison of disappointment.'

I reread Lacordaire at my father's house. I find my father as courageous, clever, obstinate and shrewd as ever. The cedar in the garden sways under the snow; one might say that it was shaking it off like a large animal, an apocalyptic beast. Lacordaire seems to me inferior to Bossuet because of his deficient culture and bad taste. There is nothing to replace knowledge, certainly not eloquence. Lacordaire hardly tries. Yet what is unique in him is the sombre grandeur, the indefinable true simplicity which Bossuet never attained, the eloquence which suddenly dies down and becomes the word and nothing else. He speaks of the Pyramids. 'Here,' he writes, 'is something solemn, calm, great, immovable, deeply simple.' That was his ideal and sometimes he reached it. To come back once more to one of his own descriptions, this time of life, mature, magnanimous, a little disillusioned (himself again): 'When soul and body have attuned themselves to the majestic motion of great events, they cannot endure the slow and peaceful succession of the days.'

One feels that he would gladly have accepted some responsibility, gladly have founded something. Sorrèze was not enough. Or take the page about St Thomas. Lacordaire recalls that St Thomas was the grandson of the Emperor Frederick Barbarossa, the nephew of Guiscard, the cousin of Tancred and of Henri IV (facts which are not as a rule noted in lay or scholastic manuals). They perhaps explain the lordly, equable, detached tone of St Thomas—the manner of a judge accustomed to weigh in order to consider, to put everyone in his place, like a just monarch: blood royal, found, in philosophy, only in Plato.

Aristotle tried to imitate this regal tone by an air of scientific detachment. Lacordaire says casually of St Thomas: 'St Thomas remains the prince he has always been, he has become the solitary he willed to be; only the character of discipleship has vanished for he has become the master of all.'

I have also been reading about Madame de Beaumont again, in books which belonged to my mother. My mother loved Madame de Beaumont. She spoke of her as 'her sort of woman'. I believe she didn't know about Pauline de Beaumont's weakness, the naked side which displeased even Joubert, or perhaps she muffled it in forgiveness, or more likely in forgetfulness? What she loved about her was her judgment, her acceptance of misfortune, her late eighteenth century culture, the culture of that age of remarkable women which has no parallel. She read me the story of her death, when Pauline wrote: 'There is no more oil in the lamp, I feel the last beatings of my heart.' My mother's last days were like those of Madame de Beaumont.

It seems to me that after the upheavals of the Revolution at the beginning of the nineteenth century in France it was a favourable time for women. Then came the Restoration and they were again shut up in bourgeois pastures, again summoned to a life of submission and endurance. When the frivolity of the eighteenth century had been expiated, and the male fury of the Revolution and the Empire had shattered home life, tradition had to be revived. It was women above all who brought about this transition. They had their memories of the old world and new visions as well: they were the women admired by Stendhal, Chateaubriand, and Balzac, Guizot, and Cousin. . . .

Here I also read Keyserling, who taught me nothing, but who made me understand the German genius, and its

48

language—not high-strung like the notes of the piano, rather the lament of a violin. Keyserling says that Kant's German style is worthy of admiration. He also says that the essence of the being is in the Kantian style which is born at the same time as the idea, and cannot be preceded by it.

The painter Ravier

19th NOVEMBER

A talk with Dr Thiollier about Ravier, the Lyons painter and friend of Corot, many of whose unknown works the doctor, an art lover, owns. Ravier was a friend of his father and he often used to watch him working.

Ravier, he told me, was well off and, unlike Corot, had no need to sell his pictures. He was 'unmethodical to the last degree'. He used everything in painting: brushes of course, but also his thumb. I will show you thumb-marks on the blue of a twilight scene which are like the devil's finger-prints. As for water colours, he would start on any paper that came to hand, sometimes a butcher's wrapping. Then he would put it under a tap to make the colours run and merge. After that he would touch it up, restore it, re-create it, using all sorts of methods, pastels, oil, and, if necessary, thumb strokes, as I have said. It is this which gives his canvases the atmosphere of wet earth, their undertones and fading light, which are unique. Ravier admired Turner, the painter of light's mystery. But Turner's light is idealized; it is the light of the seas, while Ravier's is the twilight on the earth.

He never exhibited. He had a shrewish wife and this Xan-tippe, by making him unhappy, forced him to work and create beauty. He went to Rome with Corot. From contact with Corot he retained only drawing and composition. His colour was derived from Delacroix, or, by descent, from Watteau's fairy-land. At Crémieu or Morestel, Ravier went to see the sun setting on a marshy pool. But in fact he did not look very much. He went in for blending and grinding colour, inviting the accidental, and, as Turner said: 'He never let an accident be wasted.' He had an impatient genius, preferring to rough out twenty small canvases than to give birth to one large composition.

Advice for unprofitable days

29th DECEMBER, *Nice*
Hotel Scribe

Father Auguste Valensin took charge of a conversation in which, like a benevolent Socrates, he questioned me in front of some university colleagues. The dialogue followed the pattern for all conversation, which is to touch lightly, to pass on and to return. He was the bee that never got lost in a calyx. In the long run this sort of haphazard interchange yields plenty of fruit, and I think it is the one best fitted to the capacity of the human mind. Anyone who wants to go deeply into, or to systematize everything soon comes on poison. Some time ago I marked these words of Fénelon: 'One must take the flower of every subject, and only make use of that part which one can beautify.' Beautify? I would rather say perfect, with a microscopic thought, a personal addition, a nuance.

Father V made me see that in my books there are converging lines whose focal point is not yet clear, and that from this a certain vagueness results. I told him that the centre does exist, and if time allows me to grow old it will become apparent. It is always interesting to hear this Jesuit humanist speak of his methods. We are planning to collaborate in a book on 'intellectual work'. But with his mania for perfection, his horror of deadlines, I am sure that it is in his stars that he will never go through with it. I shall write that book alone; his angel's wings would slow it down. I take note of his advice.

He much appreciated the books on Stendhal and Baudelaire by my friend Jean Prévost. They belonged, he said, to the art of living as much as to the art of writing; or rather they belonged to the art of that higher wisdom of life which employs professional technique (here the technique of writing on blank paper) upon interior unity, that is to say, beatitude. I knew Jean Prévost long ago, without realizing that this sturdy young man, so generous beneath his violence (as his death showed), was concerned about this kind of study of craft and style. But I, too, believe that his *Stendhal* is a key-work on 'creation' in style and in life, and on the ways of out-witting oneself and extracting from oneself more than is there.

'Stendhal,' Father Valensin told me, 'helps me in my moments of enthusiasm and inspiration, and when I feel young. But the method which Valéry taught me is far more useful in times of disillusion, of dust and ashes. These multiply, alas! with age, or, if you prefer, in that arid state which monks and mystics have described so exactly, and which Valéry told me was perpetually his.'

When I asked him to explain the way of aridity, he said: 'It's like this: I start with something ugly, unimaginably banal and pitiful. Then I make it a point of honour to let my pencil cover a great deal of paper, leaving spaces without ever rereading. And there must be no pause, even though it brings forth toads or monsters, as in the fairy stories. This done, I look for sequence. I cut and cut again, retaining the best. I replace wood with stone. It is engineer's work and, my goodness, it is entertaining! What you need above all is taste and a sacrificial sense. This is an unteachable gift. I say to myself: here an image is needed. I construct the image mechanically, thinking of the effect I want to produce, but with no inspiration. I let a platitude stick out. You could hardly believe the pleasure I take in these transformations. I do away with effort and inspiration and replace them by mechanical good taste. No more anguish! I cannot say that I enjoy the happiness of youth which is creative (with, however, many lapses), but a complete and calm beatitude which prevails with certainty and always.'

Then this priest, who in his lifetime had listened to so many boring lectures and dull sermons, gave me some advice about the difficult art (so often unexplored by professors and preachers) of speaking, pure and simple. To guide me I take Jules Lemaître's definition of eloquence: 'to be eloquent is to say something to someone.' 'Valéry,' he said, 'told me whimsically that to make good speeches one must have enough assurance to roll a cigarette in public; the brain must be sufficiently on the boil for ideas to spring up spontaneously without the audience's being able to complain of blundering or mumbling. It is just this possibility of a slip-up which people like, and look out for, certainly in these days of mechanical speech. Valéry said to me: "One stumbles without notes, and even with notes. And what's more, one becomes a bore." He described to me the feeling of real panic which he had often had when the audience was not alert and in harmony with him, and coughing could be heard in the hall.'

Everything, in fact, depends on a correspondence between the self and others; on a mutual waking dream; that is to say, in the total forgetfulness of self and of others. This is the nuptial flight of two surrenders. It need only last a few minutes for true eloquence to come into being, true eloquence in the Pascalian sense: the power of the word. It is for this reason that the subject of a lecture should come in a roundabout way to an act of confidence, a moment of intimacy, unexpected and unforeseeable, inviting the silent union of minds, and making impossible the vulgar gesture of applause. 'If you feel at liberty to applaud me,' said Musonius Rufus, 'it means that I have not convinced you.'

'I have a most difficult and almost inhuman ideal about the spoken word,' added Father Valensin. 'It makes me a very bad listener to lectures, and dissatisfied whenever I have to give one.'

He told me of the exercises he does every morning to keep alive his faculty for writing. He writes free verse without seeking its meaning, letting himself be guided by sound. An exercise which he commended to François, that child of genius.

Valéry's notebooks

During his lifetime Valéry never ceased analysing what he did. The 'how' of everything enthralled him, not the 'why'. And when he wrote verse, I am quite sure that he always duplicated himself—writing of course, but above all seeing himself write. Father Valensin told me that Valéry had left two hundred and fifty-four notebooks which are going to be photostated. 'To penetrate the waking dream of a creative mind, to decipher the nothings out of which he knew how to make a whole—the chaos from which has sprung the existing order—what a shaking up that will give me!'

He had seen these notebooks. And he said to me: 'Notice how in every poet (and this would also apply to a captain of industry, to a politician and to anyone who achieves something) three beings must be considered—the producer, the man of taste and the technician. The first provides the matter. The second selects. The third builds. If you are only a producer, like Eugène Sue or Dumas, you remain at a mediocre level. If you have taste only, like Mallarmé or Joubert, you will despair. If you are only a competent craftsman, like Thomas Corneille or Victorien Sardou, you will not enter the holy places of art.'

Valéry, who understood himself so well, knew that in technique he was unrivalled, and that he had the most exquisite taste. He lacked something in power. Every day at dawn he opened his copy-books:

> Dans mon âme je m'avance,
> Tout ailé de confiance:
> C'est la première oraison!
> À peine sorti des sables,
> Je fais des pas admirables
> Dans les pas de ma raison.

One day we shall follow these steps: babblings, scraps, the advice he gave himself, irritations, rough outlines, resonances, sibylline equations, poems hardly begun before they were abandoned, bitter confidences—in short, the seeds of himself. Queer fragments of the future, the bright chaos which greets your parched awakening, which one does not know how to use, yet which holds promise for a contemplative. For he feels he has the courage to bring such fragments, by force of work, to a high degree of precision, even of splendour.

The most surprising of Valéry's reflections, Father Valensin told me, was the one he wrote in pencil during his last days, and with which his work breaks off:

'All opportunities for error—worse still—all opportunities for bad taste, for facileness, for vulgarity, come to him who hates.'

Then with the same faint, slanting, slightly shaking pencil, he wrote:

'The word love has only been found connected with the name of God' (here a change of pencil and the words which follow are written in pale blue) 'since the coming of Christ.'

Father Valensin confirmed that he had read this in Valéry's last notebook which Madame Valéry kindly showed him. 'That does not mean, quite strictly speaking,' I replied to him, 'that Valéry believed in God, but rather that God believed in Valéry, since he allowed Fate to cut the thread of his life at the moment when for once his thought was of love.' 'At the close of this life,' said that genius in abstractions, St John of the Cross, 'we shall be judged on love.'

II

Anniversary of a journey to Jerusalem

Jerusalem. JANUARY-MARCH 1953

Early morning and pale dawn. Then far away on the
horizon, towards Jerusalem, brown clouds phosphorescent
with borrowed light. Rich plains, red earth, friable and rich
and suited to that little tree with golden fruit—the orange
tree. Clean new houses everywhere. At Lydda we left the
train, to go to Jerusalem along a tarred road, made for
speed. This road is bordered by pipes, or rather by sections
of large pipes placed end to end. At last the problem of bringing water to Jerusalem is about to be solved! I have forgotten
to say that the sun was up, and that it filled the sky, glittering
and flashing as in Egypt, but in air that was drier and cleaner.
They told us that it had rained two days before, and that this
is exceptional weather. The road climbs the first spurs. I
recognize this stony earth so often seen in France, particularly
in the *landes* of Garrigues and of Millevaches. Stones litter the
ground.

Jerusalem! Jerusalem! Here there must be a first thought
about the *place*. What is a place? A point in space in which
an event happened in time. The place preserves nothing of
the event. It is for the mind to make up the deficiency.

That is why history lives only in thought, and it is thought
which creates a place. Thought creates neither a happening
nor its localization. But when it believes in the first, and has
identified the second, then it unites present to past in that

place. Geographical locality retains nothing; a place where something has happened is just like all the places which have not been touched by history. Perhaps it is better that no traces should persist, for traces may awaken doubts and provoke conflict and discussion. But there are two things which time cannot destroy, and over which men have no control— heaven and earth. It is the same firmament; the same rock; the same sun.

Two sorts of people are to be feared: those who tear down out of hate, and those who build up out of love.

Yes. One place is like another, and the environment is like everywhere else. Rubbish, green grass, stale smells, urchins at play, women at work, shop-keepers, cocks crowing, the sound of the town, a blacksmith striking, a cart creaking. A lowering sky, cries, mingled noises, a town breathing, and the majority of its people content to exist. All this makes one understand the Incarnation better and also everyday human nature. It is the common play that tomorrow will be finer, for we have thrown away with our nursery books the Jerusalem of our imagination. Yet it is this Jerusalem which stirs us, as it did the Crusaders. The Holy Land teaches us that all the earth is holy, since all the world is like it.

To understand the Holy Sepulchre one needs, I think, to take the following into account:

1. One must know that Christ was crucified at the entrance to a little town on a very low hill; on a rock which was shaped like a skull. And one must realize that since all these places have been levelled and blunted by architecture and by piety, nothing now remains which can be seen or touched.

2. It helps therefore to think of a diamond set by goldsmiths in gold or some other metal, but which has suffered so much from their work that it has turned to powder, and now faith alone enables one to grasp it.

3. The various Christian denominations share this building (which had already been shared by several sites and tradi-

tions). Those who got most were those whose power of protection was strongest—that is to say protection by bullets and bayonets. The Greeks have the lion's share, and the Latins are like disinherited brothers. They may not own the stones, but, as it is in some family share-outs, they have the life and the spirit.

As soon as we arrived we made for the Holy Sepulchre. A labyrinth. Never had we seen such crowded streets: donkeys, Bedouins, stale smells which made the gorge rise. At last the entrance to the Sepulchre, and suddenly after having climbed twenty steep steps, we found a crypt divided in two; on the right the Latin altar, on the left that of the Greeks, which is on the site of the Crucifixion. No place on earth is more majestic. Nevertheless there was no one here except a dirty, absent-minded-looking Greek monk, keeping an eye on his rights. Those who own this place are no longer in communion with Rome. Yet somehow the place speaks and prays by its very desolation. The saints are more honoured than the Saint of saints. And how fitting this is since the outstanding fact about him who made glory is his obscurity, and about him who came to bring unity, the division of his worshippers.

Jesus still alone in an indifferent world! What profusion in St Peter's in Rome, and here what nakedness! Jerusalem helps one to understand Rome, and puts it in its right place, which is after all the second.

Now we are before the Sepulchre. One bends to pass under the arch which gives access to the grotto. A marble table covers the actual stone of the Sepulchre. A man kisses it and prostrates himself. The tomb is empty as it was for the Women. It is a very small vault. Fewer prayers, and miracles, less devotion than at Lourdes. A museum of sacred art which might belong to brothers at variance. Greek monks chant hoarsely. A poor woman enters.

The *whole earth*, not this earth alone, is the tomb of Christ. At Jerusalem I see one point only—the true centre. But the other arm of the compass passes through all places which I have loved.

The oriental lives out of doors and very simply. His life would be frighteningly austere were he not fundamentally idle. He makes no provision. It does not seem necessary to him to try to own more than he has; he would readily regard as a vice the Western tendency to improve one's lot and to provide for the future. In any case, an oriental would not attach a virtuous character to this. Ownership is a useless worry and too great a tie. The return to the simple and primitive life, preached by Bergson, is realized by the oriental.

Each digs himself in without a thought for his neighbour, shoving, elbowing, really living in a 'community'. That, I think, is what Renan would have had us understand when he remarked on the *communism* of the first Galileans who were close to Jesus. I would rather call it neighbourliness. I see no dividing walls, pavements in the streets, hedges round the fields, lengths of barbed wire. The people are poor and keep their belongings within sight so that they can look after them. They are not clean because cleanliness makes demands, e.g. discipline, privacy. It also needs water, which is very scarce.

Near the Damascus Gate Bedouins crowd into a corner, children play something like our hop-scotch, an old man tries to drive his donkey forward, some small-tradesmen smoke hookahs in a meditative fashion and two veiled women pass by with towering bundles carried effortlessly on their heads. The shops are so narrow, so open to the street, that one is inside them at once, and can see everything that goes on. I noticed how small the stocks were. A civilization of this kind is not conducive to wealth. But it can have a fine spiritual bearing, if the souls are upright.

We must see Jesus, then, always hemmed in and crowded upon by the friendly and the inquisitive, having no time or place in which to be solitary; in surroundings, in short, in conditions which are the least auspicious for the interior life. I think that one sees this in the Gospels. For instance, in St Mark I, 35: 'And, rising very early, going out, he went into a desert place; and there he prayed. And Simon and they that were with him followed after him. And, when they had found him, they said to him: "All seek for thee." ' I repeat that I seem to see Jesus longing to be alone, choosing the hour before dawn when his friends slept most deeply, and slipping away to pray, probably aloud. This text has been much changed by St Luke who has, so to speak, rubbed out the colour. For St Luke it was day, not 'before dawn'. There is nothing about prayer, and it is the 'multitudes' who sought him; multitudes is too vast. Simon's exclamation was 'All seek for thee,' which means not everyone seeks thee, but our group wants thee with it. Also in St Mark I, 33, there is: 'And all the city was gathered together at the door,' after sunset . . .

The daily life of the Saviour shows the Apostles as witnesses. They *saw* with their fingers, bodies, backs and limbs; they *touched* with their eyes. Life in public was unsuitable and unbearable for a nature as fine as that of Jesus. And I think that he did not prolong it beyond what was necessary. But he wished that his humanity should be steeped in our feeble humanity, becoming incarnate once in a pure body, and again, so to speak, in human propinquity, the propinquity which, when I was a prisoner, we found so wearisome.

Although they are gross and clumsy, these people did not lack a certain nobility—the nobility of a deposed king, or a mendicant knight. For here, even today, a man in tatters wears them like a royal robe. Materials which we would not use for rags become robes and adornments. The oriental knows how to let them hang and take their natural folds. He hides himself under these bits and pieces which have no beauty, yet he achieves a proud and provocative elegance.

One senses a certainty of moral equality and this is the true democracy of the East. Our democracy is built on principles and revolutions; it is somewhat uneasy, because the freedom of some always seems to be won at the expense of others. One might almost say the same thing of our wealth, and that is why we keep watch on ourselves. Here equality is an instinct of the people. We have a mere imitation of it. Amongst our peasants I see subservience and the remains of a serfdom which it would be impossible to conceive in these kingly people. The poor man is not destitute, and the basic needs of the rich man (leaving potentates on one side) are not much greater than those of the poor. The common people are in the majority. One never sees what we call the middle classes, the administrators and civil servants. Outwardly the effect is one of discord, dirt and indifference; but when you begin to think of it, it is not a bad life for man simply as man. Thus the Incarnation took place in a poor and human country, on soil where the human plant grew with that arid dignity which is natural to it.

But in this civilization of dispossessed aristocrats what a low place is given to woman! I know that in Jerusalem we have not a true picture of the Jewish past. Islam has passed by with its prudery and sensuality, the one the result of the other. I have been told that an English soldier was stoned in Cairo, because he was seen kissing his fiancée in the street. A son of the orient cannot walk abroad with his mother.

One imagines that these tall veiled women have secrets, but they are just children; not yet fully developed. The master is lord; the husband has the privileges of the male; he is the possessor. Women live shut up and confined. Having children too soon wears them out. They huddle together. I hear they lament amongst themselves, and indulge in endless palavers over the most trivial things.

Children. No sign of a well organized school except for the purpose of learning the rudiments by the rod and sheer repetition. But I do see a method which may better suit this simple existence: the child is with men from his earliest years, he is associated with the common life and his character building consists in being penetrated and absorbed by a society faithful to tradition.

Tradition. We are certainly in the place where this concept was born. Custom decrees what is done, the past gains value from the future, because what has been will be. Thus progress can only be corruption. And since some progress is necessary, there needs to be a class of men who will forcibly inject into tradition what was not there already by the device of wisdom and subtlety which they call Commentary. And if there are two rival traditions they will need to be blended together in that sacred compilation, the Book.

To have invented the Book and the Commentary to uphold tradition is a stroke of genius, for commentary without tradition could only be vegetation robbed of its sap, and even blasphemous, while tradition without commentary would be crushing, and become so difficult to observe that it would forfeit respect. Tradition corresponds to the *mos majorum*; commentary is the *opus hominum*. Out of this *mos* and this *opus*, this *fas* and this *jus*, has been made the Divine Work, the Book, the Bible, the Testament, the Covenant.

What a vast and immeasurable revolution would be required to bring these people a new tradition, a new order! No one came to change the *mos majorum* of the people of Greece and Rome. When their faith ceased it vanished. The lack of belief in tradition brought about the end of its reign, so that one might say that habit died for want of sap. But here, in the time of Jesus, the Law was at its strongest and ruled hearts. People went back to Moses as arbiter. '. . . He has said to their ancestors . . .' With incredible power the simple workman from Nazareth changed all that. He made no effort. He brought his decrees as we imagine God might bring them. If the echo of words pronounced in the depths of the provinces reached Jerusalem (and how could it fail to arrive there, in this country where everything is public, everything circulates and is made known?), the Temple authorities must have begun to foresee a struggle to the death. They could not understand what it was about, precisely because they could not conceive that the old order was an *old* order, and that it could be abolished. But they had the feeling that this was something they must crush.

Let us stop for a moment on the Mount of Olives to see the sunset over the town. Jerusalem offers herself rapturously to the setting sun, well aware that at this hour she is more beautiful than at any other. Midday shows her up as poor and small. But the slanting rays spreading from one point glorify her. The sun which sinks in the valley of Hinnom supplies the faint, fading light she needs. The places of discord are enfolded in the single light of peace. Twilight is not so sudden as in Egypt, but it has that same phenomenon of phosphorescence which astonished Loti when he saw *pink* pyramids under a moonlit sky. Earth retains a brightness and a cold light which seem to come from the soil, gentle as a shadow, yet caressing and even guiding the eye.

When the sun has set, the sky which on that side is still acid-yellow keeps to the East all manner of misty tints which are yet deep and sharp. This is why the best comparison is to a precious stone. I saw in St Anne's Museum the stones of the High Priest's breastplate: sardonyx, topaz, emerald, sapphire, opal, chrysolite. They are crystals which receive the light and change it to pale rose, to green, to faint violet, to the blue of a bird's throat. I saw this colouring again in the tint of the sky in which all the shades of the rainbow merge.

A pastoral civilization, unchanged and unchangeable. And it is the prerogative of the East to show us things which take us back to our beginnings. The sheep so often mentioned in the Gospel are like the good oriental folk, people who crowd together, who bleat and follow shepherds, who have no initiative of their own, who are unmalicious, who go where they are led, who wait when they should wait; and this is right and charming.

The beggar at the gates of the town. Little donkeys everywhere. Arguments, palaver, gatherings in an upper room. Meagre food, circular rolls shaped like *galettes*. The blind who lean backwards as they walk.

Night has fallen. It is so overcrowded with stars that one's sight is dazzled by their multitude. The stars seem much closer than in our country. Their glittering and twinkling never cease; they are alive like creatures who seem to have been surprised and captured under this dark cloak. One is astonished that they do not move or converse with us by signs, by diagrams. The Magi saw them, and saw one which moved. It is a fact that there are many like that on the edge of the horizon, a growth springing from the margins of earth. And the moon is a white chalice raised on high, as if waiting to receive something.

What glorious nights filled by unsounding voices! Science tells us that the brightness from these stars is not contemporary with ourselves. In this sky which spreads itself out like unknown tongues, numberless and without a key, there may be stars which are 1,900 light-years distant from earth. Their brightness which I now receive was projected into space at the moment of the Passion. The heavens are filled with history.

One must picture Jerusalem as a supreme reliquary; not indeed a reliquary of movable things (*res*) but of immovable places (*loca*). I have come here to see places. Places which are holy for ever, since we are at a central point of space-time; places which can only be kept and preserved in sanctuaries; but just as sanctuaries, on this earth doomed by hatred, are in due course destroyed and razed, so new ones are built on the ruins of the old. It is probable that all those which we now see will again be pulverized by guns or bombs. But one can no more efface a place than a memory. Temples will be reborn on the ruins of the Temple.

Jerusalem is the pupil of the eye. And in this lies the town's uniqueness. It condenses a priceless history into less than one square kilometre. One may imagine that every building enjoys casting an interested and peaceable glance over all the others and over the horizon. Each view of Jerusalem is unique, and seen thus from ten feet away the town keeps its original character. Its streets are rivulets of shade where people look like busy ants, many of them carrying burdens like ants. Its domes are like the mounds thrown up by moles and indicate underground workings. The terraces of its houses, palaces, churches, all are so crowded together, so concentrated, so built-in to each other that one can imagine a cargo packed into the hold of a ship, bound for a strange voyage.

The souvenirs of Christ touch each other: the Praetorium, the Upper Room, the Houses of Anne, and Caiaphas-Golgotha. Then one understands better how one should visualize the comings and goings of the Passion story: as zig-zags in a very small perimeter. One sees what these palaces, that mob, that confusion, must have been like. One sees and senses the places which Jesus loved and where he rested. The hill which starts at Olivet, and dies away at Bethany. This Mount of Olives is strategic in a sense, the meeting-place of three landscapes which were in a sense the three dimensions of the work of Jesus. To the East, the world, the universe; to the West, the town, the city, history; in fact, to the East the future, to the West the past. And, at the highest point where Jesus chose to raise himself up, the sky.

A Visit to the Temple. Now a mosque, the Temple is a jewel of gigantic proportions. The dominant colour is blue-green, which has the peculiar brilliance of glazed pottery. There on a vast scale is the world of the cabinet-maker, of the stone-carver; it is a jewel made up of innumerable jewels, all somewhat complicated and fanciful, a perfected art which displays the skill of the craftsman far more than any religious idea like St Peter's. It is not surprising that beauty and preciosity are to be seen also in details and in the details of details. The windows in particular belong to mosaic rather than to painting. They are precious transparent stone (more than glass) incapable of taking a design and thus are suited to a religion which allows no images. The only things which one is allowed to copy or imitate are vine branches with stylized leaves, and the Arab writing which in itself is a subtle decoration, with its scrollings, its sudden and complex twirls.

The dome, so wonderful in its proportion and colouring, covers a large shapeless rock, which is the top of the mountain, and a holy place, sacred alike to Jews, Moslems and Christians; it is thus the pivot of monotheism. There Solomon built a temple in the Egyptian style; in it all was pagan except for the presence of God. The true God appeared in emptiness. The emptiness apart, it was a sacred slaughterhouse. Priests with huge knives, bleatings, bellowings—not at all what we hear about in our sacred histories.

Arbitrary divisions

1st JANUARY 1953

Many of our divisions are arbitrary. They say that there are four seasons. I know only two—summer and winter with transitions which one can multiply. Pre-spring and post-autumn have very distinct qualities. They say that there are three virtues, faith, hope and charity. But is hope really distinguishable from faith? Is it not faith applied to the future? Aristotle said there were four virtues: temperance, prudence, justice and fortitude. But temperance is only fortitude applied to the body in the form of discipline. They say that there are four Gospels. I know two. The Gospels which are called Synoptic, and the Gospel of St John. They say that there are Ten Commandments. But Christ reduced them to two. He even said that these two were one.

Saint Peter and Saint Paul

The artisan of Galilee who, through *seeing* alone, became in a short time fundamental man. The Apostles—apart from Peter, John and Barnabas—what did they do? What churches did they build before their martyrdom? What do we know about them? The 'tangential' Paul, the former persecutor, who had not seen Jesus in the flesh, and had not been taught by him, operated far more effectively and understood more profoundly.

I have often observed the effectiveness of tangent-like action; the last minute which reveals everything—after one has struggled for hours, sudden and sidelong inspiration; attentive pupils who remain apathetic while you lecture to them for months on end; then a meeting with a young man, not a student of yours, who understands.

It is no great matter to be in the right

15th JANUARY

My uncle said to me that when a married couple make reciprocal concessions, the shares are never equal; one gives three-quarters, the other gives only the remainder. He claimed to have given the three-quarters, and so to have found peace. This reminded me that, a little time before her death, my mother read as wise counsel to my brother and myself this saying of Madame Svechin: 'It is nothing much to be right, to be in the right. True peace of heart is, at need, to forget this.'

When one sees family quarrels over an inheritance, endless, irreconcilable disputes over a clock in a share-out in which everyone thinks himself to be the injured party, one says to oneself that the prudent thing is to agree in advance to take the worst part; it is really the best part; and as time goes on one realizes this.

Concessions are not reciprocal. And it is impossible, when two lives are linked, that one should not contribute more than the other. Even in the best assorted ménages there is one who is more devoted, who gives up more than the other. This is seen in alliances between nations, in which one supplies money and the other blood. Paul and Peter are pillars of the Church. Paul said that he had worked harder than others. And no doubt he was right to say it.

I picture two people who love each other. They have to decide on a walk. I am sure they cannot both like the same road equally, and that one of the two will make the decision out of love for the other. In a good marriage each appears to prefer the way which he or she does not like; this mutual deception makes for good feeling.

There is no life shared between two or more without this practice of yielding. And it is a good thing to tell children that equality of shares does not exist, even in a strawberry tart. The seats in a railway carriage are not the same. And how can one divide up furniture without someone seeming to gain? For a clock is not worth the same as a console, and there may be a pedestal table which has a great sentimental value for you, yet it goes to your brother or cousin. The chicken, with his drumsticks, his wings and breast, is, according to equalitarian rules, an indivisible bird.

In days gone by good manners required that distinguished guests, whoever the first served, should be polite enough to take the worst portion. The advantage went to him who was served last. What a splendid idea! That the most favoured by fortune should come off worst! For him the drumstick and glory! For my small self the breast!

It is best to be where envy does not look sideways at one. At least one's conscience is easy because one is not doing anyone an injustice. Every time one gets some coveted promotion even though by merit (luck helping) a whisper inside one suggests that the place may have been filched from someone equally deserving. Or again, if one receives an honour, the same voice tells one that the ribbon honours others in you, your faithful subordinates, or those poor soldiers who were killed under your command. To choose what no one else wants is to safeguard that peaceful estate, a clear conscience.

It is the same thing in conversation. I do not like having the last word. I find it awkward to prove to someone that he has failed to see or understand, that he is ill-informed and, even more fatuous, to say: 'I told you so.' I think, indeed, that to say 'no' to someone is almost like calling him a liar. And to say in the American way 'OK' or even 'oke', as many do (shades of the *langue d'oc*) is to agree too resonantly.

Shares are rarely equal, and we are never grateful for receiving the larger amount. We groan when we get the lesser. We do not worry when the errors of the cash desk are in our favour. When somebody gives me too much change I take no notice, but I have often claimed on too little. We grumble at the tax inspector who makes us pay extra. But it never occurs to us to discharge some tax which is owing, but for which we have received no claim. To justify these thefts one says to oneself that they offset the many times we've been deceived, robbed, exploited; this has happened so often that surely now we may enjoy a little hidden laxity! The French reason in this way in relation to the State, and their religion does not enlighten them about it.

I think that it is better to be like my uncle, and to resign oneself in advance to giving more and getting less, to being a bit victimized, to give way just a little more than one's partner.

Where no grave injustice is in question, peace is a greater good than wrangling, and advantage is destroyed if it gives a handhold to jealousy. In an unenvious society as was apparently that of the Middle Ages, nobody was worried by a too conspicuous privilege—a tower, a turret, a gable on the street. In our time one really feels that any over-obvious superiority is acquired at someone else's expense, as in the sharing of strawberry tart.

Above strict justice stands grace. And without this idea of making concessions, which is the soul of grace, even justice is not just. For often one seeks justice from the motive of possession and to maintain one's right to have what is due to one. Wars start with the wish for that sort of justice. May humanity perish if I do not avenge my own death, if I do not get the acre which is mine!

I am well aware that what I am advocating is scarcely feasible. Even if one is not careful for oneself, one becomes so for one's friends. Concessions which one could make if one were alone in the world, one refuses as father, husband, as party member, as citizen, or European. As mayor one makes claims for one's commune, as a mendicant friar for one's congregation. Nevertheless, it would be real wisdom and a source of contentment for oneself and for everyone else if one could say right away: 'I resign myself to being the one who will always agree to take a little less in the share-out, and to give a little more in service.' Joy is hidden in the infinitely little. But how far I am from putting this into practice!

Doubles

Goethe seen through Eckermann's eyes, Napoleon through those of Las Cases; Socrates by Plato. And, lifting the situation abruptly into the infinite, there are the Gospels, in particular the Gospel of St John. Maybe in this Gospel there are two Johns: the survivor, the Beloved Disciple, of whom it was said as he passed by: 'Will he die?'—and the editor of the Gospel, younger, Hellenized, and perhaps called John as well.

Recently while writing my *Dialogues with Monsieur Pouget* I think of these texts which I call duplications, in which one sees some person in perspective reflected in the eye of another and I say to myself that however lovely a thing may be, it is more beautiful still when it is described and reflected. In the same way, however precious a thing may be, it is still better after it has been bestowed.

Does the witness-echo go further? Does he blend himself with his model? Perhaps there are texts which seem simple but are double; the master and the disciple, the general and his chief of staff, a king and his minister? And the minister himself blended with some unknown person.

Reading Lory's book about Léon Bloy: Bloy lived in eternity, but he made a mistake every time he tried to incarnate the eternal in the present; that is to say, every time he dated, named, designated. And as he planned, named, dated almost incessantly . . .

Legend and invective are the easy way!

Moulding and modulating

Don't *model, modulate.* Cézanne's saying expresses what I must try to do in this Journal. Not mould my ideas as statements or as arguments, not elaborate or highlight them, but modulate them, that is, hear them in myself and for myself alone, like inner music which comes near to poetry or prayer.

Cézanne said also: 'I like above all things the expression of those who have grown old without violating custom, and who have accepted the laws of the age.' I ask myself why the stuff of time does not fall apart, why the specks of space do not lengthen, why living species remain the same, and why I have been the same for fifty years? There is, I say to myself, something which keeps everything together, and which is evident in time as well as in space. I call this force God, in so far as it gives number, permanence and proportion. A stabilizing force analogous to patience.

Reading Baudelaire

Reading Baudelaire in the *Pléiade* edition. On hashish and *artificial* paradises, attained only by the body. Baudelaire describes what would happen to all our occupations in such a state (the vision of an earth-bound mystic), what grammar would be, and how one would see the noun, adjective, and, above all, the verb; the depth of space—image of the depth of time; what colours and sounds would be like. And also how one would find a love, not restless and exacting, but a Buddhistic and absolute benevolence. What a temptation to get all that at will by taking in a few breaths!

And the painter Constantin Guys, whom he calls Monsieur G, he is the very pattern of the amateur. He began at forty-two without a master, without preparation, like a savage or a child. He made masses of daubs without ever finishing them, to amuse himself, solely for his creative pleasure. He was unknown, he had no one to follow, to satisfy. Some of his sketches he did again, putting an outline around them as in stained glass; or he worked them up to an outlandish beauty. Thanks to his curiosity he was in advance of the taste of his time. He was the herald of Picasso and Matisse. But, for Baudelaire, Delacroix represented the eternal in art. And Baudelaire tried to combine in what he regarded as his amateur talent 'Monsieur G' and Delacroix.

Sheep

Like Solomon I was watching sheep at midday. Beside the trees they looked like stones or marble statues. Not frightened. The impression of profound stupidity (typical of many faces) came from the absence of forehead, and the fixed perpetual smile. No gaze or movement of expression. It was the true picture of the animal, and an impression of gentleness emerged from it.

Earthy bodies. The colour of pale ochre and a harmony between these faded tints and the orifices which are pale pink. A very few sheep are lying down. The rest seem not to have enough spirit to take a seat. This is the ultimate lack of initiative, the antipodes of savagery. Together they mirror the idea of tranquillity, like vegetable nature, or some utterly impassive women.

Victor Hugo's destiny

Am reading the Life of Saint Solomon (*Victor Hugo* by André Maurois).

A man whose courage and virility recall the Old Testament. Author of a Bible. I imagine the opposite. Hugo starting with vague socialism, free verse, attachment to the Emperor, then to the King, then religion, chastity, childhood, and ending up with pure prayer. The funeral of the author of *Notre-Dame de Paris*, not in Notre-Dame!

But was there ever a more abundant verbal genius: one hundred verses in place of ten, ten words for one, dimming his power of choice. Old and cherished rules kept him a Latinist, often a Virgilian. Victor often triumphed over Hugo. In prose the method was nothing more than antithesis, which alas! has not a discipline comparable to that of rhyme!

One cannot say that he lacked intelligence, judgment, dignity, courage, nor even piety. But there is a certain way of being intelligent, sensitive, dignified, and strong, which I value far above his way: that deriving from either pure scepticism or true religion. Hugo, in my view, remains common; the mind hides, the echo dominates. In Goethe I see more culture and more piety. Hugo would make a gnostic of me; he gives me the impression of a fallen angel, a particle of spirit fallen into wealth and slime and one who makes a bad job of extricating himself, in spite of desperate efforts and some sublime successes.

Perhaps he was out of his time? The French language had been set. His age should have been one in which language was to take shape. He felt himself to be a creator. But in the nineteenth century one created by way of science or criticism; Renan and even Michelet realized this.

Hugo thought that he could be creative in politics—cloud-cuckoo-land! At fifty-one he gambled on the Coup d'Etat. Was it a risky bet? It was a Pascalian bet, a true wager in which he who loses gains infinitely. For if Hugo had lost—I mean if Napoleon III had lasted, with his borrowed glory—Hugo would have lost nothing. He had his Ferney. He had his Patmos. And no doubt as he himself realized confusedly ('This evening the sun has set in cloud'), his work would have been purer if it had lacked the triumph which clouded it. It would have ended in an Apocalypse.

Madame de Sévigné

I am rereading Sévigné. And I am struck by the almost primitive vitality of the human species in that century which had scarcely emerged from the sixteenth century, and from

those barbarous days when on going to bed one never knew
if one would wake up again safe and sound. Montaigne lived
in this insecurity; it did not vanish until Henri IV, to reappear from 1790 to 1800, and again in 1944, and it will
perhaps return. Shall we be able to adapt ourselves to it?
The people of the seventeenth century, the men and the
women, have a horse-like look to me (those long noses, such
as Condé and Pascal had). They are so sturdy, vital, un-
tiring and intrinsically devoid of anxiety. It is the *Iliad* still
going on; not yet the human *Odyssey*, which heralded
Fénelon and the eighteenth century.

III

The castle of despair

The month of February brings back for me as for many ex-prisoners the memory of those days in 1945 when we were flung out on to the roads among the Gestapo and were caught between the Americans and the Russians.

This advance, during which I nearly died several times, resulted in a visit to the citadel of Colditz. Colditz is an old castle in Saxony which after having housed kings, fallen women and madmen, was turned into a reprisal camp. In it the Germans shut up the 'unconquerables' as they were called in an English film about Colditz. Chance, not merit, brought me there with some unfortunate Frenchmen on an evening in February 1945.

There is no such thing as an insurmountable barrier, a hopeless situation, a prison from which one may not some day escape if only one has patience to wait for the moment which does not come twice and which must be snatched on the wing. In the last war Colditz was the 'model fortress', the camp from which no one could ever escape. It was designed to prove that a prisoner well guarded, according to the methods of the Third Reich (which respected the Geneva Convention), could not get away, expert escaper though he might be. In Colditz the mighty Reich shut up its least fragile and most valuable possessions. Here was its treasure chest of gold, its trading reserve. And here perhaps lay hidden the ultimate weapon of revolutions and revolutionary wars—the weapon of despair: the massacre of the hostages. This was the shadow on the place—in fact it was an ennobling shadow, for under it every man relied less on his own strength than on the strength which he imagined to be in someone else.

There amongst other legendary heroes was the famous English airman, Bader. He had lost both his legs while flying, had been made prisoner on landing, had attempted a first escape and been recaptured. The Germans then moved him from one camp to another, and ended by sending him to Colditz, where his brother aviators dropped artificial legs on the camp.

Because of its central position Colditz became a symbol. It was the centre of the subject world, whose circumference passed through Brittany, the Pyrenees, the African desert, the Urals and Norway. There were about six hundred kilometres to cross in every direction before arriving at a frontier.

The fortress had medieval defences, as well as others; five successive enclosures, glacis and escarpment; loop-holes each fitted with a searchlight, illumination of the walls by night; and police dogs. And there was every modern resource in the event of escape: the telephone, the radio, and, failing helicopters, little spy-planes.

It should have been quite impossible for anyone to escape from Colditz. The digging of tunnels was impossible because of the rock on which the castle stood.

But it is just when a thing is impossible that it becomes feasible. No guard is always on the alert. He is relieved. He is not always the same person. Whereas a prisoner is always on the alert and is always the same person.

There were many escapes from the citadel of Colditz and one in particular which was among the most extraordinary feats of its kind. It lacked nothing in audacity, simplicity, surprise, the fearful risk of death astutely calculated, irony, a

77

chivalrous spirit on both sides and number and quality of spectators.

Lieutenant Lebrun decided to escape for the fourth time. He made a small bundle of his wretched clothes, and carefully addressed them to: 'Tenth Dragoons, Orange (France). Please forward.' This first step taken, he went off one fine morning, how I do not know. He was soon recaptured, and the German General commanding the fortress gave him champagne in the Commanding Officer's room before sending him to the isolation cells. In his cell Lebrun did not waste his time. He attained complete sovereignty over his body. One day while the prisoners were being exercised—in accordance with the rules of the Geneva Convention—outside the fortress in an enclosure which was surrounded by high wire, which was itself enclosed in a park surrounded by high walls, Lebrun pretended to play leap-frog, and, helped by a friend who gave him a leg-up, took a flying leap over barbed wire which was twice his height. There was still a wall to cross. Lebrun had calculated that the startled guards, after calling out the regulation summons, would fire at him, but would aim badly, and that while they reloaded he would have time to leap this wall. He therefore refrained from climbing this park wall at once. Like a hunted panther, running in zigzags, sometimes falling flat then leaping up again, he considerately offered a target to the sentries till they had exhausted their ammunition. This was where he showed the most remarkable intelligence, foresight and courage. After he had counted all the bullets, as one might count the trumps in bridge, he climbed the wall while the German sentries were rearming. They tried every means of recapturing him, they even used aircraft but they never found him. The German Colonel had his parcel of clothes forwarded to Orange (France).

A change of camp brought me to this fortress in February 1945. The Germans had evacuated our camp which was too close to the Russian frontier. After a gruelling march of one hundred and fifty kilometres, exhausted and almost starving, herded and goaded like animals by the rough Hungarian Gestapo, our wretched column arrived at the walls of the citadel.

I was to discover that it had been a royal residence of the Princes of Saxony, in particular of Prince Augustus; that Marshal de Saxe had been born here and Napoleon had slept here on his way back from Moscow; in 1870 French officers had been imprisoned here; and also the castle had been used as a lunatic asylum.

On the night of our arrival we had to climb a spiral staircase of eighty-two steps, which brought us to an empty room. I felt happy. At last, here were real and very thick walls. This marked the end of hut civilization. We were in a building older than any human span, which had sheltered others before us and would shelter generations to come. To me it seemed the difference between an oak and a birch tree! One felt that a maternal hand of stone protected one against the elements. As for windows, there were grilles and bars, which gave an outline to everything one saw through them. From our height the courtyard of the citadel looked Lilliputian. Microscopic men went round and round like rats or guinea pigs shut up for experimental purposes. A strange citadel whose successive enclosures, surrounding and enveloping each other like the husks of fruit, provided so many resting places—so many 'celestial mansions'.

Now we really lived the classical life of prisoners. Feelings and opinions from the depth of time surged up within us. Our barbed wire cages in the open country, our low barracks with searchlights, had been more like Roman camps. It had looked as though I was to have five years of captivity and never see a rampart, or the kind of spectacle which it frames. Now nature and the open countryside, as well as men, were imprisoned, being always cut up and presented to one's view in bits and pieces; it gave them a beauty of appearance which was restricted and wide at the same time. The sky, particularly, is magnificent seen through such a network. From the courtyard at Colditz one could only see the middle sky—that part which is never cut by a horizon. On fine days —which were infrequent in March—the cobalt blue of the sky flashed out between the dark bars, and the clouds which passed obliquely at one speed, in one direction, seemed like migratory creatures; one could happily endow them with some awareness, some protective glance in our direction, as one did the allied aircraft which passed this blue embrasure. If one went up into the attics, one could see through the skylight, the undulating Molde in the middle of fields which, in its silver greyness and its nonchalance, reminded the English university men of the Isis at Oxford. When we heard the sound of bombs falling on Leipzig or Chemnitz (a sort of drum roll) the English crowded to the window with cheerful shouts, as if they were watching a match and their side was winning. This saddened the Reverend Mr Heard, who told me that every year he preached, as a duty, a sermon on respect for one's enemies, but it never had any result. He told me, however, of a British characteristic very different from ours. An English officer, a prisoner at Colditz, got a letter from the captain of his Golf Club asking him to lend the key of his locker to a German officer, a prisoner in England, who wanted to play golf. The Englishman refused. And then heard that he had been expelled from his Golf Club.

At Colditz, aristocratic and military celebrities were pointed out to us, as though we were at the seaside. Amongst others was General Bor, Count Komorovski, Commander-in-Chief of the Polish Secret Army, who had launched the relief of Warsaw; a cultivated, unbending cavalryman, who always wore gloves.

Captain the Master of Elphinstone was a cousin of Queen Elizabeth, whom he resembled in good looks. Seeing me without provisions, he invited me to eat a pudding of his own making. While cutting it, he casually inquired what this École Normale Supérieure really was: several French professors boasted so strangely of belonging to it.

I tried to explain it to him in front of our fellow-prisoners, who were vaguely looking at the pudding. 'Ah yes, I see,' he said, helping me first; 'it is a school which is superior, but which is not at all normal.' Then he told us, taking great care not to hurt our feelings as Frenchmen, this piece of family history. His great-grandfather had been wounded and taken prisoner at Waterloo. He was brought to Napoleon who had him looked after by his own doctor, and even lent him his carriage. The father of the prisoner, who was then President of the East India Company, had ordered in Canton a set of chess-men carved in ebony and ivory bearing the letter N and the Imperial crown, and sent it addressed to the Emperor Napoleon, Saint Helena. Sir Hudson Lowe returned the parcel with the remark: 'I have no prisoner of the name of Napoleon, only a certain Bonaparte.'

There were, with Elphinstone, six English officers set aside as hostages, who were known as the *Prominente*. Amongst them were Captain Lord Haig, Lieutenant Lord Lascelles, the nephew of George VI, and Lieutenant Michael Alexander, nephew of the Field Marshal.

Field Marshal Haig's son gave me lessons in water colour— that moist art which reminded him of his native Scotland. He taught me how to paint flowers and fabrics, how to mix colour with water, and how to direct a drop with the brush, as though with a magic wand. He told me that his ambition was to be able to leave the Army before long, and to live among the painters of the day in Paris. One day he spoke to me about likenesses. He said that in a portrait the most difficult thing was not catching the exterior likeness. One got that by drawing. One had to bring together all the aspects, resemblances, and contradictions of one man, and from them make a new picture different from any likeness fortuitously seized, and also from what the man imagined his own face to be like . . . Haig wanted to forget that he was a son. The glory of his inheritance was a burden to him.

Lord Hopetoun was a tall young man with fair hair. He came straight to the point. He had written his ideas in fifty-two notebooks which he was summarizing so as to get them down to six. Once Lord Hopetoun had a dream in the early hours of night, in which he thought he had gained control of the universe and found the key of all things. It was a very simple idea. 'I saw,' he said, 'how everything goes in pairs of opposites, which succeed each other rhythmically, and saw that it was necessary to bring them all together, omitting none.' Lord Hopetoun attached so much importance to this idea which had come to him in his slumbers, that he felt himself relieved of all anxiety and of any need for further research.

Lord Hopetoun did not have the same kind of education as our French intellectuals. He was ignorant of many things —in philosophy of practically everything—and this gave him a sense of wonder and the capacity to form conclusions which were truly his own. If one told him that something which he had discovered the night before had been said a hundred times already, and was in every syllabus for the French Baccalauréat, he would reply: 'Really?' and wasn't in the least put out.

With Lord Hopetoun was Giles Romilly, a young man of forcible and rugged appearance such as one often sees in our Protestants of the Cévennes—those sons of the *Camisards* brought up in the wilderness on the Gospel. In spite of his youth, Romilly had almost grey hair. His furrowed face gave an impression of weakness conquered and of suffering. It was impossible to say whether this came from bodily privation or from mental struggle. He alone, in this huge camp of disarmed soldiers, had no uniform; in the mornings he wore a large brown dressing-gown. I was struck by the purity of his French pronunciation which was almost like ours, even in those sounds which are nearly impossible for English throats. He told me that his ancestors were French Protestants, as I might have guessed from the French name of Romilly. Giles was not a 'prisoner of war'. When thoughtlessly I asked him where he had been 'taken', there was a sudden silence among his friends. And he said: 'It is a very sad story,' a little like Aeneas when Dido questioned him on his life: *Infandum, Regina, jubes renovare dolorem* . . . I learned later that he had been 'captured' at Narvik. He was correspondent of the *Daily Express*, and was in a hotel during the fighting. He wanted, he told me, to know the taste of death. He went to see and was captured. Two hours later the Germans learned that he was the son of Mr Churchill's sister. He had fought during the war in Spain with the Reds. The English spoke freely of Churchill; they recognized his defects, but they also knew that these defects were absolutely necessary for the salvation of the country. They readily enumerated what was non-English in Churchill: his lively, daring imagination, his adventurous flashes (the opposite of 'wait and see'), his caustic tongue, his indifference to contradicting himself. He alone, he said, was able to rouse his countrymen from their sleep.

I recall Romilly breaking into a talk about poetry, for he was admirably informed in every way. When he did not know something, he had the grace to say: 'I have not read it —I do not know it,' even when it was a matter of people and works about which it is unforgivable to be ignorant. By this he gained stature in my sight. (R. M. Rilke confessed to not having read *Hamlet*.) Romilly described style as the continual correspondence of sound and sense, a marriage of thought with verbal matter, which required the development of a high degree of sensibility in a language, in its resources, its dimensions and its depths. I said to him that England was the land of poetry, while France was the land of prose. Prose, to be brought to perfection, demands a language of the kind that chance has made of French, something not too weighty, not saddled with susceptibility to be enriched by new words, or the capacity to invent them; musical without being sing-song or sonorous, muffled and made as it were unobtrusive by the number of mute sounds, and all that is unaccented; monotonous; furnished with many abstract words which, through use by educated people, have acquired a sense which goes far beyond their specialized meaning. All these conditions favour prose, which is ordinary speech, the accompaniment and translation of our interior monologue, as one observes it in Montaigne, Voltaire, Renan, or Gide. Whereas the very strict discipline of French verse makes it unsuited to poetry, at least for the kind of poetry which French verse can ordinarily and naturally convey. And when French verse lets itself go and defies discipline, it is always with a bad conscience or with the insolent triumph of revolt which makes poetic calm impossible.

Then we spoke of literature in its relationship to national life, to the education of a whole people. I suggested that we no longer have any popular literature and that as we go on developing there arises a divorce between art forms and forms which the masses are able to understand. Romilly related this to something more general: the changes in institutions and in behaviour which we see taking shape around us and which herald a new era in the world. It surprised me to see how universal this idea of a new age was; how it had taken root everywhere, including this *milieu* of young officer-prisoners (English, Polish and French) although they had never combined to give expression to it. According to Lord H the change affected only the physical world and the theory of knowledge, not morality and religion which on the contrary, without changing, were soon to experience a new Renaissance. *The Second Renaissance* was in fact the title of the book

Lord H was writing. In this book he said that he expressed himself as Tory and Conservative. This loyalty to a classical and Christian tradition, to common morality, he added, is what makes kinsmen of all the traditionally minded, all those who dread the rise of Communism, all those who want to work towards the ends common to their ancestors and to Christians. Not indeed by preserving these worm-eaten supports which crush the spirit of reform ('in this sense,' he said heatedly, 'the Conservatives are innovators as much as the others'), but by refusing to break with the tradition of reason, the legacy of morality.

Giles Romilly was of another cast of mind. He believed in changes so radical that they would reach to the deepest foundations. Such changes would certainly not destroy morality in the noblest sense of the word: sincerity, truth, honour; justice, the roots of self-respect and respect for others, friendship between man and woman. But they would attack everything in morality which arises from *nomos*, from law and the most seemingly sacred conventions: for instance, all that concerns domestic ties, the existing rules of behaviour between the sexes, the use of wealth, property, education, the aspirations and rites of religion; the conception of this world as imperfect and preparatory to another, the ideal of human duality and sin; in fact, all the superstructures which we have confused with real culture, real truth, because the whole of our education has been directed to passing them on to us, and impregnating us with them. One would be wrong to see these negations, these purifications as materialism. It was a reaction of the old world to call new doctrines materialist, to suspect or vilify them (as the Conquistadores did the stars of the southern hemisphere) by calling them bad names. We were moving towards a new universe impossible to define in advance, but in which the old categories would be transformed. Who knows whether the idea of good and evil, the conception of a conflict between body and soul (which we have accepted for centuries), would continue to exist? I am not sure whether GR went quite so far as this, but the expression of his face bore witness to the torment of all these problems. His mystical nature made him suffer more than the others from the perplexities of present-day youth, a youth which in this camp where physical and mental fear had anyway reached extreme limits of suffering.

The *Prominente* suffered, as we did, from overcrowding and from the fear born of great hope, the uncertainty of certitude. One had to plot to get hold of bones from which one sucked the marrow; to acquire nameless throw-outs such as a binful of peelings required negotiations and bribes. Several of the *Prominente* also ran the risk of hearing Colonel Prawitt say one morning that he was sorry but he must shoot them as hostages before evening, having received orders from Berlin to do so. For them each day was a new day gained from possible death. All the same, during this month of April 1945, in which we saw the coming of spring through bars, the Castle of Despair vibrated with hope. The bombs falling on Chemnitz and Leipzig shook its old walls. The Americans were drawing near. In this citadel filled with guards, where each day the famished prisoners grew paler but were in better heart, there was an upper room reserved for the Easter Mass and the clandestine radio. It looked out over the little town, the countryside, the nonchalant Molde meandering amidst the fields, the roads . . . one went up to it in the hope of seeing a tank.

What would they do with the hostages? Colonel Prawitt feared English reprisals, but still more the SS. He sent the *Prominente* off in the direction of Bavaria; they took the greatest risks. Romilly made a perilous escape; he has just sent me his account of everything in his fine book on the castle of Colditz.

When deliverance was at the gates of Colditz, the Germans, with a sort of irony, picked out some French prisoners from the earliest days, and sent them to the East, towards the Russians. I left the fortress; we had to cross the Elbe for an unknown destination.

The Finaly children

1st MARCH 1953

Amongst the many problems raised by the tangled-up Finaly affair—a real nest of trouble—one which requires the most serious thought is that of guardianship.

Who is my mother, and who are my brothers? Is my mother only the one who fed me with her milk, and in whose womb I slept for nine months of my life? Or is it she who wanted me; who fed me with the food of thought, and saw me through my physical ups and downs; who sowed in me the first seeds of thought; who saw my individuality blossom; who understood my first reactions? In cases—happily infrequent—in which events have disassociated these two births (those of natural and spiritual life), who is *truly* my mother, not in terms of possessiveness, but from the point of view of caring for me until I attain my majority and can decide for myself? It is self-evident that if the problem presents itself in the simplest form, if the first mother has merely given birth to the child, whereas the second has looked after it for ten years, one would leave the child with the second mother, as did the Assistance Board. Had Solomon proposed to cut the child in two with his sword, it would have been, I think, the second mother, who would have shuddered. And to her Solomon would have given the child.

In this affair which holds the impassioned attention of the public sitting in judgment, things are complicated by romantic circumstances, which future historians will find hard to understand. It will have to be explained to them that habits adopted in harsh times, which may necessitate deceiving the law, do not end as if by magic on the day peace is declared; that a conspirator remains one always to some extent, because there is pleasure in such hazards; and that in France since the expulsion of the religious orders and inventories of the goods of the Church, no one has ever thought it wrong to by-pass an unjust law under the protection of a sacred cause. I am not trying to assess whether such an attitude is a reasonable one. I have known many good people who have upheld it.

But above all these cross-currents, I see clearly that the problem of guardianship has not received—under French Law—all the modifications which justice demands. It is tragic that, after great catastrophes such as our revolutionary wars, children should be deprived of parents, whether dead or vanished. The spontaneous generosity which appears in such a case does human nature great honour. How ingenious it is, how patient, and long-suffering! Virgin mothers arise who derive their claim from strong affection. After present-day wars which kill off so many young men, one sees a strong upsurge of mother love amongst women who henceforth will have no home; young women who despair of finding a husband; one might call them nuns, living in the world without habit or enclosure, who are able to provide a gentle and individual upbringing.

After the war I lived for a year in a dedicated home in which two admirable spinsters brought up a Jewish boy. I admired the solicitude of these two sisters—a solicitude which was sometimes a little uneasy, and out of proportion compared with a mother's normal serenity. This helped me to understand certain aspects of the Finaly affair, in which one saw the excess of protectiveness to which feminine affection will go.

For a real mother derives her calm and authority from the fact that she knows she will always be the mother. The sisters of whom I speak were astonishingly self-forgetful. They knew quite well that the child would leave them, and I quoted to them Lacordaire's saying: 'It is a father's privilege to rediscover in his children his own ingratitude towards his own father, and by this means eventually to attain a disinterested love, like that of God.'

Anyway, it is natural that when a legal and legitimate family becomes aware that one of its members has been adopted into another language or a strange religion (here actual baptism counts for little—a Christian guardian would necessarily tend to instil the wish for baptism, and the more she tried to hide it in her heart, the more the children would notice it), it is, I repeat, inevitable that the 'family' by blood and by right should reclaim its progeny. Problems of inheritance may arise. It is also a question of honour and loyalty to one's race.

What should be done? I do not know. But clearly there is here a triple problem: of justice, of humanity and of religion, and it is one that will not be resolved by the outcome of the present affair.

Alain liked to quote this dialogue between a pagan and a Christian who met a poor man to whom the Christian gave alms. 'So,' said the pagan, with no doubt a mocking little smile, 'you thought he was a god.' And the Christian quietly and seriously replied: 'No, I only thought he was a man.' The fact is that outside Christ it is difficult to recognize the Man in man.

The affair of these two children could have split France into two violently opposed sides. It is remarkable that it has been explored with heart-searching and yet peaceably, with seriousness on all sides. Judaism, Christianity, Catholicism, Resistance, Free Thought, all these different viewpoints have been put forward without excessive bitterness. Put the affair back to 1910, and you will get the measure of this change. To my mind the strength of the Catholic attitude in this matter has been that it concerned itself with the children as potential men—men who are *already* in a sense free and worthy of respect. It was also in asking the arbitrator, and before him the highest Court of Appeal, to say how, in this dispute, the two mothers should divide their rights to the best advantage of the future man. Solomon, as I have remarked, long ago took action in this way, and it won him a great reputation for wisdom.

Choses vues

APRIL 1953

Reading Victor Hugo's *Carnets* on the '1848' edited by H. Guillemin. Barrès was right to prefer *Choses Vues*, model of all that is best in his great books, as their prototype, rather than his *Cahiers*. I admit Hugo's love of words for their own sakes. He evaluates like an auctioneer! The play of words circles around him, and sometimes overwhelms and crushes him. In general the subject matter is poor. The dialogues degenerate into retorts; other people's are foolish, his own sublime. *L'ensemble peint*, said HG. Yes, but often by juxta-position; St-Simon was so much better. For with him there is the flow of time, the waters of the Rhône or the Rhine, not these pools, these puddles of light, these *choses vues*, but by lightning. Hugo has the capacity to record like a tape machine, a memory like that of the Polynesians or of Scotland Yard! And the need (which one also sees in Barrès) to reveal himself, to justify and nourish himself by contact with the masses; with folly or stupidity.

The Dead Sea Scrolls

Read Dupont-Sommer's book on the Dead Sea Scrolls. In them we see once again a persecuted leader; the hope of his reappearance; a community, initiations, repentance. But this belongs to all reformist sects which spring up. The essence of Christianity is in the historical fact, the reality, the humanity, and I would say with Paul in the mildness of Jesus. In Qumran I see rigorism, dualism, a horror of what is human, 'eternalism', the roots in fact of all institutional and doctrinal purisms. I sense the intransigence of a Spinoza or a Simone Weil. How much grace (in the double sense of the word) was needed to bend, to soften and to humanize this haughty Jewish race. Truly love is indeed absent from these fine Dead Sea texts. What is strange is that as contemporaneous (so they say) with the first Christian teaching, they seem to be wholly unaware of it. Walled up in their holy necropolis, they lived without a sense of apostleship and without love.

First meeting with Claudel

1st JUNE 1953 3 p.m.
11 *Avenue Lannes*

I saw him for the first time; also, as it turns out, for the last. I knew from a letter which he had written to me on the 9th of May that my two volumes on *The Problem of Jesus* had interested him although my work was far removed from his. We had corresponded on the problem of the plurality of worlds, about which he felt a strange dread. On the 9th May he wrote to me about *The Problem of Jesus*: 'I have found time to read your book on *The Problem of Jesus* from cover to cover. It gives me a better understanding of the depth and the extent of the mysteries on which our faith rests. Even a Christian feels a kind of interior panic when the extraordinary facts with which he makes contact through faith alone are crudely forced on him through the channel of reason. I was particularly interested in the views to which you have been led about the still unexplored regions of the after-life ... The visible leads to the invisible, but it is no less true that the invisible enlightens us on the visible ...'

When one thinks about the sayings of a dead person, they take on as it were two forms of existence. We possess them twice over. First is the human form, accompanied by a distant echo of the speaker's voice, and a few blurred glimpses of his face. But the departed seems also very close to one, an inaccessible angel with silent wings. One has the impression that he leans forward and watches one writing about him; that he smiles in an enigmatic way.

I knew that Claudel did not like visitors. ('I receive,' said the King in the *Soulier de Satin*, 'for the honour done to me, and not for pleasure.') And I knew too that I would not see him again: because of his great age, and still more because of my belief that there is nothing to be gained by seeing again, by reverting to, by hearing once more (even if he is a genius) someone who can only repeat himself and pick his personality to pieces before one, a personality which is always inferior to his work: for a man's work is finer than himself.

He spoke first against the study of sources as if this were something useless and wicked. I answered him: 'My dear sir, I myself can study you in your sources and look for the secret of your parturitions. And in my opinion you yourself have provoked such research by publishing the different stages of your work. Schiller said: "When kings build, the men with the wheelbarrows do the work." '

His face was not as I had imagined it. Pictures in the papers only show the human animal in repose or in his setting. When he heard my name his glum face lit up, and I saw a *man*: the face of a country priest, a man of the soil, with a clear youthful skin, no lines or wrinkles. A dark red tie, a light jacket, slippers. Today one very rarely sees an 'old' person. He spoke unaffectedly. Sometimes he did not hear well, and said: 'What was that?' Although he has spoken so much of rhythm and of breathing, his own voice has neither rhythm nor cadence. His voice is without inflections and does not seem to nourish itself in the world. The connecting system which links it with the world must have a stoppage at some point. Bergson panted at times, Claudel speaks nasally. In this quarter of the Bois de Boulogne I could not stop thinking about Bergson. The same rug over the knees. And on his face—indefinably—the same expression; bushy eyebrows, almond eyes half open, feminine, looking inward. Sometimes a fleeting mischievous smile. But Bergson was always mistrustful of himself and of his own candour. Claudel is completely self-assured. He did not attempt to conceal his faults.

Our conversation plunged straight on to the subject of the Bible; he told me he had studied it alone, without books or guides, and he accepted it as the Book of the Holy Spirit. He could not understand the work of 'wicked exegetists, like Père Lagrange'.

Instantly I remembered the studious Father Lagrange, with whom in 1935 I had spent two months in Jerusalem. Claudel's attacks seemed to me unjust; and I said so to him. He softened before my *pro Lagrangio*. 'While I get my breath again (for I become excited when I am speaking to you, and my heart is not as strong as my carcase), tell me how you met this Père Lagrange. The *Revue Biblique*, to which I subscribed for twenty years, did me great harm. And is there anyone crazier than that good Steinmann? The Book of Isaiah, which is obviously of one piece, the Isaiah which announces the Messiah in Chapter VIII, who describes him suffering in Chapter LIII, who defines the Church in Chapter LX—well, this exegetist wants us to accept an Isaiah that has been compiled, patched up, cobbled up, amalgamated by zero-Isaiahs, by sub-Isaiahs, by servants, by copyists, masterless disciples! Isaiah has disappeared. Nothing remains. If you don't mind my saying so, this is iniquitous! And it is the same with Job. Job said: "I know that my Redeemer liveth." These idiots translate Redeemer by *vengeur* or by *goël* which no longer means anything.' I tried fruitlessly to explain to Claudel that *vengeur* was the correct translation, certainly in every sense the soundest. He did not listen to me: 'I was reading St Bernard the other day. He had a grasp of the Bible. He sweated it out through every pore. St Thomas had already lost this sense. In St Thomas you will not find a single Bible text quoted in the allegorical sense as proof. He quotes sometimes, that I admit, but only to illustrate what he has already proved by other means. It is the same with St John of the Cross. I have never come across a mention of the Eucharist or of the Virgin . . .'

Then I tried humbly—like some shepherd on the slopes of a volcano which had suddenly become active—to defend St Thomas, to say that St Thomas, wanting proof to be based only on the text taken in its literal sense, had shown a rare enough critical spirit; that Père Lagrange had proved that the Scriptures are rooted in the very soil; and that Isaiah could have had disciples to carry on his work. 'Do you think,' he said, 'that these critical quibbles have converted one single soul? And count up on your fingers the souls which your friends have alienated, because they have lost the sense of the

Word of God—a sense which almost alone amongst Catholics I have worked to recover.' 'In that case,' I said, 'you should spew me out.' 'No, I will not,' he replied.

Claudel and Renan

'You will understand me,' he went on, gulping his words as though they were large nuts to be crunched, 'when you hear the experience of my life.

'Long ago, in 1883, at the Lycée Louis-le-Grand I was given a prize by Renan.' (He articulated the two consonants in a curious way: Reunnan.) 'First of all I listened to M Renan's speech, in which specifically he said this!—don't faint: "Barbarism is conquered for ever, because everything is tending to become scientific. Barbarism will never have artillery, and if it had it would not know how to use it." Then Renan gave me my prize.'

I could picture the scene for myself: the young Claudel, a sort of stocky bull, already resolute, and Renan in his chair, limp, sinuous, debonair, with his grey gloomy flesh, its subtle yet flabby folds looking like the human brain. Claudel found himself confronted by a mind which had not the same awareness as his own. It was as if man were to see another creature on his planet, a man who had other means of perception, and was sensitive to other wave-lengths and vibrations. He stood before his opposite, as though before a cross, the sign of contradiction, to which you are compelled to face up. It is good to be fathered by your opposite; to see yourself first in a form which is yourself inverted; to receive the stamp of your own image reversed. For you only have to think of Renan for a moment to see in him the denial, the nullification, of the whole of Claudel's thought. What Renan aimed at was total knowledge; he wanted a type which would include all others, which would be both this and that, which would embrace every opposite. His scepticism and apparent dilettantism were possibly other names which he gave to the impossible search for a being who would be everything at once.

This was the hope of a purist temperament, somewhat akin to Gide's, in whom Claudel was to meet a nature related to Renan's. Gide is more sensitive to antitheses. In him there is no unified outline, no continuity of evolution, no Celtic dream, no Greek rationalism. Gide corners Claudel like some demon emerging from Renan, a Renan for his personal use, whom he found at his side, who became his life's companion. For Gide also desired to know all, to understand all, to be all, and enjoy everything.

He also had impossible dreams of being simultaneously an angel and a beast, of not being obliged to recognize any division in the inner man. That is why Gide seemed to me a *Renan redivivus*. He had a certain inability to understand the Semitic idea of the antithesis between light and darkness, of good and evil, a desire to fuse and confuse everything, to believe that it was possible to enjoy every conceivable experience without doing damage to one's personality—that, on the contrary, making use of all things would enrich it.

With Claudel we are, from the start, on other ground. He begins with precise affirmations of Being. Perhaps he had resorted to some scholastic handbook of Time and Place before he spoke, and then by an alchemy, of which he was an adept, combined it with symbolism? But he gave a new meaning to these old scholastic words—one might say a physical and *pre-Socratic* sense. He unloads them. Or rather recharges them with what Plato had taken out by his idealism, and his tendency to empty words of their content.

Renan strips words bare, and disintegrates them by the way in which he modulates a sentence. (Gide exalts them and often gives them dithyrambic impulse.) Renan uses words in a conversational way. He *atticizes* them, in accordance with the genius of the French language and of French conversation which strips from words everything which good usage does not approve or which blurs them. The beauty of Racine's verse comes from this despiritualization of words, whose worth then lies in their cadence, their deadened timbre, their dissonances. La Fontaine's words, though they keep their earthy tang, are without colour. Everything becomes like a drawing or an engraving. Colour has gone. With Claudel (and I realized it the more as I heard him speak) words are used in their original primitive sense. From this point of view, the genius of his language recalls that of the Semitic tongue, which Renan understood so well, when he said that all words have concrete roots, that they portray gestures and movements of the body.

I asked him his impression of Renan. 'I will tell you very exactly . . . a pig.' (Later I read in Claudel: 'When you call someone a pig—a *cochon*—a lot of waves immediately start up.' But he had used the word in a descriptive, not a contemptuous sense. He called Renan a pig just as on the doors of cathedrals Saint Mark is often depicted as a lion, or Saint Matthew as a bull.) 'Renan wallowed in superfluous flesh, he had blank eyes and reddish eyebrows.' And when I seemed astonished by the *reddish* . . . he added: 'I do not say that he had reddish eyebrows, I say that they *appeared* red to me. Renan did me harm. When my sister and I came to Paris, we were Catholics by upbringing. We had our routine. We sometimes went to confession *grosso modo*. My sister gave me Renan's *Life of Christ*. I was overcome. We said to each other, my sister and I: "Why practise this religion which the learned believe to have no foundation? *Jesus never said that he was God.*" Now, after sixty years, your book on Jesus has given me the answer to Renan's book. That is why I am glad to meet you. You do not merely show that one fine day Jesus happened to declare that he was God. Neither do you say, as many do, that it is the faith of the Church which has made Jesus God. You show clearly, you prove fully, that Jesus in his hidden sayings never failed to put himself forward as God, and in a way that excludes all made-up legends.

'Rimbaud saved me. He made me conscious of a patch of sky, a breath of air. Something which for me did not exist existed once more. Rimbaud was my age. Rimbaud was my compatriot. Yes, I know it is said that he blasphemed. I do not deny that perhaps there were blasphemies. But do not let us confuse prophecy with holiness. The prophets are not saints. Their message is full of blemishes. It is like birth. Something new, pure, as yet unnamed and wild, springs forth, amidst blood and excrement.

'Rimbaud was my way to Our Lady. One more word about Renan.

'Even when I believed in Renan I did not accept him as a writer. One cannot be a writer if one makes it a rule to repudiate in the second half of a sentence what one has said in the first.'—'Fénelon?' I inquired. 'So be it. Fénelon may be like Renan, but does not mislead. Therefore he has a style. But let us close the parenthesis. Satan ruled in my mind. Until the Virgin reigned there. She allowed me to do God's work. Her genuflection taught me obedience.

'After the tidings brought to Mary everything was changed. And evil which until then had splintered life became an instrument of incalculable good.

'My books spoke unceasingly of the Virgin, and that is why I have not devoted any particular work to her. After her there was no more evil, because Satan became the instrument of the greatest good.'

I thought about Claudel, for I am so constituted that, for spiritual insight, I need presence and contact: 'He has the spiritual quality of being unjudgable by anyone and of being judge of all. He has a sensual manner—sensitive, complete, shocking, anarchic, splendidly Catholic. He is the very opposite of those, so numerous in our time, who have a Christian, chaste, wise, healthy, rational, refined, pleasant, gentle and reasonable way of being atheists. Here he crosses swords with Renan or Gide and transfixes them.'

I listen to the broadcast of the ceremony of the Coronation of Queen Elizabeth. If there is no supreme power higher than the Established Episcopacy it is a vicious circle. The King appoints the Archbishop who crowns the King. Without Papacy, can there be true consecration? There is the grace of this young Queen; the mystery of woman in her; the mystery of power also. This coronation introduces us to the feminine myth, that of the abbesses who ruled monasteries of men. This is understandable, for the more power is held to be sacred, the more does it appear as transcending human frailty, as for instance in the person of a powerless or a mad King—still more so in the person of a woman, of a young Queen.

What does this mean for the masses of today? Is it a recall or a symbol? We in France no longer have the feeling of succession nor therefore of deep-rooted loyalty. With what can we replace them? This Abbey of Westminster is the only place which still incarnates the idea of a sacramental coronation. It is strange how a great silence falls upon the whole world in order that it may follow such rites.

One never knows what is seed and what is dust

Hugo tells us that he kept a box for rough drafts, in which he put papers, bits of verse, shapeless nebulae, embryos near hatching.

He jotted things on the first bit of paper to hand, the backs of that morning's envelopes, a page torn from a notebook. And sometimes he pierced them (as they pierce the ears of dead warriors) and threaded them on a string.

This is the way of a mind which never comes to a standstill . . . which cannot know beforehand what matters and what does not matter, what is seed and what is dust. Fundamentally everything is seed or dust according to the use which is made of it. And in poetry above all, here an image of life itself, a lost verse, a spoilt picture, is often the first stage of a stroke of genius. There is no gap between chaos and order; and a stroke suddenly spans the infinity between discord and beauty. Sometimes absurdity is the threshold of truth.

And this detritus can breed projects as well. It is a good thing to have plans, and a novel writer, like a War Minister, should have several plans. He can't tell in advance. There is freedom in the many perspectives between which choice is made at each moment. To choose one must have the abundant variety of a bazaar. That is why one must try to find three solutions for one problem. There is joy in this! One is aglow!

Reading 'Jean Santeuil'

5th JUNE 1953

Proust had had for a long time (without being aware of it) the knack of letting his thoughts flow gently, seriously and ironically over no matter what event or person. Behind his marionettes he prepared a backdrop seldom used by our contemporary writers: the combination of love and humour (I find this only in Alphonse Daudet, and even there at an experimental stage). Proust was preparing for it when he discovered his theme song by parodying himself. Here was 'the unhurried escape into things which do not call for genius'. What is missing from *Jean Santeuil*, which is a rehearsal, is *luxe, calme et volupté*: the indefinable sumptuousness, tranquillity, width and breadth ably unfolded and deployed, which Proust could create in his later days, and which is one of the hardest things to achieve. He already had the music, or rather the suggestion of it, but not the orchestration, that marshalling of his whole culture in the play of metaphor, which can be found in Montaigne and Shakespeare, although in a less organized form. Proust, so great a strategist in planing his work in long stretches, must have sensed something a little tenuous about his talent. He had to learn the art of 'wrapping up', the art of story-telling and the art of duration. It was an effort for him to acquire the ability to write copiously, like a woman, like George Sand for instance, or George Eliot. *Jean Santeuil* was a subconscious exercise, as was for the youthful Renan the 1848 manuscript of the *Future of Science*, his *purana*, which, he said, he should not have published after 1870. For one should not show full-length drafts. Like Proust's they should be, I won't say made into burnt offerings (that is too severe), but hidden away.

Here was naïveté, but a highly self-conscious naïveté. Here is the child genius amidst the blockheads. But the blockheads often produce very remarkable ideas, as M. de Norpois was to do later on. Proust gives me a feeling which as a rule one only gets from English novels, of the stuff of daily life, its slowness, its twists, the circumvolution of time, spiralling around for the man who remembers. It would have needed very little for this work on time truly to have embraced the real man, the common man; to have avoided getting bogged down in the sands; to have avoided the descent towards the sulphurous sea. 'A man went from Jerusalem to Jericho and fell into the hands of thieves.'

A strange page in *Jean Santeuil* is the one in which Proust tells how M. Beulier, Jean's teacher, said to him on New Year's Eve: 'I too have brought you a present.' This was Joubert. He read to him for two hours. Jean said: 'No present has given me greater pleasure.' Then M. Beulier took the book, put it into his brief-case, and never brought it back again. Then Proust tells us that M. Beulier, having given Jean all Joubert's meaning, all his soul, all his moral support, had given him everything. This was the pure and inestimable present, a gift that was entirely spiritual, a perfume, an essence which had not cost anything. It is true that one becomes inordinately fond of possessing the best, even of that almost immaterial possession, the memory of phrases or words in a beloved book. I see it in myself, for I know many passages by heart. M. Beulier shows us a higher way.

The colour of Paris

1st JULY 1953

The colour of Paris in summer, a soft black, not grey, so different from the hot ochre light of Rome, where the sun seems to be concentrated in the stone as if the walls contained some sort of chlorophyll which for centuries, since Numa Pompilius, had absorbed and held its golden rays.

In Paris the few Roman domes, such as those of the Carmelites, the Sorbonne, the Invalides, look like prisoners, imported, exposed, unhappy. The monuments of Paris seem to be poised on the earth, not emerging from it as they do in Rome, where they suggest a pagan subsoil in which Christianity grew. Paris lacks this pagan prehistory, which gives Rome so many undertones and such depth.

What then in spite of all this does one breathe in so happily in Paris? And why is it that Rome, London or Amsterdam pall quickly on me? This is hard to say in a few words. All French problems are very personal, very intimate.

In Paris nothing is overdone. No objects, however fine, demand one's attention. No more attention than would be given to a port, to an estuary or to something in nature, to a hill. The bends of the Seine and the Cité are like smiles on a quiet face. One knows they are there, and one no longer looks at them. One's attention is always driven back to oneself, this in the atmosphere of the Ile-de-France, which is half-waybetween mist and brilliance and so wonderfully designed to throw autumn and spring into relief—especially autumn which, to me, is the true spring of Paris.

Sin and literature

JULY 1953

It is a characteristic of contemporary writers that they enjoy describing sin. The truth is that art usually lives on the contemplation of sin. The ceiling of the Théâtre-Français depicts Comedy and Tragedy looking at Adam and Eve in the Garden of Eden, in front of the forbidden tree. But on this tradition, which may be a necessary convention, the literature of our day has placed a seal of its own. This seal consists in a sort of justification of sin.

Here again we need to reflect, to sum up, to distinguish. All drama is based on the idea of inevitability. The real tragedy is not that Oedipus killed his father and married his mother. It is in fact that he ended by committing his crimes without being aware of what he was doing, with hardly a qualm, because he was caught in the grip of circumstances, which gives the spectator an impression of inevitability. Oedipus is compelled, in spite of his apparent freedom and even within it, to conform to a greater design, which is a criminal one. The tragedy is that Oedipus does evil while obstinately searching for the good.

One can reverse this schema of ancient tragedy and suppose that the compulsion hidden behind history is a philanthropic will, benevolent, inventive, which in spite of every unlucky chance, in spite of the contrarieties of creatures, in spite of and through their mistakes, brings good out of evil. Since I have spoken of *Oedipus Rex*, which seems to me the supreme type and eternal model of classic compulsion, I will also recall *Le Soulier de Satin* which is, it seems to me, a drama of the compulsion of love, since in it even evil becomes an instrument for good—'a slave who draws the water'. It is true that in *Le Soulier* evil is touched but not reached. But *Le Partage de Midi* in which evil is achieved gives rise to the same observation. Here we have the *Felix culpa*; here we see the work of reparation. And this is the schema of the divine plan as we can see by reading St Paul, for God allows sin to ripen and rot on its own level, while he envelops it, outflanks it, and makes use of it on an eternal level.

What I am drawing attention to as peculiar to our present-day literature is very different from the Christian conception which inspired Claudel, and which is the spring of energy and of beauty as well.

I am speaking of the theory, the thesis, the aesthetic, latent in several contemporary writers, which seems to me false in itself, bad as a guide to conduct and also harmful to art. I have been struck by the fact that in several such works sin is represented as a means to salvation. One could quote works in which the urges of the flesh, adultery, despair, suicide, the rejection of ecclesiastical celibacy, and revolt, are represented not as aberrations contained in fate, nor as weaknesses arising from our infirmity and the conspiracies of chance, but as paths which lead to the fulfilment of the deepest vocations, the transformation of the self, and which are the gates to eternity.

The theme of the fallen angel (with that of lost innocence) is the finest basis for drama. In the nineteenth century the angel fell in order to cut himself off. But in our day it seems that the angel falls in order to reach heaven by a short cut.

Some thoughts of the same description on germane subjects:

It is assumed that it is better to err in company than to be good in isolation, cut off from one's fellow men. A soul, when it feels an impulse towards conversion, hesitates and draws back, reluctant to abandon friends who do not share its light. And we praise such scruples, seeing in them a more sensitive love. I am not here probing the secrets of conscience,

105

but I think it is strange to endorse the maxim that perfect love comes before truth. It is also said that it is better to sin in good faith and sincerely than to be half-way between good and bad, like the bourgeois, the mediocre, and indeed like most people; that all faults are equal; that there are not big and little lies; and that if one has not resisted temptation at the outset it is better to go on to the end because everything should be tried, and it is better to be Adam than Tantalus —Adam having occasioned the Redemption.

One is also told that the word suicide is ambiguous; that suicide can be a duty (to avoid giving away a secret); that a crime may also be a duty (doing away with someone who might reveal a secret). And that there are suicidal love-pacts which are akin to vocation, a way of attaining to God by a direct route.

Graham Greene, whose English temperament permits an alliance between casualness and faith, has shown most vividly the springs of such behaviour in which the reversal of God's plan becomes a maxim for mankind. He has pushed things to a startling extreme in *The Heart of the Matter* (it is indeed the root of the problem seen in human terms) in which Scobie profanes himself and commits suicide to find salvation.

If you look at these propositions, you realize that they fail because they try to extract from a particular case (one in which, however worthy of respect it may be, human frailty has played a part) a rule of general morality and virtue. This is something which should never be done in this world.

I feel keenly that the error of such ideas lies in transposing God's point of view to man's without making the necessary adjustment. It is true, a divine and transcendent truth, that everything serves the purpose of mercy—everything, even the greatest sins; and those already in the light of eternity, as at that last moment when we shall see history completed, are 'blessed sins' once they have been redeemed. *But it is a source of error to aim to transform into rules of conduct these long-term arguments which only hold good in order of the predestination of God.* For instance, it would be wrong to imitate Magdalen the sinner, or the Penitent Thief, in order to get into heaven before the righteous.

It is true that God sees everything, even the future. It would be wrong to let this inculcate fatalism—that is to say to do nothing on the pretext that 'everything is determined'. Everything is written indeed, but in divine handwriting. To interpret aright, 'everything is determined', I must act as though everything depended on my own effort, on my own free will. This transposal of the divine proposition into the human proposition rules our existence in time; it stands for the honour and the worth of our lives. Always, through an obscure hope which is no deception, we know that God watches us to the end. And it is so, more so even in the lives of Christians. We hold through faith the sublime idea that all things work together for good for those who love God. But from this divine maxim we must, like St Paul, draw the decision to work out our own salvation in fear and trembling, at the same time confident of success and perpetually vigilant. A wonderful combination, which it is impossible to express satisfactorily, but which gives life an uneasy yet triumphant charm when one knows that God loves one.

Our mind, however, tends to simplification, and above all to justifying even our misdeeds. Then it becomes very difficult, as Bossuet said, to 'hold the two ends of the chain', and to preserve simultaneously the power of God and the liberty of man. It is so tempting to put oneself already down here into the divine perspective—to imagine oneself at the end and, in spite of all vagaries, to equate maxims of human behaviour with the mystery of simultaneity and mercy. Such fatalism was a Jewish temptation; one can see it in Islam which is in relation to Israel a simplified heresy. Jansenism has been a temptation and a deviation in Christianity; it has fascinated many great minds. I seem to find traces of these ancient errors in the idea that aberration is the most direct route to God.

I shall be told that my criticism may be all right from the point of view of a metaphysical moralist, but that aesthetics do not involve such considerations; that the need to sin in order to be saved is a source of pathos and that, if it is true that beauty consists in 'surprising us by a fine excess', it can bring forth beautiful work. But I draw a great distinction between the necessity of sinning to save oneself and the idea which I have noted as inspiring Claudel. In Claudel man does not turn to evil that good may come. God remains the first and total cause which, while giving human freedom full play, either repairs the wrong done, or ingeniously halts it, as in the request which Dona Prouhèse made to the Virgin when she offered her her little shoe.

Beauty then makes its appearance because there has been no manipulation to change the rules of existence either in relation to nature or to grace. Sin can abound and superabound, but it remains in its own order. The essences are not confused.

One might say the same of Dostoevsky, where, in a Slav setting, man is thought of as reaching good by a road which passes through an excess of sin. 'The hideous toad,' said Claudel to Amrouche, 'suddenly becomes a kind of angel.' There is here just the abrupt mutation from brute to angel who until then was asleep.

Although he allows little play of freedom between these two magnets of the flesh and of grace, Mauriac also breathes the air of St Paul and St Augustine. This is not at all true of the works of which I have spoken. I cannot believe that they please solely because they are beautiful. I think it is because they seduce by becoming an accomplice to the crafty and sensual part of ourselves. Beauty must not connive if it is to enrapture me.

When a fine mind, friend to man and to being, a respecter of mysteries, perceives in the springs of a novel, a play, or an intimate journal, some pure error (which is worse than a gross one), then an emotional impact on his judgment prevents him from experiencing the 'fine excess' of which Keats spoke, the yielding to ceaseless surprise . . . That is an aspect of the danger which art runs in our time. In different ways it risks being put to the service of something other than art. In certain countries we see it used in propaganda; that is gross and recognizable. But one can also profane beauty by demanding that it should clothe us in a false innocence, as no doubt Adam and Eve dimly felt when they sewed fig leaves to cover their shame. Whenever art is used as clothing, it is no longer pure.

IV

View of a life and of a valley

Arrived about ten o'clock at La Pensée in the rain. Kant was
waiting for us at a turn of the road. The leafy countryside
looking specially lovely in the fine rain. Everything is more
beautiful veiled. And water is a veil of moisture and
fecundity, a silken web shaken by the wind. My countryside,
which is flat like a plain, has a woman's face, mournful and
gentle. It weeps and veils itself like destiny so as to give
an extra richness to the sun's smile which is no doubt in
reserve for me, and which will be once more the glory of this
holiday.

Last year I had to give a lecture at the Sorbonne on
Creuse, the countryside in which I grew up.

To begin with, what does this word *Creuse* mean? It was
first given to a river which hardly hollows out the ground
except for an occasional gorge. Should one believe the peasant
of my village who said to me: 'Where it is empty inside, it
sounds hollow'? Long ago one of my first teachers who was
a geographer and a poet in the manner of Lancelot, the
author of the *Garden of Greek Roots*, taught me to memorize
in verse *Quand la nuit vient, l'affreux chacal va d'os en os*,
which gave me an alarming picture of Normandy! Then
coming to the Creuse: *Creuse un profond sillon, tu feras bon
guéret* suggested labour in depth.

But I did not wish to speak of this *département* (Guéret)

for I want to speak only of what I know, and the older I get the more I see that I know very little.

Even an *arrondissement* is too wide a horizon! It is not my countryside. For anyone who lives on a given spot, far from any village, five kilometres from the nearest church belfry, the word 'countryside' means very precisely a circumference of five or six kilometres, drawn around a central point—your home. Pascal said that the world is a circle whose centre is everywhere, and whose circumference is nowhere. I would say that, like every man, I belong primarily to a countryside; in my case the centre is the Commune of Champagnat, in the place marked *Fournoux* on the Ordnance Survey map. This circle encloses and contains all living creatures 'after their kind' as Genesis says: men, animals, vegetables, rocks, also all the stars of heaven; everything inside a great circle of soil bounded by the hamlets of Puy-de-Mergue, Marambaud, Théollet, Épinasse, La Châtre, and Pont. The river Tarde crosses it. One might draw the circle wider and then within it there would be some churches: Lupersat, Saint-Sylvain, Bellegarde-en-Marche, Champagnat, Saint-Domet, and Mainsat. If it were further enlarged, about twenty kilometres away would be the stations of Aubusson and Auzances. In addition, or rather to be explicit, I will point out that this countryside like the Creuse of which it is the imaginary heart is in the heart of France. It is placed at an almost equal distance from the Arctic Circle, the Northern Hemisphere, and the Equator, and not far from the point where the meridian of Paris intersects the 46th parallel. Before we based ourselves on Greenwich, we based our calculations on the meridian O on the planisphere. Even maps of the world show the place of which I am speaking. So it is in a very central position, far from the sea and the mountains, far also from great centres of population and of culture. I am grateful to it for not having produced many great men. One is aware of this when reading histories of La Marche. The reasons suggested are odd. I have read that it was because there was no university. And I have read also that the Limousin Popes skimmed the countryside of its élite when they enlisted them for the service of the Church, in Avignon. Clement VI said: 'I will plant in the Church of God so fine a Limousin rose tree that after a hundred years there will still be buds.' And it is a fact that our people, because of their common sense, their humanity, and their sort of lively unconcern, make excellent administrators. They have the Creuse and Creusois characteristic of being neither this nor that, and of being at an even distance from almost every extreme.

Creuse is the country of the golden mean, of neither too much nor too little, and so is on a man-size scale. An eroded relic of primitive Hercynian strata, it was lucky in the Tertiary Period to be at a safe distance from the upsurge of the Alps which so altered the eastern parts of the Massif Central. And it has been only slightly affected by the volcanic upheavals which have given Auvergne its tormented appearance. In geological maps—authorities for the third dimension of depth in every countryside—I have always liked the garnet colour of the Precambrian, the lovely archaic red which is like rose petals with a little touch of the violet of the Juras.

Creuse remains a witness to far-away ages on this planet, to the ancient and long-enduring marriage of water and stone from which it derives its rather poor arable land of decaying granite, hard to work because it lacks depth, but which, scalloped with rivers, riddled with water holes, and magnificently green, provides landscapes 'full of grace and truth'.

In comparison with its sisters, Limousin and Bourbonnais, Creuse has a charm of balance and reserve and a sort of poverty all its own. In Creuse charm is born of the renunciation of beauty.

I have read in Felix Ravaisson's *Testament* that Leonardo

da Vinci held that every object in nature had its own way of curving, and that the secret of drawing was to reproduce this *serpeggiamento*. Ravaisson and Leonardo, and also Bergson and his daughter Jeanne who loved this definition, would have been happy in our country, because here everything winds: the pink roads, the trunks of the willows, indeed even the dry stone walls. And this Leonardo (whose name is so Limousin) would have loved as well as the *serpeggiamento* of the outlines, the moist colour due to the ever present rain, which gives so much charm to Creuse, and makes it an ideal country for painters of the school of Corot-Turner. It reminds me of a girl who has been weeping:

> *Mon enfant, ma sœur,*
> *Songe à la douceur,*
> *D'aller là-bas vivre ensemble:*
> *Aimer à loisir*
> *Aimer et mourir*
> *Au pays qui te ressemble,*
> *Les soleils mouillés*
> *De ces ciels brouillés*
> *Pour mon esprit ont les charmes,*
> *Si mystérieux*
> *De tes* (vagues[1]) *yeux*
> *Brillant à travers leurs larmes*
>
> *Là, tout n'est qu'ordre et beauté,*
> *Luxe, calme et volupté.*

Did Baudelaire guess that apart from the one adjective which I have altered, these verses did not apply to Holland alone?

Compared to Cantal celebrated by Malègue and Auvergne sung by Pourrat, Bourbonnais by Guillaumin, Jacques

---

[1] *Traîtres* in the original text.

Chevalier and Charles-Louis-Philippe, and beside Giraud-oux's Berry, Creuse is an enclave unknown, voiceless and echoless; this is because it is neither primitive nor wealthy. So here again it is at an *equal distance*. Poor. Ordinary. Earthy. Creuse! Nothing romantic. It is Attic, and the only prayer one could say before it would be Renan's before the Acro-polis, which I recited from memory in my youth:

> *O noblesse, O beauté simple et vraie.*
> *J'arrive tard au seuil de tes mystères . . .*

Pools here? Perhaps—yes indeed—but no devils in our pools, George Sand . . .

I would like to take you into the past. And I have chosen the date 1912 which, in so far as transport between station and village was concerned, was as old-world as the time of Louis-Philippe, in fact as the days of Charlemagne, King Numa or Rameses! In many ways the rural world changed more be-tween 1912 and 1952, than between 1952 B.C. and A.D. 1952. So let us consider 1912, look back before the atomic age, be-fore the world wars, even before the motor car, and at a spot remote from any railway.

One must remember that, as far as I was concerned, I re-discovered the Creuse each year when I left a part of the world which was its opposite. The mining town of Saint-Étienne, the black town, was my father's native place; Creuse was my mother's. Without entering upon Freud's learned and tiresome follies one might imagine that a mother, rather than a father, has the power of making her sons love her childhood's home. And again one might imagine that holiday places gain by comparison with the working places of winter. I attach far more importance to the last suggestion, which colours and which perhaps even distorts my feelings about Creuse. To me, the Creuse has always been a 'reward' (and in the exact definition of the term, which for a believer means the 'promised land') left behind, rarely 'possessed', except in what my mother called 'those visits to which memory alone leads us'.

For six months we would talk of going to the Creuse; our departure would take place about the 25th July—which was prize-giving day, at that time. Up to Montluçon we were still in France. But at Montluçon station, when I saw, at the platform marked *Direction d'Aygurande et du Mont Dore*, the engines of the Compagnie du P.O., I felt I had landed in another universe.

The single-track train was sometimes broken-winded, sometimes it speeded up and on the twisting gradients it made sounds like a moaning violin. After crossing the viaduct over the gold mines, and passing through various cuttings and high granite bridges about four o'clock in the afternoon, it expired at the station of Auzances. (This has hardly changed.) At Auzances an ancient hired cab engulfed us; it was very badly sprung, its windows rattled incessantly. There were two horses, as tired as we were, which, except when going down hill, were not allowed to trot, and there were our trunks piled on top, giving the conveyance the look of a skyscraper.

This went on for two hours. Eventually the light of the sun withdrew but the countryside continued to smile silently upon us. One was aware of the crowding trees and stone walls, the solitary fields. Then, at a bend, sculptured, milky white above a wood shaped like a dome, we saw the two un-symmetrical towers of Fournoux. For the last twisting kilo-metre we had lost sight of them, then there they were once more as though trembling a little with the joy of welcome. We lost them again as we went through the Fournoux woods, along an avenue from a fairy story. Then we arrived and my grandfather who had been waiting ten months for this, held us in his arms. To understand just what I felt I must tell you that I was alive and sensitive to mystery. I had been made to read the *Legends of the Middle Ages* by Gaston Paris, the novels

115

of Walter Scott, *Ivanhoe*, *The Bride of Lammermoor*, *Waverley*, those stories which Fournoux had in its bones.

The walls of Fournoux date from the thirteenth century. We heard of mysterious underground tunnels and were shown the entrances to dungeons. One might even see, and I once very clearly saw it—the ghost! Although we were welcomed by dogs, horses, cows, and ducks, the isolation of the place always made us feel, especially towards evening, an odd fear, an uneasiness at the dangers of the hours of darkness, which I have never lost in Creuse. I had a room hung in blue, to which we went up with candles by a spiral staircase. In the evening before closing the shutters I looked at the Fournoux woods deep in shadow. And I heard the clear rushing sound of the Tarde which reassured me. I do not know if it is a result of this early childhood experience, but for me happiness is always associated with tremor.

Next day, the sunshine poured in and chased away all such terrors, and then came the great splendour of day. But away from time and space, and in a very hidden spot. Since the Middle Ages Fournoux has hidden itself in the valley of the Tarde, between its woods and its river, its horizon being bounded by two adjacent estates to right and left. It was a kingdom without a frontier, without neighbours, far from anywhere. The station was seventeen kilometres away, the nearest village five kilometres, the nearest hamlet one kilometre.

A car passing on the road was a much discussed event. Whose was it? And if we could not identify it we felt that our privacy had been violated. I remember the first car very well. We were astounded to see argonauts in clothes which nowadays one associates with interplanetary travel. And you will scarcely believe me that even, today, if a passing car is no longer an abomination, it is still a surprise, and if you can identify it you feel as though you have been rather indiscreet.

You will say that the Creuse of my youth sounds improbable. I am being truthful. I lived in a Kingdom, like a Crown Prince, encompassed, as were the children of that time, by total affection and by a strict code. This mixture of tenderness and prohibition recalled the Paradise of Adam and Eve as described in Genesis. It was a tightly woven net which both protected and imprisoned me. Creuse was woven through with prohibitions. No walking on certain garden paths because of ponds or snakes; no sitting on the grass in case of possible colds, no sitting on stony places because of the remote possibility of vipers. No reading books in the library which 'were not for me'. No touching my grandfather's cartridges which might suddenly explode. No going off too far for fear of meeting the mounted policemen Gauvin and Dulac or, worse still, thieves, hawkers, strangers. No going into the big drawing-room because of its perfect tidiness. No going up into the attic because of its disorderly state which might set me a bad example!

In this way I was moulded by a Woman and by a Land which were inextricably intermingled. I think that in France certainly, and perhaps everywhere (Pearl Buck), this is a fairly usual occurrence. In the nineteenth century it was the case with plenty of Europeans. When later I read Proust, Balzac and Mauriac, I understood them better.

I myself rediscovered what Balzac wrote in *La Grenadière*. In this one sees Madame Willemsens bringing up two boys. Her life is ending, knowledge is deep, she is weak but her affection is perspicacious . . . and there is the countryside. And I also found in Fournoux a picture of that Charentais establishment which Fromentin has described in *Dominique* under the charming name of *Trembles*.

But it is Balzac rather than Fromentin, who has made me understand the bond between the development of the feminine spirit, the solitude of the fields and the capacity to teach. In *Le Lys* Henriette de Mortsauf wrote a letter to

Félix which drew its teaching from her loneliness in the depths of a valley. The fact is that however perfect a countryside may seem, you can learn nothing from it unless it is brought to life by a human being, in particular by a woman, for women are more in tune with nature than men, more capable of recognizing the spiritual power in the plants in the furrows of the earth, and the past which is incarnate in a place. My mother had never been to school and had had no other education than the Book and the Creuse (the Book hollowed out by study, if I may put it that way, and the Creuse open like a book before her). She bequeathed to me the ideal of a species of humanity removed from every academic, administrative, clerical or university convention, from every attitude and system. This conception, so difficult, even impossible to define, is at the basis of my tastes, my friendships and of my decisions, it is linked with Creuse and is summed up in it as by a source or a symbol.

I have found a letter which my mother wrote to a friend when she was eighteen which expresses the same idea, so far as this can be done by a shy girl who was already conscious of these abstruse things:

' For country-lovers nature is always charming even in mid-winter; the dry branches, the play of light and shade, everything, even the wind in the heather, can tell us something of what we love . . . I have rediscovered old walks with true delight. It is certainly really pleasing to explore a countryside or some familiar place but I think that there is a greater pleasure still. It is to find oneself as a girl where one has been a child, and to make a kind of excursion into the past. I like reading with a wide horizon before me—fine thoughts seem to go with the finest places, and in the evening, above all, I read with intense pleasure. On Sunday when we had a glorious evening it was delightful. Sometimes I read, then often I shut my book to read something still better in the deeper and more mysterious book around me. But that is

the story of the good days. We have others in which the loneliness of the country would have been almost too much were
it not for the endless consolations of work. . . .'

The Creuse shows an extraordinary power of preservation.
I have said that the way of life there in 1910 had not changed
much since Louis-Philippe; that in linking the *département*
to Paris the railways had brought little change in customs,
and that the two transforming powers which have spent
themselves on the countries of Europe—War and Revolution
—have by and large hardly affected this quiet place. No doubt
this comes from the placidity of the Creusois temperament
and also from the central and remote position of Creuse.
The Creusois did not belong to Auvergne or to Bourbonnais,
or to Berry, not even to Limousin. So they were out of the
commotions, out of the battle front, on intact ground. The
great Revolution, apart from transferring the properties of
the nobility to the peasants who have owned them ever since,
does not seem to have troubled our countryside. Conscription
which in the last years of the Empire left many memories in
Cantal and Auvergne, where men on the run took refuge,
does not seem to have weighed too heavily on Creuse. Pourrat,
the amazing author of *Gaspard* (that *Iliad* of the Centre), succeeded in collecting in Auvergne many stories relating to the
First Empire. I have sometimes tried to do the same, but
without success, even though the author of *François Buchamor*
who charmed me as a child was Creusois. Perhaps I landed
on an island which, like my grandfather, was allergic to
evocation. Creusois on both his father's and mother's sides,
he never spoke of the past. I cannot imagine the possibility
in our country of such a scene as that in Balzac's *Médecin de
Campagne* where a Napoleonic veteran of the Dauphiné re-
surrects his god before admiring peasants. In Creuse
suspicion would be aroused at once! In the last war the Germans never defiled my six square kilometres; they never
came that way.

The most definite historical memories (I do not say the most correct ones) which I hear of an evening are those of the Hundred Years' War, when the English occupied the country. At Puy-Ferrat and Courtiat, I am told, there are traces of battles and sieges. After that one has to go back to the Gallo-Roman times and then to the menhirs to find signs of the past; these show that even then the Creusois had a cult for the dead. The plough still turns up Gallo-Roman tombs, small spherical cavities cut into the stone, which held the ashes of the dead. Even today the cemeteries of my country-side, in their solidity and their piling up of firmly jointed grey stones, remind me of Luxor.

On the other hand, if the countryside has taught me little of the past, I have learned a great deal from it in poetry, and poetry holds a mirror to the future. It was there too that I learned by using my hands and by reflection the little I know about drawing, painting and colour. I will tell you about these beginnings. My mother had some drawing lessons from her mother, and also from a general of the Second Empire, General des Portes, who had retired to the Château of Pey-rudette. He had commanded a regiment of the Guards in 1870 and been taken prisoner at Sedan. A little sitting-room in his old house (hidden in the depths of the Peyrudes valley) held the relics of his campaigns: pistols, decorations, en-gravings of the war in Italy. This veteran helped my mother to study the Crosses of Creuse. Every two kilometres or so along our sunken Creusois roads one finds a granite cross above a stone seat. These seats mark the stages for the relay of coffin bearers. The distance between them was determined by the amount of united effort needed to cover it—the capacity of four men to bear one dead man on their shoulders. A noble measure of exhaustion, grief and peace! These crosses give to the scenery of our countryside a measure of inner distance within the dimensions of death. Their perpendicular lines provide a frame which is mysteriously open. To the apprentice artist the building of these crosses, simple, crude, easily reproduced, gave a solemn yet encouraging schooling. It was by looking at these crosses of the Creuse that I learned the proportions and values, and also the harmonies which (at almost all seasons) exist in the improbable alliance of earth, fields and passing clouds.

My mother, who in her childhood had put together an album of Creusois crosses, told me that she had had from her mother, who had had it from a grandmother, this profound and simple thought. 'Notice,' she had said, 'that what is so remarkable about the crosses of this countryside is that they resemble the trials of life. A day will come when you in your turn will experience these trials. And then you will see that they are all quite simple, all different from each other, that they are hidden at the turn of the road and rather unexpected. All different, I said, and yet all alike.'

I have often thought about this resemblance of the Creusois crosses to the difficulties of life. It has never seemed artificial to me, and I have even discovered other likenesses. This, for instance: our crosses are hidden and one doesn't see them at a distance. The crosses of Creuse are proportioned to our vision. They do not overwhelm. They are not too heavy; they are on a human scale. They are not ostentatious, but made of granite and covered with moss, and bear a Christian inscription which is partly rubbed out. Our human trials have the same characteristics.

The crosses were the straight line; the road the curving serpentine one. Here is divine geometry, which is straight, and man's, which is winding. In the Creuse they were united. I loved to draw the crosses long ago and then the roads in their perspective, their lonely line, and especially their curves. I liked drawing at the corners of these roads and was always ready for a surprise in the shape of a donkey-cart emerging from the foliage, or a flock of sheep complete with shepherd-ess and dog, or of a lonely walker whose heavy, anxious tread was like that of an exiled king. One must remember that in the days before tar, days when road-menders wore blue spectacles, the Creusois highways were made of pink granite, flecked with mica, which shone with a dark gleam. And this colour of ochre-madder into which I slipped a hint of burnt sienna set off the heavy greenery of the countryside. A Parisian painter, a subtle student of colour, taught me that in order to get the true tone of a tree floating in the air (like seaweed in the sea) one must mix red with the green. After that I had a better understanding of Corot's greens, which are grey or blue and sometimes pink, but never green. The pink of the Creusois roads hazily reflected on the greenness gives it the support of a neighbouring contradiction—without which the eye is never satisfied, for one needs contrast.

Then too I loved painting a road bordered with birches. This tree with its pale white trunk whose heart-shaped leaves are always shaken by a breath of wind (like the broom, the heath, and the great beeches) seems to me when I shut my eyes to be a symbol of Creuse. My mother loved the motto on an old shield: 'A trifle shakes me, and nothing loosens me.' This motto was applied to the oak, which is not uncommon on our poor land . . . The perfect tree would be a mixture of the oak and the birch. Sometimes I bear the Creuse a grudge for not having produced it.

Besides crosses and roads, I had a third incentive to drawing—the young shepherdesses. These shepherdesses are now grandmothers. If some have come to the Sorbonne this evening I shall find it difficult to recognize them. But no one can help detecting a relationship between a familiar countryside and the human beings who frequent it and are assimilated to it. I imagine the Creusois scenery, like all woodland and moorland, as belonging to the female sex. There is an affinity between such landscapes and the faces of young women. George Sand saw this in Gargilesse, which is a continuation of the Creuse into Berry. I have retained the idea of feminine beauty as being a little withdrawn, a little defiant, very resolute, and sometimes even slightly hard. And I would venture to say that in Creuse as I knew it, and as I feel it, the old women—I mean the very old ones—have more grace and femininity than the young, who because of their shyness are like buds in March. The old women are adorable, Angéline for instance, of whom more later.

I have found in an old letter from my mother an account of an expedition made before 1914 to Aubusson which shows how eminently placid and matter-of-fact a Creusois woman can be. 'The great event of my week was a journey to Aubusson, where I went with my father. This picturesque little town always enchants me for a time. We were welcomed in the street by our cousins who kindly invited us to lunch in a house where I should like to end my days, a charming unpretentious house, with a wonderful view. I did not dare be too enthusiastic before my cousin. She is a woman of such excellent common sense and so very conventional that romantic raptures over scenery might well have upset her. So instead I let myself go about the coolness of the cellars and the capacious storerooms.'

Leaving Creuse for the 'black country'—for regular work in town—which happened during the last week of September, was a wrench, an example of pointless suffering and therefore of unqualified misery. It was the moment when the generous autumn of Creuse began, when the rumbling moan of the threshing machines resounded and when, though the country was misty and bluish, towards evening it seemed to be invested with a golden spring-time.

The scenes which I described to you were now unrolled in reverse—the long slow cavalcade led away from Fournoux, which appeared and disappeared above its woods. Next one arrived at Montluçon, to be again for ten months immersed in everyday France . . .

One never knows when what one calls the past will spring up again; as though the former things were the first image of the future. For every human life has moments, when after long forgetfulness, *longa oblivia*, as Virgil calls it, the past lives again in a new form. Creuse, from which a pressure of events had removed me for nearly thirty years, has come to life again in an unexpected way.

In the Gospel stories about the Resurrection which I have studied for so long, there is a mysterious passage. It is not the root mystery which is the Resurrection, but a secondary mystery. Why did the angels say to the women on Easter morning, 'He is not here . . . behold he will go before you into Galilee. There you shall see him . . .'? One has to remember that for Peter, James and John, Judea was a hard barren country, while Galilee had the charm of its lake, its rich green lakesides, far away Hebron and its snows, and Thabor isolated like our Puy-de-Dôme. For the friends who followed Jesus, Galilee (and Galilee itself comes from a root which means 'stony') was the countryside of their early upbringing, of their development and of their first calling. Jesus could only appear to them in the original Galilean setting, in these their earliest surroundings. It was there that he would go before them; or better, following the translation which Monsieur Pouget suggested to me on his death-bed, it was there that he would lead them, that he would guide them.

It seems to me in fact that it all happened as though Jesus felt that he must come back to life for his followers in this provincial place, in this countryside which had seen their childhood, near to their mother earth.

In the same way I sensed that in Creuse (my Galilee) I had a chance of seeing time. Sometimes my mother said: 'It is in the Creuse that you will find me again.'

When I was a prisoner, sometimes in spirit I walked through this countryside, finding the old roads, and in my mind's eye seeing all my belongings. I learned then the possessive power of memory. How sweet is this grey gleam of colours brought together, and how sure is memory's groping touch! For I came to see with a vision, different from the normal one, yet keener. I could certainly not have counted the trees. Alain says that a man remembering the Parthenon never knows how many columns it has, and on this fact he has built up an entire theory of memory. It is true that the picture retained by intimate memory is not an image which one can see; but it is not imaginary; it is a picture which is within me, and which instead of being seen, helps me to see and to grasp.

So in spirit and in fact I took carefully planned and intentionally circuitous walks. I used to say: 'This evening I am going to Puy-de-Mergue, and I will go past Deveix, and say good day to Germaine.' And I imagined what the weather was like and what the light was like—both so important on a walk.

Between 1905 and 1920 I had often contemplated from the other side of the Tarde a hamlet which stood against the leafy horizon; it was within range of voice and shotgun. Contemplated: yes, that is the right word. For in those early afternoons of overpowering heat, or even in the evening a little after dusk, at the time of the first stars, when the body is relaxed and the mind at rest, I was overwhelmed by what I saw, and I breathed it in with calm and beatitude. At Deveix-d'en-Haut there was a cottage which I had drawn because it was so completely a cottage . . . weighed down by its protecting roof as if by a heavy eyelid. I thought in the words of the song that it must shelter at least two hearts. The antithesis of a castle in fact.

This cottage housed simple good people, in particular a little mystic hunchback who had sold her land to become a pedlar and to act at times as sacristan—she was the soul of the countryside, its Fadette: Marie Vergnaud was a friend of my mother, who consulted her on several occasions.

In 1949 I heard that this cottage was for sale. No one wanted it, because it was too primitive and also because thatched roofs were not liked in this land of stone-masons. Helped and inspired by my wife, whose vocation is self-forgetfulness, I committed madness before a lawyer.

Having spent the first part of my life in coveting a thatched roof from the window of a château, I hope to spend what is left of it in contemplating woods, walls and towers from the window of a cottage. I will then really have been round the world.

For me, it is the completion of life to see the same thing from another angle. Sometimes this other angle is that of privation. Sometimes it is a different form of presence. For me this change of view-point, this glance, wheeling like a constellation over the same valley, this change from ownership to a modest station, this place of my upbringing now become the place of my thought . . . all such peaceful contrasts never fail to teach me about the nature of *being* and *having*, and even more about that law of perspective by which Leibnitz with his monads sought to explain the existence of matter.

It seems to me that when chance has favoured you to some degree, the best use you can make of it is to exalt what is lowly. Awake, little Deveix! This evening the hour of remembrance has come for you!

Deveix is a primitive hamlet of five hearths, six when we are there; without a church, chapel, village store or access from the road. And it is almost invisible from the highway. This hamlet is a witness to the first settlements of early man. It stands on the brow of a rock, not far from a river. Sometimes even now, the plough knocks against Merovingian tombs, stones hollowed out in the shape of an egg, to receive ashes. For Creuse came into being in the days when they burned the dead, therefore before the coming of the Catholic religion.

Let us imagine then that to avoid the highway you are wandering along the side road from Bellegarde to Mainsat, which for lack of customers has no bus service. This rolling road was built at the end of the last century to allow the mounted policeman, the yeoman, the doctor, and the landowner to go at a trot. After long bends which slow you down, you come to the bridge of Deveix. You are now at the end of the Gabelle country. There, long ago, the carts stopped so that salt might be measured into granite containers which still exist. Where salt was once measured, the cow now drinks.

The first living creature is Germaine's donkey. He looks at you with concentration and has a peaceful air which is not foolish; he has not got the silly pride of a horse, nor the stupid silence of a cow; he lacks a dog's affection or sense of partnership; his is a scholarly attitude of withdrawn and peaceful knowledge. He is the real master here. One recognizes this in wartime: while unmobilizable but not immobile, he enables one to move at will from place to place. After the State and the war have taken everything from you he carries on and gives you that freedom which is the ability to move about. He can cross these distances which make up his countryside (the six kilometres which I mentioned). He is called Pascal. I call him Kant, not to debase Kant, but to honour this animal who never laughs, who has no wish to do so, who seems to doubt the tangible world and who is so alert. If Kant sees you, he hardly bothers to move. He is set on what he is doing. Beyond Kant's ears, you will see in profile the sprawling sheds of the mill, once monumental, the size of a small factory, but which grinds no longer. The wheel remains, a well worked wheel, which no doubt gave many generations an idea of the power of invention. For the wheel is the first example of technical intelligence. (Following on the wheel came the grindstone, and that is a wheel too.)

The invention of the wheel indicates man's capacity for abstractions. Nature makes lines, angles, curves indeed. But never except in the full moon does she exhibit such equality of radii, such perfect and inhuman outline. Now the wheel is motionless, a wooden ruin, covered with mosses. In this barracks, of which she occupies only the guard-room, Angéline camps. She looks after her hens, a few cows, a goat. Angéline has a musical and sibylline voice. I don't know whether she prophesies correctly, whether she can enter the guarded kingdom of things to come. But I do know that she has the right sort of voice to convince you that her predictions are sound. It is a voice which emerges sharp from the depths, and continues in a sigh which pauses and wavers. Then come sonorous, grave notes which are neither amused nor hesitant.

One should observe her hand twisted around a two-pronged stick. This reminds me that the Etruscan oracles used a crooked stick, of which the Bishop's crosier is a survival. According to the rules of divination, earth must be linked with heaven: so based on the ground you point at the sky (or at a cloud). Angéline looks up; her heavenward glances punctuate her prophecy, her request for aid, or rather her protestation that what she says is true; for I can detect no doubt in her. Diviners do not doubt; science does that.

There are peasants who are born story-tellers like those whom George Sand described, Étienne Depardieu for instance, with his quiet pleasant-spoken eloquence. But to tell a story is one thing (our Germaine tells stories), and to predict is another. Germaine's style is that of the Book of Kings. Angéline's is Isaiah's when she predicts, and she is certainly a Jeremiah when she foretells the worst. Angéline does not narrate. She is too lazy for reminiscence, and long-drawn-out stories do not befit prophets. Angéline does not make allusions to the past; she secretes ideas about the future. I notice that she is very cunning in that what she says can always be taken in two ways, so she cannot be caught out whatever happens. Sometimes (as when the Pythian sibyl said to Socrates 'Know thyself') she enunciates words of pure common sense which are also verities, revelations. Monsieur Pouget, who was a peasant saint, also prophesied, thanks to a common sense higher than that of the scholars and wise men of this world.

The last time I saw Angéline I asked her her opinion on the international situation, and whether there was danger of war. She did not jib. First she looked over her shoulder, as if to make sure that her husband was not on the prowl and that there was no interloper who might interrupt what she wanted to say to me alone. She leant on her stick and took a second glance towards the sun, which blanched her face, then after heaving one or two long sighs, she said: 'War. Ah, war' (as though compelled to utter this hard word war, already so familiar in towns, but still dangerous in the country), 'not yet, Monsieur Jean, not yet.' 'You are certain, Angéline?' I said. 'You are really sure? In Paris they are not as sure as you are,' I added to test her. 'No indeed,' said Angéline, not in the least upset, 'there is nothing to be frightened of, nothing at all.' 'And how can you know, Angéline?' '*They* are not yet rested. You know, Monsieur Jean, you cannot be rested in a day—they need time for it . . .' I insisted like Joan of Arc's judges, when they wanted precise details about St Michael's doublet or about his sex. 'How long will it take for them to get rested?' Angéline jerked her head. She waggled her chin. 'Ten years?' I asked. The stick swung to my right, away from her. Angéline spoke no more. She seemed to say: 'Perhaps less, perhaps much longer . . .' What did she mean by the 'they' in they are not yet rested—who were these vague beings, these *nonulli*, these *quidam*, these *illi*, whom she did not name, and who no doubt represented for her the class of the 'have's', the Owners, the Top People, those of whom Monsieur Pouget also spoke, and who are always against the 'little people' (of whom she was one) in every popular epic? These 'they's' like wars, when it does not weary them. These 'they's' represent that part in every one of us, which at bottom likes war, and makes it, when we have ceased to suffer from the exhaustion of a previous war.

If one wants the whole picture one must visit every home: Alfred's—he is the only craftsman in the place and finds his fulfilment in sabot-making; Alexander's—whose height proclaims the leader; Germaine's, with her two brothers, Léon and Félix, who are simpletons; and finally Robert's—he married Odette for love and his cottage has seen the birth of Yvette[1], the sole hope of this village, which is in danger of dying for want of births.

Here we are at last in front of the cottage. It is called *La Pensée* because of the modesty and velvety look of the flower name, and also because its owner was called Marguerite Pascal. The family were Pascals by descent. (It is not improbable that Pascal may have seen the house on his way from Clermont to Poitiers.) And finally I called it so because to me it spells quiet.

It is the only thatched house in the district. And as such it is a luxury. For I have found it very hard to find a real thatcher. One such, Monsieur Catelot, a real craftsman, kindly came to help me. All the village co-operated. All trade guilds were represented according to their fancy. But solitary, the thatcher craftsman, mounted on a ladder, wove tapestry of pale gold.

The inside of La Pensée is poor; it is certainly the poorest

[1] Since 1952, a second daughter has been born in this house, Renée, and then a third, Bernadette. I write their names so that they may read them later and that this may be a part of their dowry (note of 1959).

house in this poor hamlet, and in my eyes poverty is the choicest wealth. Poor but well proportioned and beautiful. It is far from the road, and particularly from the water, which is about two hundred metres below us: hence the constant chores which teach me the essential weight of things. This water which is so light, so fluid, and always so heavy when I carry it up to the middle of the gorse field!

The best moment is when one has to lean over the well to draw, sometimes from a great depth. Half-way down the spring is muffled in greenery; it is well faced with stone. The water slumbers in its depths, and seems dense and heavy. With us this is not a meeting-place, as are so many wells of the west and east. My fellow citizens and citizenesses do not meet there. One waits to come until the other has gone. I am always alone there, and alone I plunge the bucket with a ritual gesture—crouching, kneeling sometimes, so as to dip further like the Spirit in Genesis, who covered and fertilized the abyss on the first day of creation. This well is truly the Spring, the Source of the thousand-year-old hamlet. No cult or superstition has grown up around it, because the people hereabouts are sober in their beliefs and images. But from it rises, at various levels, dependent on the drought, the subtle element of life, of freshness and sweetness, the cleanser and quencher. O pure spring! This water is like those profound thoughts which one carries deep inside and which one becomes aware of at various stages of life, but on different levels.

From La Pensée, one sees one thing only: Fournoux and its woods. I have hung a bell, and at midday this bell rings. And at Fournoux my little cousins ring the bell at the château in answer to me. The little bell of La Pensée, and the more solemn bell of Fournoux meet in a marriage of voluptuous sound above the valley. Midday, it is midday. The angel passes over. It is the hour at which Joan of Arc heard her voices, which she said never sounded clearer to her than in the clangour of bells. Then Robert and Odette say to each other: 'Monsieur Jean is ringing—it is midday. One more truss and we will go home.' And Alfred says to himself: 'It is midday; I hear the bell. Just this last sabot.' And Germaine calls her brothers: 'Ohé! Léon. Ohé! Félix. Midday, midday.' And the aeroplane to Algiers goes over, along the meridian, linking Paris with Africa.

When I look at my roof and see that it is undulating like the back of a dinosaur or again that it is sprouting corn at the top (as though to tempt the scythes of angels), I feel uneasy. Three weeks ago I shared my anxieties with one of my two simpletons, and he said with irrefutable wisdom: 'Mustn't worry, Monsieur Jean, roof's solid—'e won't fall, 'e won't fall, no risk of 'is falling.' Then turning towards me and shaking his head (as the traditional manners of these parts demand) to show that he means the opposite of what he has just said: 'It's what shouldn't fall that does, Monsieur Jean, it's what shouldn't fall.'

This made me think of the advice given me long ago by Monsieur Roustan, Inspecteur Général, and President of the local Jury d'Agrégation to which I belonged. 'My dear Guitton, you will never make a career. You don't know how to write like a civil servant . . .' 'How is that?' 'It is very easy. You say something in the first sentence. Then you start a fresh line, and let the sentence following insinuate the opposite of what you said in the first.' I should have taken more notice of Félix's advice so as to fit myself for a government post.

It is a remarkable thing that every one of us in La Marche, and in the whole of France, has an imaginary circle of which he is the centre, and which he calls his countryside—a countryside which seems to contain and sum up his whole nature, and with it the rest of the world. Man is made that way and can't be changed. His affections are restricted. No doubt he can extend his affection to a whole country, to a motherland. But to draw the circumference of the motherland (which is an extension of our attachment to a single corner) one arm of the compass must be fixed. And this is precisely that love of one's countryside, of the chosen six square kilometres which one pretends to regard as the hub.

This little region helps one to understand that other people have their own, and to respect them for it. And there is a strange trait of our nature in this. I think you cannot love others without first loving *one* chosen being. That is why Henriette de Mortsauf, Balzac's heroine in *Le Lys dans la Vallée*, said: 'I love it less than I love you. But without Touraine, would I perhaps not go on living?'

Having tried to explain the bond of love between one's countryside and France, I want to add a word on the relationship which I feel exists between Creuse and Paris. It seems to me that, of all the *départements* of the Centre, Creuse is the one which links itself with Paris in the most natural way in the world. Something about Paris sucks in the masons of Creuse, and somehow also Creuse inhales Paris. There is a harmony between this country of stone and proportion and the capital which is stone and proportion too. I do not remember who said (I may have read it in Rilke) that the colour proper to Paris, the one which suited it best, was grey, the colour of moderate gravity, of resistant and hard stone.

When I am in Creuse I dream of the Louvre and the famous Ile around which Paris and France have grown up. And conversely, when I cross the meridian in the Luxembourg Gardens I have no difficulty in extending it three hundred kilometres, and seeing it cross my gorse bushes. I can even say that I project the Creuse countryside on to the streets of Paris, and this helps me to find there a wide unchanging peace. And I sometimes think that these two solitudes are alike; the one you feel in Paris amid its enormous traffic and the one that one enjoys in the countryside of the Creuse.

These two solitudes are wedded. Pressed to the limit they turn out to be one. For all of us are sons of the land. And the Creusois are so in a particular way, because like the Romans they are peasant masons, able both to work the land and to build an Eternal City.

There, ladies and gentlemen, are the few ideas I have to put before you on this Saturday, the 20th of December, on this Sorbonne evening. It is like a Christmas Eve on which we come together in a common devotion to the places of our birth—places in which our graves will be dug. My grandfather arranged for his tombstone in Champagnat cemetery to face towards Fournoux, no doubt so that by raising himself up a little on the Resurrection morning, he might see the top of the Fournoux woods. It is a profound idea which gives to our love of countryside some likeness to the love we feel for our own limbs and bodies. One day we shall all be dust of this gentle earth; it will be our glory and our mystery.

Yesterday

Yesterday is as far away as the beginning of the world. Although yesterday hooks itself on to me with very sweet or very bitter links, I cannot act upon it. It is as unchangeable as the first day of creation. Yesterday has become an object of contemplation. It is just a thought.

'I am not a prophet nor am I the son of a prophet, but I am a herdsman plucking wild figs. And the Lord took me when I followed the flock . . .' Amos, 7: 14-15.

Compensations

The goodness and even the tenderness of hard people. The stupidity of intellectuals. The sectarianism of sceptics. The courage of the timid. The sudden fears of the strong. The hypocrisy of the sincere. The superstition of rational-ists. The naïveté of the clever. I have names and memories to fit each of these phrases. There are exertions which make you lose ground; times of sleep which explain and reveal. I would like to write a treatise: *De labore infructuoso, de somnio fructifero*.

On the superfluity which stupefies: it can be found in books, memoranda, texts—in knowledge even. It is useless to carry documentation beyond a certain point. Politicians understand this. Set up a commission of inquiry and it will multiply view-points and produce information, it will pro-duce a dead level, even everything up, dilute it and dis-solve it. Till one can no longer know or see anything. There are no more actors, no more opinions, no more culprits.

Sartre, like Zola (and Hugo sometimes), uses mass effects without paragraphs, pauses or gaps. *They* know that mass, block, substance, hides weaknesses. They trust in the future which will be sure to preserve some valuable bits and pieces amidst the rubble. This way of writing is an act of faith in the future. Valéry was the opposite. He made his own museum. In his written work he left only ruins, fragments, truncated images, like the Parthenon frieze in the British Museum. He edited himself.

Alain

Alain taught me a craft, that of making, of self-making. The best thing about him was his workmanship, his craft, the craft of being a man. It sets me thinking of Goethe, Montaigne, Socrates . . .

The son of Parmenides (Lagneau), he had no philosophical ability. Of his father he preserved only his obscurity, a formidable obscurity! Every day, inspired or not, he worked his 'clay', two pages of it. Sun and chance dried it out. Now and then the result was lovely.

But he and the blockheads were contented for different reasons. Daniel Halévy told me that he knew Alain—the pre-Alain. Alain he described to me as a Thales, a primitive man, wielding supremacy even then, and not accustomed to being interrupted. He spoke of things, of people, of periods, as if they had the transparency of ideas, and conversely of ideas and philosophies as if they were tangible objects. He shared with Aristotle or Hegel the rare gift of reducing thought to something in nature, and nature to a state of thought. All inner life (as in magic) was virtually abolished. He spoke of his horror of the interior life, of his ineptitude for the life of the spirit—it was the same with Valéry and so many contemporaries. Halévy told me that while Alain was speaking a gardener passed by. And Alain broke off his train of thought (as my old teacher Monsieur Pouget would have done, even in the confessional, to question his penitent about his bag if he found he were a sportsman). Alain then went off to talk to the gardener about seeds and cuttings. After the meal, when the night was ablaze with stars, Alain spoke about them and the planets. He could spell out the constellations. And he filled up the spaces between them with verses from Homer which he recited from memory. This was that 'first Alain', the 'M. Chartier' of whom Bridoux and Massis spoke to me with enthusiasm and affection. Then, from the soil of Chartier sprang an Alain, who was, I think, rather different; it was Chartier knowing himself as such, a little too much so for my liking. I realize that: this was his vocation, as it was with Pouget, with Thibon, with Heidegger, a return to simplicity, to the formless, to pulp, to the tangible, to the rudimentary, to nature, and to man, apart from our conventions.

And then there was the Tree of Ideas, the magic forest, the thousand and one exercises collected by his disciples, the sort of lay prayer every morning, the peasant furrow passionately hacked out in all weathers. I see two Alains struggling with each other, like Jacob with the Angel. The Alain with thoughts of heaven and earth (I do not say of God and man) and the Alain who acknowledged no authority, the radical anarchist who is often insolent, obstinate, limited, deliberately limited, so that he might feel free. This Alain is easy to imitate, because, at root, rebellion is a lazy attitude, and also a very usual conformism in our day. Who can separate these two Alains and who will rediscover Émile Chartier, the thoughtful peasant, under Alain the magician? The *homo* beneath the *artifex*? Is such a distinction possible? Is it not the *artifex* who has sometimes revealed to us the *homo*, and the ponderous prose (nearly always misfiring, as he realized) which attains moments of sublimity? Who will ever know? Montaigne, Balzac, Claudel, Stendhal, belong to the race who never erase, leaving to others the job of sorting out.

The growth of wisdom

On wisdom. It can increase and in its growth is the worth of old age—that age which is so ill-considered but which should be (for the spirit) a time, not of decline, but of summing up and of the savouring of delight; savouring the pleasures of former times concentrated and reduced to their essence. Hugo said that to grow old was to possess all ages—all ages and the essence of each one, particularly that of childhood; that which the child represents to adults, something he himself does not understand or experience: newness, and the sense of existence in the process of both, the idea of a new world about to be born. (Written on the 6th of July in the early evening of a specially radiant day.)

Joubert

On the 23rd February 1799, he said that pride was the result of 'too much *spumosity* and the capacity to inflate and stimulate that part of our being which makes us aware of our personality. By exercising continence the sensualist directs all his humours towards a single kind of pleasure, and this when contained and mingled with others becomes gentleness, charm, joy of life and habit.' There is more truth here than with Freud who hunts over these same territories, those of repressed emotions.

Jesus and the doctors

6th JULY 1953

Finished a picture in which I showed 'Jesus in the midst of the Doctors'. I gave the Doctors the faces of various philosophers. I copied Pascal from the red chalk-drawing by Domat, and the death-mask, which shows eyes of which one almost sees the globular form, and half-shut eyelids, and lips which in the mask have been quieted by death, but which in the living man were, I imagine, avid and hinted at fierce attach-

ments and had little tendency to smile. His is a face sometimes glowing, sometimes white with concentration. I tried
to light this face from below, by a radiance coming from the
Child Jesus. Georges de La Tour, who is so clever in depicting
reflected light, would have done this admirably. Beside Pascal I put Spinoza, as I imagine him: an aristocrat, severe and
single-minded. His fire unquenched, his zeal consuming him
from within; reserved in his view of Jesus, profoundly unbelieving, contemplating Jesus without arrogance, but with the
severity of one who knows by the proof and has no need to be
disdainful. Behind Pascal and Spinoza, I put Descartes, the
gentleman geometrician, interested, but lacking any strong
feeling on the subject. Above, I put Plato, Aristotle and
Plotinus. Plato like the foreman of a jury, laden with years,
sympathetic but enigmatic. Aristotle a pure intelligence, but
authoritative, curt, soldierly, the type David portrayed when
he painted the head of the young Bonaparte. Plotinus,
absent-minded, evasive, awaking from some enigmatic
ecstasy.

Below on the right is another group comprising Bergson,
Brunschvicg and the 'unknown disciple' of the Gospel story
of John. Really this unknown disciple, dressed in red, forms
with Mary and Joseph part of another trinity. These are on-
lookers hidden in shadow, and in joy. I would have liked to
have done pictures of this kind, paintings filled with hidden
meanings, allegories which hold pointers to things of the
deepest significance. Paintings which would make full use of
the artist's privilege of being detached and independent of
time and so able to show everything at once, without the
clamour of words, in that silence which respects the mystery
of the object and the freedom of thought.

Faith and love

This morning I set myself a problem. Given that faith and love are one and the same thing, and that the one leads to the other, which of these two words has for me the greater power and the least illusion? I answered: faith. Because for me love is a vague word. In the liturgy of baptism how admirable, simple, deep and pure is the interrogation: 'What do you ask of the Church?' Answer: 'Faith.' 'What is the fruit of faith?' Answer: 'Eternal life.'

And I asked also, between these two counsels: 'Love that man as your son,' and 'Love that man as your brother,' which moves me most to action? I answered: 'As your son.' Is it that the word *brother* has been too much abused? Paternity seen as the greatest of all forces.

I asked myself: 'Why have I been brought up so strongly to *desire*, and so little to *receive*? To make, to invent, rather than to welcome and acquiesce?' Our education is Pelagian, but one needs to have reached fifty to recognize this.

Difficulties in art

Oil painting is too simple compared to water colour, fresco, sculpture in stone, copperplate engraving, to all the arts in which one can virtually make no corrections. In the glaze of oils there is nothing which cannot be undone and started again, it is as if one were working in clay. But if an effect seems happy to you and you then try to harmonize everything else with it, you destroy the effect and all has to be done again. The world of prose or of poetry does not call for such desperate expedients. In a painting everything is always an open question, and everything is spoilt or saved by a single stroke of the brush. The other arts are more definite. Which do you prefer? By temperament I like the implacable arts.

I had a letter from Claudel in which (mixed up with many unfair things on the subject of M. Pouget and of exegesis) there was this lovely sentence: 'The Gospel is shot through by love, as the *Iliad* is by the wrath of Achilles.'

15th JULY 1953

The country is eternity. 'Paris,' said M to me, 'is time.' A little provincial town is neither time nor eternity, it is filled with gossip, worries, business, things which melt away in Paris in all the bustle and festivity.

Solitude

In the country, in the complete solitude of the country (which some of my family used to know) there are two lessons. One is morose, stoical, and tells us that man's state is as precarious as that of vegetables or of animals; that everything which he does or desires will fade. My grandfather, who lived at Fournoux, felt this very strongly and said it too often. The other lesson is that the secret of everything is peace, abundance, calm, measure. Here beauty and the goodness of beauty (that quality which is almost inexpressible in language) surge up on all sides, in every season, at every hour of the day. And what a renewal of beauty! Each hour is a universe with its own atmosphere, its own balance, its fulfilment, its sufficiency. There is no death, but transformation from one beauty (itself a surprise) into another—and this is so, above all, in the Creuse, when the skies are cloudy.

These two voices of the country are its *mors et vita*, its latent

141

religion; the religion of the earth and of the changing sky, that of King Numa (so dear to Pater), of Eudore in Chateaubriand's *Martyrs*, of the earthy pagans, on to which, about the fourth century, Christianity was grafted.

As soon as I draw near the village these two voices die down. There are comings and goings, greetings, politenesses, a beginning of décor and shadows. Here is the end of religion. Here are the frontiers of the world.

It is true that I find solitude also in Paris. But solitude which is a perpetual reverie about history. Paris is a thought which awakens many other thoughts in me; every moment in Paris is a constellation of events. It is like a dream, stimulating yet lacking connection with our stolid substance. And yet I need it also in order to be.

Morning of 23rd JULY 1953

Morning well-being, that getting up with the lark, has never been real to me. My body and mind are far apart. The dovetailing, the concurrence, the inspiration (which are indeed essential to me), only come in the evening. I suppose many other people are the same. But there is such an urge to praise the morning and to discount the evening! *Aurore*—what a magic word! *Crépuscule* conveys something lugubrious. If one could only speak of the *aurule* and the *crépuscore* ... one might be able to express what I vaguely feel: the sadness of the beginning of day, the joy of the day which ends or rather fulfils itself. For just after sunset comes a moment of completion which recalls the words from St John's Gospel: 'Consummatum est.'

The optimist

Yesterday we met an optimist. He had broad shoulders. His eyes were bright blue, like transparent marbles. In 1940 three days before he was taken prisoner he said to me: 'The Germans have had it.' Can one say he is mistaken?

The French countryside

Dijon is proud of having reared Roupnel, that little-known poet-historian who wrote such a fine book about the French countryside. In it he shows that what we call the countryside is an achievement, quite as exceptional in its way as an oasis, a Greek city, or an Oxford lawn. For instance, he explains that fields have not come into being by themselves; they have been actually reclaimed and formed from clearings along the primitive roads which are the origin of all tillage. For furrows started with roads. At the dawn of history the plough had already carved out these strips measured by time and human effort. This is why our countryside looks like a variegated fabric, whose stripes are sometimes dark red, sometimes yellowish-green as they are at this moment.

Gripped in a rigid framework of roads, the countryside has in fact changed little over the years. The fields have contracted or broadened a little, a faint movement which has hardly changed their shape. And new roads generally follow tracks that have ceased to be visible. Contemporary man treads in very ancient footsteps! Despite machines, road and field are still part of each other. The road is still a dimension of the field at right angles to it. Still the ploughing team or

143

the tractor turn round upon the road from which the furrow still starts off again. So the countryside, which one might think of as a wild garden which has come into being without human labour is a condensation of history. One thinks of it just as so much space. But it holds within it an unforgettable venture. First of all it is a work of art. Beauty is always the result of work. Courage, serious consideration of setbacks, fresh beginnings, wear and tear, bereavements: all these are included in the objects which we call *things* and to which our spirit gives a patina. But we keep the expression 'work of art' for those tasks which man carries out in a studio or in places which are set apart. We never think that a forest, a road, a port, a garden, and still more the countryside, the French countryside, are also works of art, and works which have demanded an incredible amount of patience and decision. With the difference that this collective art spreads over generations, or should I say millennia? Oh, the classic courage, the obstinate courage, which made the furrow and which indefatigably turns and returns upon its track!

Here is the difference between our Gaul and those great countrysides where nature has not been cut up into strips; where the eye is only halted by the horizon, where there are prairies and no countryside. There you get extension, dilation, production. With us it has been a matter of endurance, patience, creative mediocrity. And who can say that man will not take fright when some superabundant crop has saturated the whole world with its product, or when mechanization has suppressed small holdings and villages? Who can say that he will not feel nostalgia for the bygone countryside? Who can even know positively that the land which will last until the end will not be the one which has been worked by craftsmen from the beginning?

I write these things in a tiny hamlet in the heart of France. Six hearths huddle together there, unchanged since their stones were first polished. Work calls, scythes are sharpened and the little gossips hold forth. Light comes and goes through the clouds. The sun smiles down on this one field as if it had a particular affection for it. But fickle . . .

And I gaze out over these eternal fields. I am amazed to see how alone, precarious and frail is the man moving about in the distance, almost a stranger in his weighty kingdom beneath the sky (so wet this summer) and its great dome which is too vast for him. What is he thinking about? He doesn't think. It thinks in him. He breathes in a past of which he knows nothing. He is an artist unaware, like those friends of George Sand who was my neighbour. In such a countryside sentient beings feed on the land, and as Roupnel says reap their harvest of light in fields of death.

AUGUST 1953

Raphael said that to be a painter one must think about other things. Novalis also recommended angelic idleness as an aid to inspiration. This means: evade the spasm of the mind which leads to an impulse to turn back, to reconsider, to reflect, to feel (in terms of self-love), all of which are the devil's constant counsel. Nevertheless, one should always attend steadily to one's subject, go back to the beginning again and, as Joubert said, 'chew it over'.

May my thoughts be inward but not over-selfconscious. May they accompany me without being a hindrance, as thought in conversation goes along with speech.

Baudelaire said, à propos of Delacroix, that a picture is made up of several pictures superimposed. It is true that at every moment of his work a painter (and no doubt a sculptor also) makes a new picture which he decides to discard. 'Always complete but never finished,' said Ruskin, I think about Turner. A motto for work and thought which is appropriate to this environment of non-achievement which we call time. This, for me at least, is the answer to the problem of the sketch. In one sense everything is a sketch. And with the exception of Ingres, who wished to bring his painting (this is not true of his drawings) to perfection, giving a mechanical impression of finish, I notice that most people call a halt before reaching finality. Bernard Grasset (who paints when he feels like it, and better than he writes) told me the other day a saying of his chauffeur who, cigarette-end in mouth, was watching him at work. 'This time, sir, please don't niggle at it!' Oh, the temptation of that last touching up! The secret is to run like a hare from one's composition at the first warning shudder, to go no further, to break off, to die to the world before the world abandons you.

In oil-painting there is work on top of work. A picture destroys itself and remakes itself all the time. No doubt this is also true of a poem.

Robert d'Harcourt told me that Goethe had a keen sense of the value of time. With a sort of tactile urgency he longed to arrest the swift flow of its chary waters. A daily paper however futile and insignificant (the fact of noting the day, the hour, and the weather) was one of his ways of escaping from its flight. Amusingly enough he made the worthy officials of the Weimar Library set down the trivialities of each day, just for the satisfaction of duty done.

21st NOVEMBER 1953

Visit from a financier who told us about his rules for life and for speculation. When for three months there have been frequent setbacks in some enterprise, it is a sign to pause and mark time. Conversely, if three months have passed without too many upsets, it is a signal to carry on. He quoted as illustrations the '14 War, in which he said that by October one could foresee that the Germans would not win, just as in '40 after the invasion of England had been checked one could foresee their defeat. He applied this rule to three months of recent history. He thought that the United States was wise not to persist in Korea.

Pinay, he believes, is about to become a symbol. He pointed out that Millerand, Poincaré, were in the trenches before Clemenceau. Nevertheless Clemenceau alone is remembered. Men endure in people's memories only because of some brief moment of their lives, a moment which coincides with a deeply felt need for a symbol. A great man is one to whom such a coincidence happens. He has only a short time; after that he disappears. But in his transit he has done something which remains and enters into the stuff of things.

Corot painted landscapes like the faces of young girls; and painted faces like landscapes as well.

Catastrophe Paris-Saigon

Death inflicts on each of us a wound which is our own. I want to write about the way in which I am affected when I think of those who are no more. I remember what was most individual about them, their tone of voice, a line on their face, their bearing, the way they raised their little finger. What I remember best is what was human, natural and homely about them—even more, their way of speaking, of laughing and of smiling. And I say to myself: Yes, I know the spirit persists, the individual person; the self at its deepest level has not been done away with, it lives on mysteriously. Indeed, these people are more alive than we are in our mundane existence, busied with self-destruction and self waste.

But where are you then, oh friend of yesterday? In what light do you see me now? And what do you think of the little things with which we were preoccupied, you who are so suddenly outside gravity, disembodied? What has become of the things which were a link between us? I well understand Valéry's anxiety when he wrote:

> Où sont des morts les phrases familières,
> L'art personnel, les âmes singulières?
> La larve file où se formaient les pleurs.

It is no doubt because the idea of a continued and familiar existence has become impossible, that some people doubt the existence of life after death.

All these thoughts come to me with greater distress after the accident of the Paris-Saigon plane in which my two cousins and their child perished. Nine o'clock at night . . . Orly and the everyday talk of travellers. Eleven o'clock. Fours-Saint-Laurent, the cryptic village of the Basses Alpes, which I had visited. Nothing, nothing left of these human beings, not even remains. It seems to me that the destruction by fire of modern aircraft gives one a better understanding of the separation of the soul from its familiar body, and of the transformation by which death, out of a mortal man, suddenly creates an eternal being.

Air crashes have given back the meaning to the old expression, *perdus corps et biens*. And no doubt the atomic era has in store for us death by volatilization, which will leave no traces. Bodies, funeral rites and burial will be dispensed with. My mother worried about leaving a body behind her; she thought this the height of bad manners. She would have liked an assumption. The total disappearances of bodies throw into clearer relief the abrupt parting with everything, the sudden identification of our selves with what we essentially are. Here we face the depths of the mystery of death.

This disappearance of the familiar is almost unbearable to

me when it applies to others. And for oneself one thinks: 'How shall I pass from my poor useless life to that world of souls in which God is all in all? What a strange birth into the mystery which will fling me in the midst of my distractions into the outstretched hands of the living God! Here I am irritated by trivialities; afraid of influenza, worried about the strikes ... Then suddenly ...'

Only great contemplatives are prepared for this transition, because they live at the heart of the mystery, as an embryo lives in its mother's womb, always alert and each day readier for birth. 'Lord,' said the great Teresa, 'it is high time to see Thee.' (But the other, the little Thérèse, said more humanly: 'Mother, shall I know how to die?')

It is wrong to place an impenetrable barrier between the visible and the invisible world. The city of the dead which imagination sees as above the skies—may it perhaps be here —between you and me, between me and myself? I know it is. We cannot communicate this, I know, but there is a gentle understanding, a sort of presence, perceived only by love.

I read in the *N.R.F.* the strange testimony of Drieu la Rochelle, that perverted mystic whose life was seamed from childhood with an almost constant temptation to commit suicide. Why? Through an excessive love of solitude, an impious wish to pierce the veil, 'to reach like a drunkard the last ruinous drop at the bottom of the glass'. He described his last day in the Paris of August 1944 before his first unsuccessful attempt at suicide when the trees and the sky and the beautiful avenues had struck him with their decrepitude; when people seemed like puppets, while he was about to set sail that very evening. The unhappy man saw no link between the two lives, those of time and eternity. For him the life of this world was shot through with absurdity, while the life of the other world seemed ineffable and unconnected with this. He was at home in neither the one nor the other because he saw no link between them, he wavered between the two. In this world, a stranger; in the other, a lost soul.

If the Faith has some solid, even though cautious, teaching about this (Christianity is reserved about death for fear of necromancy), it is certainly to remind us of the great inter-mingling of the two worlds. Our dead are there around us, they await us, they brush by us with smiles of peace, assurance and amusement. From the angle of the living and of those who have not made the great journey, the absence of the dead is more than a sorrow. It is so incomprehensible, so ironical, to see them no more, not to be able to communicate with someone who was a substantial part of one's life, and who seems to have gone away one evening in a fit of madness leaving no address!

The cemetery where we shall honour his physical husk is to my way of thinking the place where we may least rediscover him, because when he was with us he never lived there, and also because there he has far too many fellow-tenants.

I try in the perspectives of faith to hold on to what har-monizes with this deep human experience. And it seems to me that on the subject of the presence of the dead in our midst, within the very stuff of our lives, one could have an experience such as this:

After the death of a friend the heedful soul is aware of the help of a being which introduces itself almost imperceptibly, like a visitor who comes into the room in which we are sit-ting, but who obstinately stands behind our backs. He is cer-tainly not there to watch us and still less to speak to us, or even warn us, he is there simply *to be there with us,* to give more substance, more gravity, more serenity, to what we do and to what we are. Sometimes to give a good twist to events, as Captain Nemo did in Jules Verne's *L'Ile Mystérieuse*—a novel which Claudel loved and in which he saw an image of life. You will remember that Captain Nemo was there at the heart of the island's mystery, but he was invisible, only mani-fest by his kind offices to the shipwrecked. Of course I may

be told that this impression of the presence of the dead is
an illusion. I do not ask for proof.

Man deceives himself when he takes steps to communicate
with the dead by turning tables. In Guernsey Victor Hugo
received nothing but silly messages. It is only by thought and
prayer that we may communicate with the dead, and by
following their counsel. It is if we do this that we come to
realize that they are still present in our life, preparing us dis-
creetly for that higher life into which they have preceded us.

Encounters

When reading the other day about the friendship between
Einstein and Louis de Broglie, I thought about the strangeness of encounters. It is hard to think of a life which has not
been changed by some meeting. Who does not think that,
but for some crossing of threads, his destiny would have
been different? Everything seems to originate in these knots
which have been tied in some completely unpredictable way.
Love is often a risk which the heart takes and which endures.

Deep-rooted habits, tastes, vocations (even for martyrdom),
may spring from a single word in a book. Reading the Lives
of Great Men, one often perceives that their consecration
sprang from a single meeting—sometimes rather comically as
at Port-Royal when Mother Angéline decided to reform
everything after hearing the sermon of a travelling Franciscan: now this Franciscan had in fact run away from his
monastery and was about to unfrock himself in foreign parts.
The wretch, so Racine tells us, spoke forcefully about the
beauty of the religious life! And it was this last almost blasphemous sermon of his which founded the Citadel of the
Just.

I have often noticed that the most casual encounters have
the greatest repercussions. You unburden yourself to someone

you know you will never see again (and that for worse as well as for better). The wandering prophet has more prestige than the old bishop whose mannerisms everyone knows. It has happened to writers, teachers, actors, to find their true and sole disciple, not amongst their regular readers or listeners, but in someone to whom they have spoken by chance. The orator facing a crowd often has the feeling that he is making an unknown convert. The journalist and the broadcaster too understand this gift of the fortuitous. Mothers fear it—they who have given so much humble and continual love know that it will all be snatched away from them one evening by an unknown girl at a dance.

So, in meetings there is far more than the meeting itself. Because of this one sees very clearly that we are all to some degree explosive substances which go about the world seeking someone who will inadvertently light our fuses. We are dormant substances whose 'fission', as they say in these atomic days, must come from outside ourselves. Meetings are a little deceptive. We think we have discovered an enchanted kingdom in another's face. But really it is only a screen on to which we project ourselves, and the more flexible and vacant, the better the screen. That is why the great intellectual passions (*vide* Dante and Goethe) seem to be focused on girls who are still immature.

I think also that in encounters which are the spring of great enterprises (one recalls that of Foch and Weygand) a symbiosis is immediately created in which each gives and takes, though obviously in very different proportions. For instance, we do not really know which awakened the other, Socrates or Plato. And we shall always argue whether Mallarmé formed Valéry or whether it is rather a case of Valéry re-creating Mallarmé, who therefore derives from him. And as for myself, who think I am as solid and substantial as an indestructible solitaire diamond, I am really but the result of very unlikely combinations and crossings in each generation.

My parents might have given birth to two hundred and twenty-five billion different individuals, all equally possible. I emerge from this multitude as if I had been drawn in a lottery during the night. My heredity, my character, my face, my being, all derive fundamentally from absolutely chance meetings. In the tenth of a second or less, I would have been someone else, or not been at all.

When we were prisoners, to pass the time, we amused ourselves by telling each other how our father met our mother. I remember the oddest trivialities providing the circumstances: a smile, a lock of hair, a jest, a glove picked up, a lost train, a look! Our game did not go on for very long because everyone became serious, awed when he realized on what a pyramid of chance he was poised. Existence, sweet and enjoyable existence is thus woven of improbable threads! And in my view this is what gives it its strangeness, and its attraction.

Wait and see. Who knows, who will ever know, whether the meeting which is to be an illumination to me has yet happened? The meetings I have been conscious of, however important in themselves: may they not prefigure some other which will be more important still? Meetings in youth are important and one might even say that youth, ever ready to ignite, is more than any other in life the age for meetings. But youth lacks continuity and is very subject to illusion. A meeting between an old and a young man is, of all meetings, that which comes nearest to fatherhood: but without that inevitability by which a son isn't free to choose his own father and a father too is surprised when he looks at the face of the son he has not chosen.

One recalls the fascinating meeting between the young Mistral and the old Lamartine, during which poetry was recognized and transmitted by a species of divine ordination. It was a meeting which resembled a consecration. It consoled Lamartine for growing old and reassured Mistral about his youthfulness.

It is through these encounters between the very old and the very young that tradition is carried on. I have observed that tradition often skips an intermediate link as in families in which the grandfather and the grandson are the only two who are able to understand each other.

Acknowledging the amateur

DECEMBER 1953

The other day I read the unusual and magnificently illustrated book in which Mr Churchill has recalled his experiences as an amateur painter. An English friend sent it to me, knowing that I too am a Sunday painter. Churchill tells in a spirited way how, when over forty, he discovered brushes and oil paints, thanks to the advice to be bold, given him by a young woman. (What the amateur lacks at the start is self-confidence.) He tells how he found peace and total relaxation in painting, also the art of controlling his temper at trying moments. Churchill says that painting calls for the qualities of the strategist, first long consideration, then strokes quickly made; the call on reserves, which in painting are represented by a sense of proportion; the lucky chance quickly seized; set-backs recovered or concealed: all these resulting in that juxtaposition of colours which one calls a picture and which gives its creator satisfaction. This suggested to me that the amateur has the advantage of grasping secret analogies between the arts, of seeing, as Descartes said, that they are all rays of one single constant wisdom.

On the other hand, since the whole truth must be said, if an amateur comes to see me and, timid but assured, shows me his verse, his reflections, I realize how difficult it is to say the right thing and to give him good advice. Instantly my professorial mind is aware of an indefinable *lack*: of mistakes, of excess or deficiency of that facility which is so hard to achieve. Corot said about a picture that it had taken him a second *and* all his life to paint it: it is that depth which the amateur lacks. And then a perfidious voice says to you, 'This novice, this youth, this Sunday-man! How can he achieve effortlessly what has cost me so many sleepless vigils? Even if by chance his work justifies itself, do not let us be misled. Between such attempts and the work of a professional there flows an abyss of time and patience.'

But what should one say to the amateur who awaits the verdict in silence, and above all if one detects in him a gift which is undeveloped for lack of opportunity, or if one surprises in his sensitive and anxious expression his belief that he has drawn near to truth and beauty and his regret at not having been able to devote himself more completely to art? One advises him as best one can (and always it is only *as one can*, when one offers consolation). I tell myself that one day I also shall be, in another sphere, an amateur, knocking at an artist's door with a miserable sketch. Or I see myself appearing before a Cordon Bleu with a home-made ragout, or worse still propounding my inarticulate prayer to a mystic. An urge to 'condescend' runs through my veins. I remember that one must do to others as one would be done by. And I tell the amateur that there are mistakes here and there, but that his verse is good.

After this the amateur asks me to show these good verses to my publisher. And what chance is there nowadays that a publisher will publish the verses of someone unknown? Would it perhaps have been better to tell the amateur that his verse was not good? But then can one ever be sure that certain poems are not good? Valéry admired this line from Racine's *Esther*: *La nation chérie a violé sa foi.*

If an amateur had written it, no doubt Valéry would have

regarded it as bad. Who knows if the amateur has not a virginity, rare intuitions, which we have lost? In philosophy Maine de Biran was an amateur, but of his epoch he alone survives. Pasteur was a chemist who did biology when he felt like it. And Louis de Broglie was a student of history and was initiated into research in physics by his brother.

Then one reflects that an amateur sins by not being a true lover—that the word *amateur* which he applies to himself betrays him. His sin is that he does not love—he only 'loves loving' and does not go on to the vow of consecration. The amateur's gaze instead of going out to an object turns back upon himself. He takes for seeds of genius those erratic efforts that are mixed with tares. At heart it is himself whom he loves.

What of it? We have all been amateurs before becoming true lovers. Each artist starts in this way and only later gives up everything else to follow his true bent. Rilke wrote to Kappus, a young Austrian officer who in 1903 had sent him some poems: 'You ask me if your poems are good . . . You have sent them to literary reviews . . . From now onwards, since you have asked me to advise you, I beg you to give up all this. You are looking outwards, and it is just this which you should no longer do. No one can give you advice or help, no one. There is only one way. Get into yourself. Discover the need which makes you write: see if it thrusts its roots right into the depths of your heart. Confess your sins to yourself. Would you die if you were forbidden to write? And this above all: question yourself at dead of night. Am I really compelled to write?' And Rilke adds that if you can say 'I am', then life must be built upon that assurance. And then one will no longer ask whether one's verse is good. One will delight in it as in a possession. A work of art, born of necessity, is good.

The Cathari and St Francis

A talk with F, the eminent mediaevalist, about St Francis of Assisi and the Cathari. At that time, he told me that the Cathari were tremendously successful in the towns. Their problem was St Francis's also: the eternal problem, that of perfection in an imperfect world—the same (I said to him) that faced the Church as soon as it mixed with the world. This is the practical problem of the *permixta ecclesia* or that of knowing how far in fact one can insist upon the perfection of the precept: 'Be you therefore perfect as also your heavenly Father is perfect,' in spite of the human condition and universal frailty. And then there is the problem of the good and the better. Can good be distinguished from better? How can I say that I am not committed to the better, when the better is clearly known to me and I feel capable of it?

The Cathari according to F decided the question in a curious way. The *perfect* were few, but they were committed to the Better, like religious who have taken the vow of the 'more perfect'. The others could do what was generally done by the people of that time. But at the moment of death these imperfect members received the *consolamentum*. Regard this, said F, as a mixture of baptism, the Holy Eucharist, and extreme unction. Recall the baptism of the Emperor Constantine on his death-bed. At the moment of the *consolamentum* the imperfect member was made perfect to die. If he recovered, he was not afterwards allowed to return to his former unworthiness, but was committed to perfection. In fact, all believers were potentially 'perfect', but did not become so in act until the moment of death, which is the moment of true entry into religion. Something of this still lingers, I think, in Russian piety.

With the Cathari there was also (and this is what developed the dualist gnosis in them) a radical division of the human species between the 'perfect' and the sinners.

St Francis addressed himself to the same problem. He thought that the world could not be reclaimed save by a return to the Gospel, and that the road of this great return would be through poverty. But he saw his disciples as laymen. And I am convinced, said F, that Third Orders were his great ideal: a laity poor and evangelistic, going about the world working like labourers and dressed like them in homespun and sandals. Innocent III had seen something of the kind in action in Milan during his youth, people who were called the *Humiliati*. This was a society made up in equal numbers of clerics and laymen. He imposed this formula on Francis, who was obliged to form an order of priest-friars to serve as a cadre for the Third Order. But Francis himself did not wish to become a priest. He remained a deacon.

Priest-artisan, worker-priest

9th DECEMBER 1953

Alain drew the line between worker and bourgeois at the point where the art of persuasion begins. He said that a bourgeois is essentially one who seeks to convince by the spoken word, whereas the worker distrusts it because he works in material which is not susceptible to persuasion. Alain never told me what he thought about the vexed question of the priest. But I imagine that a priest, in his view, was bourgeois, since he seeks to persuade.

Following up these divisions one might add that there are two ways of treating refractory material, of which the first is that of the artisan. The thought of antiquity and the Middle Ages about free work is fundamentally concerned with craftsmanship. This is artist's work. When the village shoemaker makes a sabot he is thinking of an individual foot. Often his shop is the family living-room.

It is quite another thing for the operative, and particularly for the industrial worker, as described by Marx. He has been snatched from his home. The inexorable factory thwarts his enjoyment of the natural link between the man and the work of his hands. He does not touch the sabot. 'Il ne le fait pas beau', as the song goes. He never knows the person for whom the sabot is made. He never even sees the shoe completed, he only sees one bit of it, a nail perhaps, to which he is riveted as though he were an extension of a machine.

If one is prepared to admit that a priest may come down from the heights of Consecration to join the world of men, not only in the office of an evangelist or minister of Grace, but also as a man like all others save for his consecration and his powers, then a new chapter opens in the history of the Church. And I do not know how far back one must go to find the first example. Is it St Francis of Assisi who so much wished to mingle with our poor human clay? Francis worked in the fields, but he did not wish to become a priest and he did not earn his bread with his hands—he begged for alms. Is it the monks of the West? But these monks worked together in an almost liturgical rhythm. Or shall we quote St Paul who was a tent-maker and who gloried in his craft? But Paul was an apostle before all else, and he did not become a slave. The Jewish prophets? They were often workers (Amos was a shepherd of Tekoa). But the prophets were distinct from the priests.

In the idea of the worker-priest I see a new conception, that of a consecrated man, incarnate amidst men. Will it succeed or fail? I do not know. But when I witness such beginnings I share Newman's emotion as he described the birth of a great idea. 'Whatever may be the danger of corruption which threatens it, the trial must be made. The idea gropes its way. From time to time it makes trials which fail. It wavers; then finally launches out in a definite direction.'

Definite? Not quite that as yet. The future of a priest pledged to work in the world might take two possible directions. There could be the artisan-priest who would participate in work which is almost that of an artist, work which links town to country and takes the middle way between manual labour and sculpture. (It is also a trade to write a book.)

Worker-priest? That is quite another thing. The worker-priest is plunged into the mass, he has none of his own colleagues, only the comrades brought to him by fate. He is like a missionary who sets sail for a far country (although this one is around him), and we do not know whether we shall see his face again. He is so assimilated to the working world that one wonders if the priestly image (as twenty centuries have defined it) can survive in him. Without wife, children or home, he is obliged to do the same work as other people, under penalty of forfeiting human authority, while at the same time he is subjected to the Rule of the priesthood under penalty of forfeiting divine authority.

The artisan-priest makes one think of a Trappist. Like him he would profit from contact with material things, with the earth, the rhythm of the seasons, the slow passing of time. The worker-priest makes one think rather of the rootless man, the man of sorrows, whom Isaiah described as being without form nor comeliness, as a root out of dry ground.[1] Both look back to the same pattern, but in different ways. Here is an incarnation; there, something more akin to redemption.

[1] Isaiah, 53; 2-3.

Meditation on mother and child

The curve of ivory invites the sculptor to carve a leaning figure, such as a mother bending under the weight of her child; for these two beings complement each other so well. Even when they are not smiling at each other (and then one never knows which smiled first) one feels that they are but one body. At Christmas I love to see this perfect couple—this time they are a little apart. The kneeling mother contemplates the reclining child, as though she were gazing at a work of art. It is true that this babe is a 'beginning' and there is nothing else which can be so tenderly disturbing.

For 'beginnings' hold promise and great uncertainty. So many ways open towards the future, but they cannot all be followed. This child cannot be the man whom his mother dreams of and also remain hers forever. He cannot be both his mother's joy and that of another woman. There must therefore be choice, and that means sacrifice.

The mystery of Christmas is the mystery of origins, which are always incomprehensible. What seems to be making its appearance now has already returned from a long journey. This is true of the child with his nine months of prehistory and his stock of chromosomes, on which his character and future are written and which define the boundaries of his freedom. One was aware of him without being able to know him: his sex was unknown right up to the last; one hesitated between two Christian names, two faces . . .

He was born unfinished. While in the anthropomorphic monkey, the brain becomes mature within six years, man has to wait thirty for his nervous system to be perfected. As has been said, he is a primate of retarded growth. The reasoning animal needs time to develop mental power and to blossom. He has arrived too soon. He has arrived prematurely. And that is why he needs swaddling, care and education for so long. He needs a mother.

At this first stage one does not understand the role of the father—a character who seems almost useless in our nurseries! I excuse Doctor Freud for having announced that the child, like a modern Oedipus, longs to marry his mother and kill his father. I would say that the child who is obliged to judge by appearances, between the suckling mother and an enigmatic man, would (if he could think for himself) imagine that he was born of a virgin.

Meanwhile there he is—the image of all humanity—a species recent to our planet, hardly emerged from the slow evolution of species!

Like a child, humanity, which itself is new-born, seeks for the wrappings which we call city, culture, the motherland, religion. Quasi-maternal wrappings which protect the young growth and prevent it from being too wild, from developing too fast, from being violent and destroying everything by excess; wrappings which give it confidence and prepare it for that last birth when it will be suddenly shot from the womb of things into the divine mystery. I often fear that our modern age no longer understands this and that it will reject as impediments those things which nourish and protect.

What a slight hold he has on life! How vulnerable he is, this little wizened brick-red creature who already clenches his fists and dreads the gentle light! But this is just why one loves him. For human love is given by preference to that which may vanish, to that which it feels is threatened. The gross things are robust. What is unusual, or unlikely, or satisfying, hangs by a thread. Everything threatens it from within and without. Our life, so indisputable and so fine, depends on the meeting of a man and a woman, which is often the result of pure chance. I like this thought of Simone Weil: 'To meditate on the chance which brought my father and my mother together is more salutary than to meditate on death.'

At root this child of man is sound. He is the colour of red earth. He is a living rock on which everything rests. The beings who last the longest are not the least shaky. I think of states, enterprises, even one hour of my life. Everywhere I see this mixture of the precious and the precarious. I see seeds and dust together, risks to be run, yet great hopes. No certainty about the moment just ahead, yet great confidence. Flowers amidst ruins. It is catastrophes and the very small remnants, as the prophet said, from which a fresh innocent world begins again! That is what one calls being in this world. Never doubt it.

The child who knows all this unconsciously smiles.

Towards Christian unity

Oecumenical Week

In this week in which Christians of all denominations pray simultaneously that by the mysterious paths of his choice Christ may bring about their final unity, I think of Lord Halifax, who was called the knight errant of Christian hope.

I remember a Lent which I passed alone with him, twenty years ago at Hickleton Hall, and those evenings during which I explored his long memory. He had been a friend of the mother of William II; he described her as a remarkable woman. He had seen Napoleon III defeated at Sedan, and he remembered having been presented to the Duke of Wellington in 1844. I questioned him eagerly about this, for it seemed to me as though I were in touch by oral tradition with very remote history. If the Duke had said something which I could pass on to a great-nephew in about 1980, how few links would be needed to join two or three centuries! But the Duke, being in a bad temper, merely gave the child a coin for luck.

Lord Halifax's relations with Edward VII (his knowledge of the private religion of Edward VII) are well known. His vocation to work for the Church—for 'the highest call'—caused him to give up his political career. 'On King Edward's marriage,' he said, 'I sent him a little pious book, *The Treasury of Devotion* ... Perhaps you remember the death of the King?

I went at once to the Palace. The Queen took me in. The King's body lay heavy on a small bed. On the bedside table I saw my little book, which the Queen told me had never left him.'

Born an Anglican, Lord Halifax remained one. He never had any wish to imitate Newman and be converted to the Roman Church. He was as near to the Church of Rome as it is possible to imagine, and yet very far from conversion. One day he told me this. At the time of the Conversations of Malines, while the Abbé Portal had gone to post a letter, Cardinal Mercier spoke to him about conversion. 'Eminence,' said Lord Halifax, 'I am so old. People would say: "He is such an old man," or "He has always had this up his sleeve." Yet if my conscience had seen this as a duty, I would never have hesitated for a single day.'

While the logs flamed and I was half afraid some familiar spirit might appear (for Lord Halifax had a romantic bent and would have liked his house to be haunted), he instilled into my youthful mind the simple and profound ideas which kept him ever young, and which made his long life a pattern of succeeding adolescences.

When reading the Gospel of St John at Christ Church, he had been impressed by the prayers and yearnings of Christ: 'That they may be one as we also are one.' And again: 'That there shall be one fold and one shepherd.' He reflected that the problems of division could be overcome, since that was the Lord's wish and universally recognized as such. He dreamt of a great Pope who would surmount custom and officialdom, and deal directly with the heads of the separated Churches on the conditions of reunion. This was the method that his son (then Viceroy of India) tried with Gandhi. Perhaps in the realm of faith where the idea of pure truth reigns it is too diplomatic a method. While waiting for this im-probable Pope, he suggested that unofficial conversations should take place between separated Christians. This is what

Cardinal Mercier organized in the famous Conversations of Malines, in which for the first time since the Reformation Catholics and Anglicans discussed their difficulties in a spirit of unity.

Lord Halifax himself had the faith of Abraham which sets hope against hope. He thought that if conscience said that something was necessary a sufficiently ingenious use of the imagination could make it possible.

He excelled in finding a small point of agreement between men of conflicting views which could be enlarged almost indefinitely, and which might eventually absorb their differences. He was clever at translating difficult propositions into acceptable language. When his father, like Gladstone, waxed wroth on papal infallibility, he said: 'Father, would you be prepared to agree that the Leader of Christ's Church could lead the faithful into error on a question of faith?' 'That is inconceivable,' replied his father.

Since Lord Halifax's death, conversations between the Churches have been adjourned. But (and this Lord Halifax did not foresee) oecumenical councils have come about in the Reformed Churches in which Christians of all denominations (outside the Roman Catholic Church) have united to think and pray in common; a supreme act of faith, particularly when one thinks of the autonomy of these free consciences.

And (this is perhaps even more remarkable) it has become customary, between the 18th and the 25th of January (the date of the Festival of St Peter's Chair at Rome and of the Conversion of St Paul) that the Christians belonging to different families should simultaneously offer official prayers for their unity.

This would not have surprised Lord Halifax, who used to say that the unexpected always happens, and whose love hoped all things. I heard him say: 'Unity—if all willed it, with a total will, well then, it would not be far away.' This is why at ninety, dressed in a long cloak and wearing buck-skin gloves, he went about the world to rekindle the flame of hope which is always inclined to be faint.

One would have thought, seeing him so plucky despite his great age, that he carried a talisman! 'Now,' he used to say, 'we are off again.' His fine face, shaped like a downward-turned flame, made me think of Greco's figures.

It is known that on his death-bed Cardinal Mercier sent him his pastoral ring, the ring which is for a bishop the token of his marriage to the Church. One day I was brave enough to ask him to show me this ring. He opened his collar. And I saw the pale gold ring hanging from a little metal chain, quivering over his heart.

No one was more like a saint, but no one, in certain aspects, was more Puck-like. Life for him was the most stimu-lating, mysterious, delicate, romantic, variegated and zestful thing imaginable. To me he was all Shakespeare, and I pic-ture that enigmatic writer as being like him. 'Isn't it exciting, isn't it strange?' These were his formulas and his constant exclamations. He got up at half-past five, and went to Mass at six o'clock whatever the weather, and then spent the day planning and working for unity. In extreme old age his motto was that to avoid growing old one should not do things like an old person, and one should prove that one was alive by taking some risks. At ninety-two he used to hoist himself on a pony to go out hunting.

Every morning he meditated with a little book written by an eighteenth-century bishop called Challoner, who wrote a series of meditations, one for each day of the year. He bought me this book so that I could meditate every day on the same subject as himself. But in the evening he never went to bed without reading some story about ghosts or phantoms. He liked to associate others with these fantasies, for he knew that nothing cements friendship so much as being in collusion. There was something of La Fontaine or Musset about him, but a La Fontaine brought up on the *chansons de geste* or a Musset who had absorbed Walter Scott.

He was headstrong about what was right. When he thought that something should be done, that some decision was good, he would not let himself be put off by any obstacle. The question of possible or impossible no longer existed. A setback was only a better opportunity to go forward.

I felt the affinity of this winged nature with the English countryside, which always has something of the sea about its wide stretches and its mists, and its even breathing which comes from the coast.

His face was really a *holy* face, and I suggested to him that this was the true etymology of Halifax. A face shaped like a long triangle, with a little Spanish beard, a very fine forehead swept by white hair, and behind his thick spectacles a glance which continually changed from withdrawnness to alertness. He dressed in an ordinary way, but draped himself in a long cape. In winter, to go to early Mass in the village, he carried a lantern at which Gyp barked. His only extravagance was buckskin gloves which went over his cuffs.

He was attracted by what one might term psychical research, the coincidences of telepathy or foreknowledge, to which he attached more importance than he did to ghosts. Once I asked him if he believed in all this and he answered: 'In this particular case I can't say, but there are so many cases that if one did not believe there was something in them, one could not believe in anything.'

His son published a book in which Lord Halifax had collected the best ghost stories he had been able to find: *My Father's Ghost Book*.

In his last days he always had with him a dog that was the most understanding of creatures. In defiance of all rubric, Lord Halifax thought of having him buried in the churchyard. Gyp survived him for a short time. One day I asked him if he thought that Gyp had a soul. 'I don't know,' he answered, 'but to the extent to which these little creatures have an impulse to love, I believe that they have a future.'

Clarity and obscurity

It seems to me that nowadays too many people resign themselves too easily to being obscure. At the very moment in which we wish to make higher education available to everyone without exception, the books which deal with it become more and more hermetic. Thirty years ago one could still study alone. Reading the books of Henri Poincaré, of Boutroux or Bergson, with a little concentration you could end by understanding what they wanted to say. Reading certainly demands effort, for of course a serious author does not treat in a facile way what is difficult by nature. But he should speak about it distinctly, and in such a way that a reader's endeavour to understand it will in the end make the text clear. Short of this, writing is not worth an hour's effort; it is so good to be silent. In my view the purpose of speaking or of writing is not to mystify, but to explain. Such at least used to be the French ideal. And the prose of our language lends itself very well to this. A French writer is never alone. He is always engaged in a dialogue; one might say that he is always talking. And one knows that in talking to someone one adapts oneself to his expression, which is an animated looking-glass. If one sees bewilderment or raised eyebrows or a frown, then one changes one's approach. One lets oneself be interrogated and then it is one's turn to question: 'Have you followed me?' One cuts an over-long idea into two when one cannot force it through the little opening offered by human attentiveness. Talking to a woman is a help here because women do not know how to pretend not to understand. An uncomprehending woman immediately becomes ugly and she knows it. While the plainest woman, in the instant in which she has understood, is beautiful to behold. Renan's sister Henriette cured him of his vagueness by teaching him that one could say nearly everything in the plain old words.

Even the mind needs to have the right touch to give a new polish to these old familiar words which have become so dulled by use and our unimaginativeness. Pascal did it for the word *cœur* and Bergson for *durée*, stamping them with a new and original sense which yet harmonizes with their first meanings. It is so tempting to forge a technical term in the style of the German language—to say 'cephalalgia' for headache, 'phenomenology' instead of a description of appearances. Especially as obscure words have their magic; as everyone knows they heal and they replenish; and they help towards mastery.

It is possible to be lucid, concentrated, crystalline, and even a stylist, in treating the most difficult matters; this I know from the writings of scientists. They always express clearly what they have learned by heroic research, when it is a matter of imparting this to a wide public. Some people call this popularizing. I would rather term it *ennobling*, for I think that it is a fine occupation to imitate, if one can, Louis de Broglie or Jean Rostand, and to hoist others up to one's own level. It is thus, it seems to me, that the inequalities of fate and genius are redeemed, by allowing the lowly to share in pure knowledge, sparing them the thorns and offering them only the flowers, or even only their scent.

This is true democracy as the Greeks conceived it. People will be less distrustful when they no longer feel humiliated by technical arrogance, or penned into incommunicable specialization.

But how can one be lucid? I will try to explain. Weygand tells in his *Memoirs* how, when he presented a report to his great military chief, Foch made him start by reading it aloud. If Weygand had to put down his papers on the table to amplify it by a comment, this was, Foch considered, a sign that the thought was obscure. 'What did you mean to say?' he asked. 'Such and such.' 'Then say it bluntly.' A golden rule which makes for style, wit and audacity.

Conversation about Nietzsche

29th MARCH 1954

I met Daniel Halévy in the rue de l'Université. He thrust his white stick before me like a radar. He said to me, as we were going up the red staircase of the *Revue*, that he had met Nietzsche, thanks to chance and a Hungarian lady. Meeting Nietzsche had been a shock. 'It was so different from what I had heard.' I said: 'I imagine what delighted you was his pessimism in so far as it was a condition of creativeness.' We were at the end of the first flight of the red staircase. I guided him as did Antigone, and as I have often led Monsieur Pouget, with sympathy and respect, and the joy of learning something every time he stopped. 'I knew someone who had seen Nietzsche. She said to me: "Nietzsche took me into the countryside. He himself was a river." '

It seemed to me that Daniel Halévy's life was inspired by an ideal of nobility, of magnanimity in the sense which Aristotle gives to the word. In a world which is decadent, vulnerable, perhaps doomed to perish . . . The need to rescue those who are creative! Spot them wherever they may be hiding. The élite are not necessarily the aristocracy, or those endowed with nobility in the narrow sense of the word, any more than the 'master' is necessarily a professor—he may be a peasant from the Centre, a writer who is ignored or gagged, a young man, a refugee, or an outlaw. There is Nietzsche, then there are Péguy, Louis Hémon, Émile Guillaumin, Henri Pourrat and many others.

I walked back with him. He spoke again about Péguy who

had said to him: 'If I am condemned by the Church I will go down on my knees ritually, and I will speak.' This is what Péguy used to do when he had the feeling that the other person was in the wrong, and that he himself was right—as he did to me—and as he imagined Joan of Arc did.

Then Halévy spoke to me about an officer called Mayer, whom he had known in 1910 when he had written an article which had been rejected by the reviews. In this he had said: 'The next war will consist of a line of trenches from the North Sea to Switzerland.' In 1930 he wrote another article in which he said: 'The next war will be a struggle of aircraft.' Mayer said that when Bonaparte arrived before St Peter and asked to see the greatest general of all, St Peter took him to a cobbler. 'There,' said Peter to Bonaparte, 'there is one who during his life was the greatest general of all time. Only there was no war.'

Daniel Halévy told me this in the rue de la Seine, amidst an inextricable traffic jam, of which he took no account, thrusting on with his white stick.

The unrecognized great men

MARCH 1954

In Montesquieu's *Cahiers* I found this thought: 'Talent is a secret which God has given us; we reveal it without knowing it.'

A definition certainly, but one which does not apply to everyone. No one could deny Victor Hugo's talent, and he was hardly unaware of it!

Following this train of thought, I asked myself if there have not been and still are unknown geniuses; for instance, unsung poets, unemployed thinkers, strategists who would have made superb generals—had there been a war. These unknown people remain inactive for want of opportunity, perhaps because of too little ambition, the lack of that spreading reputation, that tide of praise, which often is so essential.

One can imagine that morose young woman making an admirable mother if somebody had discovered her. How many minds wilt because they have not found an audience to bring them to blossom!

Such a one without doubt was Louis Aguettant, of Lyons, Valéry's friend, who confided to Henri Rambaud: 'Virgil would have liked to start again on Lucretia, but he satisfied himself by praising the obscure (*inglorius*) rivers and woods; that is to say, those with no wish for fame. But what poetry there is in that obscurity! Not the shadow of a desire for reward; only pure love.'

In our epoch of almost indecent publicity, when a king cannot shave without the risk of appearing in the illustrated papers, when a priest cannot work in a factory without the entire press saying so, and when, contrariwise, there are so many who suffer from being obscure or who occupy the stage undeservedly—what compensation there is for these sublime unknown people who give up publicity to enjoy the authentic taste of truth!

I like to think that there are in the world (perhaps close to me) very secret poets, young men who are working for pure science, old men who are learning a new language, hidden dedications, saints whose names will never be known and who are greater than the ones we venerate. Which is the better part, silence or speech? The work which unfolds itself silently or that which moves forward amidst acclamation?

I firmly believe that in the world of the spirit, and still more in that of love, it is true that nothing is lost. Moral life is founded on this truth which cannot be verified, yet which is the most certain of all. Sooner or later these splendid unknown spirits will emerge out of the divine memory, and they will be our lights. Do not let us pity overmuch those who have a vocation to obscurity! Let us leave them in their shadows, these unknown ones, and may their thoughts help us to persevere in our daily work, when it is dull, when no one sees us; work which no one knows about or ever will know about.

The universe of minds is made up of people like these. Apart from a negligible handful, these men are great unknowns who pass on.

This is even more true of women, since history ignores them, and they live in the shadows. And in this age in which everything, even in quiet households, is projected on to a screen, these unknown people stand for the only thing which counts: *being*, not *appearing*.

Monsieur Pouget and Simone Weil

MARCH 1954

I wanted the book of *Dialogues* to be an echo of my first book *Le Portrait*, and wished it to carry on the communication of our minds beyond death. The *Portrait of Monsieur Pouget* appeared in the review, *Van*, which Victor Carlhian published in Lyons just for his friends, and for which the recipients (oddly enough) paid no subscription. I wrote and delivered it instalment by instalment, not knowing that I was producing a book, which was a good thing, since the urge to finish spoils things. I think I have put into this book, in the form of seeds and images, all my thought. My model was the *Phaedo*: a man and a thought so closely united that one cannot separate them. From this mingling of Man and Idea, one may draw deductions that reach to infinity.

René Poirier noticed this book; he made Jean Grenier read it, he passed it on to Camus; and thus *Monsieur Pouget* was born many times.

I am often asked who Monsieur Pouget is, and it is hard

to answer. I say a learned peasant, a Christian Socrates, a constructive critic. But nothing of all this satisfies me. The best definition would be a wholly natural man. But no one would understand that. Later when I came to know the works of Simone Weil, I found this thought which revealed to me what was individual and almost irreplaceable in Monsieur Pouget:

'The existence of science gives Christians an uneasy conscience. Few of them would dare be certain that, if they started from scratch and considered all the problems without prejudice and in a completely impartial spirit of research, Christian dogma would appear to them as manifest and total truth.

'So that religious feeling should be proved from the spirit of truth, one must be absolutely ready to give up one's religion (even though by so doing one might lose all reason for existence) in the event of its being anything other than truth. Only by this disposition of the spirit can one see whether or not the truth is in it. Without this one cannot confront the problem in its full rigour.'

I reflect that religion is essentially a kind of knowledge which is not taught. Therefore it becomes a collection of heteroclite propositions to which one adheres by an act in which despair has a part. Some accept this faith though it is inconceivable; others because it is inconceivable to reject it. Both are troubled and have an uneasy conscience. And since time is short and life moves forward and they have no time to learn, they commit to silence, forgetfulness and lack of attention this very important problem before which all others pale.

Monsieur Pouget faced it.

The religious orders are like living species in which there are fresh starts on the same pattern, burgeonings and new departures. Monsieur Pouget was like Monsieur Vincent; he was entirely without system and in this respect he was completely contrary to the Jesuit type. Is this complete lack of worldliness perfect? Is there not too much indifference amongst the Lazarists? Through Anne of Austria Vincent de Paul touched a mainspring of the world. This certainly resembled the Jesuit method which consists in coming to terms with power and influence.

The questions which he tackles are the essential ones; the foundations. If God does not exist, if Jesus does not exist, then everything that is based on the existence of God or the reality of Jesus inevitably collapses. It is unnecessary to say more. Our epoch has posed these fundamental problems. It has cut the tree very near to its roots.

How few thinkers seek to re-establish these foundations! It is not enough to postulate them, to affirm them or believe in them, or even test them by way of mysticism. There is a crisis of intellects, a sort of semi-fideism is about. The will to believe. The wager. Demand substituted for proof. Illumination in place of reason. Poetry, mysticism or politics in place of intellectual work.

Monsieur Pouget was against all this, he did not criticize, but in obscurity he laid foundation stones.

Sadness of the spring

22nd MAY 1954

He said: 'How sad the spring is, above all because it is uncertain. One never knows where to go for the holidays, nor how to dress. Country houses are uninhabitable. Also, spring is transition. One is too aware that it will end. The flowers are so vulnerable, so irrelevant. The month of springing shoots reminded the Jews of their flight.'

He said too that the spring was woolly and tired, that it attracted adjectives ending in *ish* (*-âtre*): bluish, softish . . . Whereas autumn, all gold and tenderness, was the true spring and no deceiver and that, like Stendhal, he preferred *le rouge et le noir* to *le rose et le vert*. I replied: 'Can you imagine your astonishment if you had never seen the spring? Who could imagine that this tree which one rightly calls "dead" could flower? If we had not become used to seeing it, spring would typify unexpected joy. It suggests that nothing is finally lost, that everything may spring up again and as St Paul said "be raised to life".

'Easter is well placed in this unique season. It is the time of the Resurrection, the time of that unexpected hope, the hope that relates also to death. We all need such hope. As we penetrate further into the future which once lay before us, we need the thought that, at the bottom of the abyss, something better will germinate in a form which no one can predict. And I would add that spring in our countrysides is not that abrupt transition of an eastern spring in which one passes straight from the rains to languid heat. "Arise, make haste, my love . . . For winter is now past, the rain is over . . . the voice of the turtle is heard in our land."[1] Central Europe hardly knows springtime. In our camps in Silesia we went from cloying mud to eternal summer, almost without a pause.

'The East does not recognize the young girl. The child suddenly nubile leaves her toys for the arms of a grown man. The *jeune fille* is a Western conception; she symbolizes a time of delay and of waiting, of the uncertainty of choice between possibilities, which so charms the mind . . .

'Springtime delays the harvest. Like all delay it is very beneficial, and like all delay it is beautiful. The flower proclaims it with its purposeless colour and its purposeless scent. Let us accept this: that there is no true happiness except in the one that has been long awaited, long expected. There is no true good save that which has been promised.'

[1] Song of Solomon 2; 10-12.

Without arms or armour

JUNE 1954

I once said that the layman fights without arms or armour, because he has no Rule or Office to shield him. I have been called to account for this idea and I want to defend it. Office is a powerful help. One recognizes this as soon as one puts on a uniform, as soon as one is under orders. People look at you and see, far beyond you, the man vested with authority, the man whose mere words will be effective: to punish perhaps, or to forbid you entry here or there. A policeman with his baton stops a whole stream of cars. A guard can make one get off a train. It is a brief authority which he takes off with his red cap to become himself a man under authority. But while he wears his cap, what strength he has! He is fraught with mission; the entire power of his trade union is behind him. Here too is the idea of order on which every society rests. This does not derive from the uniform, but from authority. In Russia I have seen a people's commissar who wore no insignia, but had full powers; he was a happy man.

I have hardly ever held office, for fate and temperament have led me towards states of life in which action is linked to status by only a very slender thread. A professor does not need a gown, and I prefer a virgin visiting-card. Whenever I have had to hold some small office, I have enjoyed getting rid of it. As a teacher, I used to leave the platform to walk about the aisles, sometimes speaking to the child population at close quarters. As an officer I liked to chat in the lines. In this I was much mistaken, because the separations due to function are part of the function itself. And even if one can sometimes oneself ignore them without harm, such neglect harms others. One weakens the office of which one is only the humble trustee. That is why, more worldly-wise, I shall now be neither professor-friend, nor lay priest, nor Little Corporal. To a subordinate who removes his hat (an uncommon enough event nowadays when we all go bare-headed) I shall not say: 'Put it on.' This helps me to understand the layman's difficulty in the Church: barefoot, bare-headed, and, as I said, without breastplate, coat of arms, crown or any charter to help him.

The advantage of office is that it allows one to be half-awake, preoccupied, absent-minded. The Army, the Civil Service, the Church, speak through you. If ever you make a mistake they will defend and avenge you, except in the case of very grave dishonesty. An academic friend, regretting his retirement, said to me, 'I was able to wear out all my old clothes under my gown.' This is a symbol of the benefits of office, and one observes that it applies also to oratory. A layman must interest his hearers, a curate less, a vicar less still. It is clear that the higher the authority, the more it has a duty to be imperative, personal, like the truth of which it has charge and the less it feels an obligation to convince or please.

But a layman, seen from all sides, and without office or protection, is obliged to be simply himself. He presents himself as he is. He reveals his inner feelings. And as he is not obliged, by office in the Church, to teach the whole of the doctrine, he speaks only of what he knows, or has experienced. Moreover, people do not ask him for a list of dogmas. They ask that he should say if he holds them sincerely, and up to what point, and in what sense. They do not ask him for theoretical reasons, but how he reached conviction. Under these conditions you will appreciate that he cannot refer to a higher authority, or shield himself by a great name, nor even adopt a tone of authority or be didactic.

Whether in a barrack-room, a factory, or in the hall of the Sorbonne, the present-day layman is asked: 'And what have *you* to say for yourself?' In a way it is easier to talk about what one has experienced than to communicate doctrine. But to be able to speak up well for oneself, one must have reflected, meditated, endured, and become engrafted with the truth by experience—which is a long, hard business.

The lily in its valley

I wanted to see the spreading out of those valleys whose beginnings are before me in the Centre and in the circling Loire in its full maturity. Above Saumur, the Cher, the Indre and the Vienne enter the Loire—they are streams which come from the plateau of Millevaches, having flowed across our granite rocks and through some little-known towns before deciding to turn towards the Atlantic.

This Loire country holds for me the memory of Madame de Berny, that woman to whom Balzac, towards the end of his life, was so harsh, but who had intimations of his genius and moulded him, who knew how to draw out the seeds of greatness hidden under his coarse nature—in its origins prolific, but without measure or a sense of taste. Madame de Berny's discernment helped Balzac to move on from his first grandiloquence, from the novelette stage, where he might have stayed for ever, like a kind of Eugène Sue. She helped him over that threshold, so hard to recognize in oneself, and still more difficult to cross, which separates the mediocre (I mean what wells up from inside and can always be produced in quantity) from the element of perfection which will endure. It was she who incited him to the real break-through, to recognize the duty always to go further; it was she who gave him the urge to fulfil himself, the courage to be self-critical.

I visited the Château of Saché, where Balzac wrote *Le Lys*, the novel which to me is a thing apart, less for its own sake than because of its overtones. (Claudel and Alain agree in their admiration for *Le Lys*.) No doubt it was at Saché that Balzac wrote those pages of the second start and the penultimate climax which make this book as lovely as life. The description of the valley and of its spirit, Henriette de Mortsauf's letter on the theme of noblesse oblige . . . and then the slow sacrifice of Henriette as she dies of thirst at the time of the grape harvest.

From the little room at Saché where I am at this moment I can see in the distance the Château of Chevrière, which Balzac was to change into Clochegourde; an ambivalent word, in which one first hears a clear sound which then turns dull and a voice which turns into matter.

In the spring of 1830, Balzac, aged thirty, had brought Madame de Berny to Saint-Cyr, near Tours, on the banks of the Loire, the village where Bergson was to live during his last years. They went down the Loire as the current took them. They saw Langeais and the Château d'Usse, and all the princely houses which are like the few notable books that mark a writer's life as it flows along like a stream.

In that valley I see a symbol of another valley, my own, whose waters make towards the same estuary. These two valleys have a relatedness similar to that between a woman, a type of upbringing and that form of culture now reaching its end in Europe (unless it revives after a final crisis). I once knew this relatedness which is free of the impulses of the flesh; these are avoidable, and, whatever people may say, they cloud thought and distract or bog down art. Alain called this a novel about the Hundred Days seen from the side of the émigrés, though I would describe it rather as one of the Restoration, in its clandestine phase. It is also about an education, which is not 'sentimental' but 'willed'. Once the romanticism is pruned away, there remains the story of a development in magnanimity, as Aristotle or, better still, mediaeval chivalry conceived it, and as Nietzsche also conceived it in an aberrant form. There is the sense of the difficult, and the hidden longing for it; the pursuit of elegance even in sacrifice, the quest for what is pure. In *Le Lys* with its delays, its stages, its gifts, there is an initiation. And the drama of faithfulness, of married chastity victorious in the end though wounded and dying of the wound. *Le Lys* heralds the *Soulier de Satin*, and retains the perfume of the Song of Songs; that at any rate is how I have presented it in my book: that is, as the original drama of conjugal fidelity and thus the vindication of the moment of creation, in which Jehovah-Elohim launched into existence and for ever one man and one woman. 'I am the lily of the valley,' says the young peasant bride of the Bible.

Before me, sinking into peace beneath the great triangle of prismatic rays with which the sun crowns the earth before sunset, is the actual valley of which Balzac spoke.

Surprise and disenchantment! This valley is not wild as I had imagined it would be. It is not the gorge of Fournoux and La Pensée. It is a quiet, thickly wooded valley, very green and luxuriant, which gives on to the great widening of the river, whose banks are thick with houses.

Le Lys is the last of the novels of chivalry. One sees this in the progression of love, in a certain feudal feeling which runs everywhere through it, in gestures, in names, in the transformation of people by a change of name, which Balzac also did in the world of symbolic flowers. The ideal of the transcending of self rather than of sacrifice (in this *Le Lys* is more mediaeval than Christian) makes itself felt amidst obstacles of illness, temptation, passion, disillusionment and boredom, that great boredom which the countryside secretes.

At the close of her life Madame de Berny was able to read the story of Henriette's death. 'I can die,' she said then, 'Balzac will get the "Couronne".' She made one criticism only. When she came to the end of the novel she thought that Henriette should not have clouded her purity, so heroically cherished, in a kind of regret. At this time Balzac was travelling in Italy. It was the 27th of July 1836.

After overworking or getting into debt, Balzac used to take refuge in Saché. He worked there by night, starting at two o'clock in the morning. I have made a drawing of his lamp and his coffee-pot.

The solitude of the servant

Churchill said to the Queen: 'Don't worry, Ma'am, and be happy. If I fail it is I who fail. But if I win it is Your Majesty who is victorious.'

Thiers said the same thing to Louis-Philippe. And in every constitutional monarchy, the Prime Minister alone is responsible for what goes wrong, while what goes well is attributed to the Crown. Such is the Prime Minister's privilege and no one can complain about it. The noble and necessary relation between the ultimate authority and the servant is something that has to be faced. One cannot expect authority to give cover and approval in advance; nor demand from the layman the passivity which loses battles. His virtue is bravely to accept in advance the terms of this fine contract, whereby it is stated that if things go wrong he alone is to blame. On the other hand—and here is his true glory—if one day he is right, it is the Church that is right in him, and not he in himself. Empires are founded in this way. The colonist or the conquistador merely asked approval for setting sail. Often, like Lyautey, they added a country to the motherland as a bonus. Had they failed, they would have grown old in solitude, and their names would have been spurned or ignored.

A marriage without a bride

During the fourth year of our imprisonment one of my companions got married. It was on Easter Monday of the year 1944. He had been engaged since 1940. He had a feeling that marriage was a grace which would enable him to bear and to sublimate absence for them both, changing it into presence through the virtue of the Sacrament. It was a strange wedding in a wretched army hut, and with no woman present. Beside the bridegroom a chair had been placed as a symbol. At the almost non-existent meal which followed, I was in the right of the bride's empty place. The impression was not one of sadness but solemnity. A Presence was around us. And I have never understood better that the essence of marriage is in consent.

It was Easter Monday and a breath of the Resurrection passed over us; this marriage was surrounded in its intimate and transfiguring light. I have found in my journal the page on which I noted my impressions. For listening to the Gospel about the disciples at Emmaus, I recognized the link between that experience and certain aspects of human experience.

Marriage of G . . . The story of Emmaus in this nuptial context set me deeply musing. This morning's Gospel seemed to me so consistent with what life offers us. These discussions with ourselves, which are so full of incertitude about the things which concern us most; our doubts about the meaning of great world events; the feeling of failure out of which so often springs a renaissance; the irresolution of the good, and our facile attempts to refute our best guides; the need we have of a saint for a friend and simultaneously our bad manners towards him (like our need for a saintly wife, and at the same time our crude treatment of her). Then the coming of God into our lives which happens naturally, and imperceptibly through some unexpected meeting, or some everyday and yet very improbable happening, as the scholars would say. Our inability to recognize the presence of Christ in the very moment in which our heart is full of it. A meal taken together after a Sunday evening walk. The delight of having a friend full of wit and intelligence, of feeling that for ever he will strengthen us, of realizing his faithfulness, and all this when that very morning one did not know him. The dying day; night around us, the fear of a possible absence, of death, of solitude. Here is the mystery so sudden yet so long awaited, the moment of divine irruption at the simple gesture of the breaking of bread. The supreme Presence in supreme absence.

A nuptial mystery as well, this betrothal on the way, this love rising up in hearts, unavowed and unseen. Then the full and fleeting moment, so quickly shattered, after which there are only fragments of broken bread to pick up, jobs to do, monotonous rhythms of joys and sorrows interlinked—in other words, daily life. But that life will not be the same. There is an indefinable memory at its heart. Each day, each evening meal, will revive it.

It is a law of human life in that the great joys of life are not usually appreciated until after the event, until they have been withdrawn. One does not fully realize love until it vanishes; not until after their death does one understand one's parents and often awareness comes too late. Presence is too much for our sight—we cannot bear it. It must turn to absence for us to enjoy it. Then memory is liturgical. What bliss to enjoy indefinitely what eluded us by the excess of its presence.

But to come back to the story of the prisoner and his strange marriage, I would like to add this. During the days and weeks which followed Easter Monday, I had the chance of talking to the new husband who was as solitary as before, and asked him smilingly if anything had changed in his life. I remember the tone of his answers very well. He said that the difference was enormous. Not only because he felt he was in a definite state of life, founded on the rock of promise, but because he felt the presence of two persons and their substantial union which had been effected by the sacrament of marriage which they had received.

Suffered under Pontius Pilate

LA PENSÉE, APRIL 1954

The countryside has been opened up by the winter. I see it as a space within space, the one more open than the other. There is a hint of autumn in the spring. (In Touraine too, the poplars at Saché had those russet tints, this withering to pale or dark gold.) And I know that in the autumn it will look just the opposite: like the spring. This April evening, the Fournoux woods are russet. The sap has scarcely risen, numbed for so long by the winter which this year reached its peak in February. Nowadays there is no snow at Christmas, and it seems to me that Christmas loses a lot by this staggering of the seasons.

The Creed passes without pause from birth to death. It places them both in history. Jesus was born of the Virgin Mary; he is therefore not a myth, not a symbol, not an eon. He died under the Roman Governor, Pontius Pilate. His passion was an event in the history of the Roman Empire. All this places Jesus completely in the human story and into the historical stream. Jesus suffered. The Creed tells us that the Son of God could suffer, and that is all it says of Jesus. There is no reference to his miracles or to his sayings, but just this—he suffered. That was his great work, and that is why he came: *Passus sub Pontio Pilato*. This 'under Pontius Pilate' is something on which I place such great significance, because it affirms the historicity of Jesus. My old friend Couchoud always used to say: 'All the Creed is true, except under Pontius Pilate.' A Polish proverb says 'to come like Pilate into the Credo', meaning to come without necessity. How wrong this proverb is! There is nothing of greater value in the Creed than the mention of Pontius Pilate.

When suffering is the result of circumstance and does not become self-centred, or at least does not exact too much self-pity, it is a centre of life and light which is never lost. The suffering of Jesus was the suffering of a martyr. It was the result of his preaching, his energy, his courage in proclaiming the truth, in spreading the Word, so that his sufferings were not as ours are so often, the result of weakness, but the mirror of his being. His suffering summed up what he was. That is why we meditate on the Passion, regarding it as a diamond which concentrates the light; the Eucharist being itself the memorial of the Passion.

To take the cardinal virtues: first, Justice. How clearly justice is realized in the sufferings of the righteous man, in the Passion of Jesus! Prudence: I see him retaining his sense of proportion under torture, neither complaining too much nor being too resigned. Temperance: since he had no earthly food, only thirst. As to Fortitude: this is seen in the form of extraordinary endurance. Then Faith amidst darkness; Hope despite everything; and certainly Love. There is also in the Passion that gentleness and meekness of heart which Jesus said was his own. Never did he appear more gentle—a truly divine characteristic, for it is unusual amongst martyrs. Lowly of heart and loving humiliation. And Jesus is humble, not in the sense that he is sorrowful or that he is unaware of himself, but in the sense that he is full of admiration for the work of his Father which is being accomplished through himself, and forgetful of his own courage. He suffered with intention, concerned at every moment of his oblation to fulfil its every part as though it were the task of a craftsman. This enabled him to say at the end that all was consummated.

I do not feel in complete sympathy with the commemoration of the Stations of the Cross. Even as a child they did not satisfy me, and now I suffer more consciously from the discrepancy between the formulas and the feelings which should correspond to them. Just as those who are far from the danger of war cannot describe its perils with the simplicity and the near indifference of eye-witnesses (for rhetoric grows with distance), so the images of suffering become excessive the further away one gets from the Gospel. What I shall never cease to admire in the accounts of the Passion is the tone of impassivity, the plain statement, the care never to exaggerate, I would even dare to say, their speed. All literature fades before these lines from which all colour has been banished.

I can never forget that the Resurrection is close at hand; the Way does not speak of this, nor suggest that the Body which endured the Passion is the Body which will not suffer corruption; which bears already (as I think Velasquez and many other painters have felt) the marks of its approaching glory, now so near. Jesus appears as a victim truly without blemish, in perfect *nettezza* and beauty. The Passion passes. Incidents crowd one on another as happens in days of catastrophe, as for instance in June 1940. That was the impression which St John retained, and which he put into the mouth of Judas, when Jesus said to him: 'That which thou dost do quickly.'

Holy Week

My mother had an affection for Easter and the Easter season. Early on she taught us to follow the offices of the Easter fortnight. Holy Thursday, Good Friday, Holy Saturday, were unique days in her eyes. She wrote to her friends for Easter and said: 'It seems to me that it is a breath of the risen Christ which unites us.'

After the preliminaries of the first days of Holy Week, when the Masses are almost as usual but with a heightened peace, on Holy Thursday everything falls apart. Everything reverts to primitive simplicity. Holy Thursday, the day of the Last Supper, starts with the sweetness of unbelievable companionship; of friendship attaining its greatest imaginable height. When I had reached years of discretion, my mother gave me as a motto the text from St John: 'Before the Festival day of the Pasch, Jesus knowing that his hour was come, that he should pass out of this world to the Father . . .' ('This,' she said, finger on lips, 'is the definition of death') 'having loved his own who were in the world, he loved them unto the end.'

In this way also is realized the Johannine saying of St Thomas: 'Spiritual sweetness is tasted as the spring at the source . . .'

But already at Vespers things are changed as though to remind us that joys are brief (how brief was the journey of our Lord) and that the shadows draw near. The soul strips itself at the very moment when the Altars of Repose abound with flowers and insipid perfumes, and one paid those 'visits' which tired my mother and which seemed to her vain repetitions. Together we read the prophecies of Holy Saturday, rather lengthy, but which with the *Flectamus genua*—*Levate* conveniently placed, reproduced all the Jewish hopes that came before. Then the Blessing of Water and Fire, evoking the creation of the elements, or rather their resurrection by Grace. Water which instead of being suffocating, uncontrolled or perverse, becomes a spring of purity; fire, which instead of burning, purifies and illuminates with gentle brightness—as when I saw, at the back of the church near the baptistry, the new flame caressing the honest old priest and the solemn child.

A pure spirit

29th APRIL 1954 (5 p.m.)
Centre Universitaire Méditerranéen, Nice

Père Valensin was acclaimed by Émile Henriot, André Billy, Doyen Lépine, Père de Lubac, in a way which would have pleased him. Roger Martin du Gard was hidden somewhere in the hall. Homage from minds by nature close or remote—which a trifle can separate.

Lépine, the Doyen, rightly said that Père Valensin's idea was to wear down unbelief on the diamond of faith.

Here is what I read: 'The last time, the only time, that I spoke at the Centre, was in 1939 on the eve of war—uneasily enough I admit, because I had seen, at the back of the hall on a bench to the left, the ovoid skull and the enigmatic (Goethe would have said demoniac) smile, the sensitive, musical, articulate, but already dissenting, hands of Père Valensin.

'After the lecture he rushed me into a green tram, and took me to his room in the Avenue Mirabeau. He expounded two points to me. Firstly, that my theme was excellent, secondly, that it was valueless. He took me to pieces as one takes a clock to pieces, then he put me together again, and made me strike the right hour. Thus was renewed a friendship which had already long existed between us. I have always enjoyed being taught, and he was an incomparable teacher as regards methods of thought.'

In his personal notebooks he once described himself as follows: 'I am a wonderful mixture of an intelligent man and an imbecile, with the imbecile predominating. This is my strength and my weakness. My strength when I explain a difficult point to others. My weakness when it comes to

understanding what others are trying to explain to me.' And
he added: 'The difficulty I find in catching the meaning of a
hint, in getting over an expression which does not translate
the idea exactly, in crossing the barrier of a wrong conjunc-
tion, in filling in transitions that have been taken for granted,
in keeping under my eye the various parts of an argument—
all this means that, once I have grasped a theory, I can explain it in a way that saves others the struggles I have had
myself. That is the secret of my clarity. I pay dearly for it.'

He explained this same mental characteristic of his in a
vague and less modest fashion on the occasion when he tried
to explain Paul Valéry to readers of *Études*. He said that there
are two kinds of intelligence. First the magician's, that of
Henri Poincaré for instance, which grasps without difficulty,
by intuition or instinct. But he at once qualified the remark
by saying that this kind of mind is often very specialized, apt
for geometry or business, for music, or perhaps for chess.
A sleep-walking intelligence whose operation is a miracle.
Then there is another type of intelligence: 'That which is
destitute so to speak of talents, being absolutely nothing but
itself (though without diminution), and which finds in its
own resources the means of achieving by hard work what
others do by nature.'

Père Valensin was thinking of Descartes, of Leibnitz and
still more, of Edgar Allan Poe, and Paul Valéry. These people
are able, he said, to give you what you want. Through
mnemonic technique they supplement memory. Do you want
feeling? Love?

They will manufacture it for you by intellect alone. Do
you want a poem of genius? Void of inspiration they will
compose it mathematically, as Edgar Allan Poe did in *The
Raven*. Do you want a battle? They will win it for you without being strategists; this Jomini did for Napoleon. They
will give you what they have not got.

One day Père Valensin said to me apropos of Leibnitz

and his calculating machine: 'Though I can't add up for toffee, I feel sure I could invent an adding machine.' He could hardly forgive Valéry's sarcasms about free inspirations, and those many poets who, he said, were only the Muse's shorthand writers. He took to himself the sorrows of the Pythia:

> *N'allez donc, mains universelles,*
> *Tirer de mon front orageux*
> *Quelques suprêmes étincelles!*
> *Les hasards font les mêmes jeux.*

For Valensin as for Valéry, nothing was valuable which was not lucid. Nothing was lucid unless it had been calculated. In fact he was interested in workings rather than effects, in a subject more than an object, in art more than science, in the action more than in the act. (The day he criticized my lecture at Nice, we did not for a moment talk about his own theme which was St Augustine.)

And this is why, like Valéry, he felt compelled to write only very little and then solely to meet his obligations, and with a very painful feeling of incompleteness. His mind was like a sun which was invisible to himself, and from which he could receive only a few sparks. It was hard to imagine what a mind so capable of self-instruction would have gained by being tutored for any length of time. On the other hand, it was obvious that a mind so gifted for elucidation, and at the same time (like those of many old priests) so fresh, always so eager and of an almost perfect candour, would have benefited by finding a disciple; I mean a malleable disciple and less lazy than Plato's Theaetetus.

It was through a chance encounter that in François d'Espinay he was offered such a disciple. D'Espinay was alarmingly precocious in wisdom and Père Valensin moulded him after his own image. The Father—then truly a father—was able to see himself being born; in 1935 he witnessed (in what seemed to me a strange and mysterious way) in François's death the presage of his own.

During these last weeks I have reread *François*. It is a unique book, because one cannot imagine anyone else writing it nor could one imagine anyone else having this genius as a disciple.

In *François*, I recognized Père Valensin's personal method; it consisted in studying the secret machinery of all things, in moulding the spirit to 'the poetic' (the *poiétique*, Valéry would say) rather than to poetry itself. He moulded it to grammar, to a sense of metre, to fulfilment and ultimately to a complete and unconditional surrender of the soul to God beyond all perturbation. And this is in fact in relation to piety what 'adorable severity' is to poetry. Whence comes this line from *François*?

Idées conduisez-moi: tant de soleils m'égarent!

Père Valensin taught François his craftsman's technique, his scales, the daily exercises of pen and verse, so as always to have something to chew on, something by which to judge his daily progress, to give himself the pleasure of work which was precise, elaborate and difficult. One day he told me that Gide had confided in him that he too needed such gratuitous work. Comparing Père Auguste Valensin with his elder brother, Père Albert, whom also I knew well (it was to him that he dedicated his last book), I said to myself that possibly what attracted these supple and free minds to the Company of Jesus was, at root, the idea that to attain liberty in that somnolent mass which is man's body, exercise is vital and method indispensable. Let us not forget that Descartes was brought up by Jesuits.

I think that here I have touched the crux of the problem of Père Valensin's Mediterranean mind, which was so akin to Valéry's and which suffered the same torment. There is this likeness between them: that they left not one work, *opus*, but works, *opera*.

Also, they did not set forth their teaching, but the by-products of their work: inscriptions, epigrams, programmes, propositions, positions, 'carmina', theorems. Valéry was more of a poetician than a poet; Valensin was less of a philosopher than a constructor and destroyer of philosophies, actual or potential.

And their secret models were not teachers, but the unmatchable geniuses, near-monsters of excellence. For Paul Valéry, the model was not Racine whom he was content to admire, not even Mallarmé, who only provided him with the first and necessary push, but Leonardo da Vinci. For Auguste Valensin, the models were not Lachelier, Kant, or St Thomas (though he admired them also in some ways) nor even Maurice Blondel, to whom he owed his awakening, and still more his philosophic and religious vocation. But as Valéry, looking beyond Racine, beyond Stéphane Mallarmé, perceived the unattainable Leonardo, so, behind Maurice Blondel and beyond the masters, Valensin fixed his archangel's gaze on the incomparable, the inimitable minds: Dante and Plato; not masters but gods! Yes, in order to reach to Christ, he needed gods.

This explains his arrogance, always so charitable and polite, towards many modern and even classic authors. The dweller on Annapurna cannot be much astonished by Mont Blanc. After Thabor, Mount Gazirim lacks colour. When one is attracted solely by what is supreme, one can only hold oneself in disdain, and prefer silence to productions that must inevitably be mediocre.

It is true that, thanks to Maurice Blondel, Auguste Valensin did not give way to the vertigo which caused Valéry to take non-existence for the stuff of his action and as his consolation. Nor did he fall into the abyss of Fichte or Hegel, his true tempters, which was to reconstruct the individual from his own dialectic material. But after he had passed his thirty-third year he was, as he passed amongst us, rather like an angel with broken wings, the victim of his ideal of excellence.

To the extent that one can extract a philosophy from those of his own thoughts which have been published, I would willingly sum it up in this way: 'It is not the truth of the object of faith, but the necessity for belief which requires to be demonstrated.' But this saying does not come from Père Valensin. Do you know whose it is? It is from Joubert, whom Jules Lemaître called the Seraph, and about whom Émile Henriot has written such fine pages; Joubert belonged to the same rare genus.

Père Valensin had deeply meditated, elucidated, probed, and, if one can so put it, perfected Pascal's wager. He made me understand that real gamblers do not fundamentally wager anything and never run risks. Their method is the reverse, and consists in finding a position in which even in the event of losing everything, behold! they have lost nothing!

Had the impossible hypothesis that God did not exist been valid, Pascal would yet have made an almost total gain, since he had renounced the false pleasures which bedevil existence, and prevent one from enjoying the sunlight of the present. But Père Valensin went even further than Pascal, and, in that famous passage which so struck André Billy on the 'unthinkable hypothesis', he says that if at this last day he were to realize that nothingness exists and not Being, all right, he would not have made a mistake. 'I would not regret having believed,' he wrote; 'I would feel that I had done myself honour by believing, and that if the Universe is something absurd, then so much the worse for it; the fault would not have been with me for thinking that God is, but with God for not being.' And with this we left Pascal for Descartes, and St Anselm. I do not know any profounder transposition of the celebrated ontological argument.

I said that we have left Pascal for Descartes. This is incorrect. We have gone back to the springs of both one and the other. We are very near to Plato, the living source, from which Père Valensin also drank. Before Nietzsche (inspired by the village of Eze, rather than by the Baie des Anges) attempted to dethrone him, Plato had stood for the whole of philosophy in the West. From Aristotle to Lavelle, and even up to Husserl, what Western philosophers have been aiming to do is to build out of the ruins of the Parthenon a dwelling for the mind. But how right Père Valensin was to see Plato always looming behind Dante! He who could not see a difference between reason and love, between science and art, between asceticism and ardour; he in whom Plato's maxim, 'I see as a God him who can accurately divide and define', must have echoed strangely. He, who finally, like Valéry, thought that perhaps the most adequate form in which to present a many-sided thought (thought in a state of development, and always in travail to fresh corrections) was dialogue. But the author of *Balthasar*, like the author of *Eupalinos*, found out how difficult it was to recreate, in these contrived dialogues and in a Europe grown old, what Plato alone, in youthful Greece, was able to do. It is very understandable that of all Plato's dialogues, Père Valensin liked the *Symposium* best, because in this alone, this Greek 'Song of Songs', Plato first adumbrates Pascal's over-intellectual saying: 'Reason has been inopportunely deprived of the name of love, and they have been placed in opposition on no good grounds, for love and reason are the same thing.' Just before his death Père Valensin was preparing a lecture which he was to give here, expounding and explaining Plato's *Symposium*.

The last conversation we had coming down the slopes of Mont Boron, and seeing all the lights of Nice shining below us like a second heaven, was on the question whether the universe and history existed before Adam. I made some reflections on the hypothesis of the plurality of inhabited worlds, and questioned what consequences the existence of other human beings in space and time (pre-Adam's perhaps) would have for the doctrine of the Incarnation. He gave me one of his dry burning looks as though he were the Angel of the desert, and said that my question *had no meaning*. 'Because,' he added mysteriously, secretly, 'I do not think that the world existed before the emergence of consciousness.' And he developed for me what I had read some time ago in Berkeley (an Anglican bishop) as follows: 'Before Adam, that is before the first birth of consciousness, there could not be a world, only a memory, an idea, and the possible history of what in fact had not existed.' He made this comparison: 'When you go to the theatre, you hear in the first act, from the lips of a confidant, the story of what has happened before the curtain went up. But what this confidant relates has not in fact been enacted; it has not really taken place; it exists only in the realm of thought and story-telling. So it was with the beginning of the world before the seventh day.'

I protested. I declared that I could not accept this view. I affirmed that the universe and space and time were in existence before the emergence of consciousness. Geology, for instance, proved this.

But it was an impossible dialogue. I saw from his sibylline smile that he was going to treat me as he did after the lecture I gave in 1939 and to regard me as a novice, not yet initiated into the great mysteries.

As we entered the shadowy, lighted town, I reflected that chance had made me acquainted with the two most opposite of religious minds that it is possible to conceive of: Père Pouget and Père Valensin.

Père Pouget, a son of the land, and of the peasantry of Auvergne, whence he drew his method of 'groping for being', his horror of eloquence, art and system, hardly tying up his sheaves, bothering no more about the form of his thought than a reaper would care about the curve of his sickle pro-

vided it cut; Père Pouget, too, did his mathematics every
day, but regarded them as an exercise for the mind to be
worked out on a scale which he had invented, 'a special case
of logistics'.

Père Valensin, who was always concerned with reconstruction, with going up Jacob's ladder step by step, who was devoted to art and method and discipline, to number and
grammar, dared to write these two lines:

> *Je suis Esprit, le monde est en moi, je le porte,*
> *Je définis le Nécessaire et l'Impossible . . .*

Valensin the last of the Greek Fathers, the last of the sons
of Plato and celestial Aphrodite, who came to flower in Nice
—that part of France which is nearest to Greece.

Pouget, the peasant of Gaul, the rough-hewn Celt, the
minder of flocks, zealous for knowledge and tangibility.

One, the son of rebel lands, conquered by Caesar; the
other a Greek, rather oriental in his subtlety, his 'idealism',
and in that mixture of spiritual fervour and pure reason
which informs Plato. One blind, the other living by light.
One a follower of Jesus Christ, the poor workman of Nazareth; the other following his counsel regarding the principle
of divestment.

> *Dépouille-moi de tout, Jésus, sauf de Toi-même,*
> *Je veux n'être plus rien sinon celui qui t'aime,*
> *Éteins mes facultés. Souffle sur mon esprit . . .*

What a sacrifice for a man who knew himself to be and
wished to be pure intellect!

So, starting from two divergent points, one a son of the
world of men, the other a son of the realm of ideas, one a son
of Monsieur Vincent, the other of St Ignatius, they reached
a point of stability and concurrence; that in which, as St
Paul described it, all things are ordered under one head,
sustained and summed up.

When mentally I considered them together, they made me think that all ways lead to this end, even (perhaps) the most difficult and arid of ways, that of Paul Valéry.

Joubert

4th MAY 1954

On the 4th of May 1824, Joubert died at Mass, not at the elevation like Montaigne, but like Pascal after having received Holy Communion.

My meeting with Charles du Bos

In an old journal I have found some notes on this teacher, who becomes daily more and more present among us. A Celt, of English, Nordic cast, whose face was delicately lined because of a cruel disease, which had caused him to undergo many operations. He told us about them there and then as we covered the grass-covered expanse leading from his cottage.

He said that suffering gives the mind above all else a certain gift of *discerning nuances*. People today place their trust in precision. But above precision there is nuance, and the intuition of nuance.

He quoted the work of my friend Peyre on Shelley in which he strips Shelley of everything that has been written about him, and writes a chapter in which intuition is his sole guide. One can see in this that the immense erudition which we consider essential had not revealed anything of real importance to him. Next, we spoke of Sainte-Beuve. Charles du Bos remarked that what had brought about Sainte-Beuve's downfall was his desire to judge. 'One sees very clearly,' he said, 'that the fatal moment, the critical point when Sainte-Beuve betrayed his true vocation was after '48, when he was carried away by his readers, and by the form he had chosen.'

Du Bos considered that one should never seek to judge. True judgment is implicit judgment and emerges unintentionally, simply by the manner in which events present themselves to one. Sainte-Beuve exercised true judgment in his first style. Du Bos also said that Sainte-Beuve lacked breeding. He was a bourgeois, with bourgeois vices, noble in intelligence only; and his life proves that intelligence is not enough.

That helped me to understand du Bos in the quality of a gentleman. He had the real affability of a gentleman, which is devoid of irony; detachment and a mind naturally sure of itself, yet without self-assurance, which is a bourgeois characteristic.

He spoke slowly, lengthily, precisely. He thought in circles, curves and spirals. That would have been the height of preciousness had not one's mind's eye been always riveted and seduced by the conscientiousness of du Bos, conscientiousness pure and simple, entirely engrossed in its labyrinths and its quintessences by the search for the last decimal, the ultimate nuance. He was subtle, he was not precious. I never felt I was on his side on this point, for I love the quick straightforward grasp, the dagger-thrust to the heart. He would have been a marvel as an executioner, for he would have made his victim tremble, without killing him.

Unlike Joubert, he needed ten pages, not ten words, to express himself. And even the quotations in his books run to several pages. If it is true that French thought presents the agile reader with only the residue, the glaze without the slow firing, then du Bos is no more a French writer than Proust. Is he rather a European author?

We spoke of the *moment*, a theme which is dear to me. He willingly agreed with me that the spirituality of the moderns lies in the sense of the moment. Because in the moment they strive to find a substitute for the whole spiritual life. At bottom, he said gravely, spiritual life is essentially a continuum . . .

There is an affinity between my thought and his. He said he too had recognized it when he read my theses, which Gabriel Marcel had introduced him to. He had bought them from the publisher that very evening, whilst crossing the Place Saint-Sulpice diagonally, in the direction opposite to that which Renan took on the evening he left the Seminary.

The solitude of woman

A propos Madame Régnier's book, of her death and of her *Journal*, I have been reflecting on the problem of the solitude of women and of what they suffer. There are, I believe, two kinds of solitude. One in which we feel that all our ties are falling away. This kind of solitude is better named *isolation*; it is as if, with the approach of the sea, we found ourselves islanded in a watery emptiness. The other solitude is different. It is a feeling of change in ourselves, and only in ourselves, the feeling that we are unable to communicate with those who crowd round us and who yet don't seem to be present. A sensation of fear comes into this isolation.

Having said that, I wonder if women understand these two states in the same way as men. Women seem to me to be less isolated than men. A woman has ties with life, with children, the ties of dress, of providing food, of housekeeping, ties with other women . . . A woman is also better adapted to solitude of the second sort. Her 'amphibious' nature helps her to pass easily from the world of social relations into the higher world of contact with mysteries. Madame Acarie for instance had her ecstasy while turning an omelette. The easy transition from the frivolous to the sublime is part of a woman's ordinary nature.

Why then are so many women all at sea in the world of today? It is because it is not yet properly developed to make women happy. Of course women have been emancipated and an end has been put to their servile position; but our present-day world is a masculine one, thought up by men for men, with its masculine institutions and a culture which is masculine rather than 'human'. The universities admit women to all their competitive examinations, but these examinations are planned and organized by brains that are male brains: logical, mathematical, or rhetorical. Women I know can excel in these studies. They can outstrip the men, but this is due to their faculty for perseverance, for imitation, they can achieve it out of defiance, coquetry, emulation and passion. All the same, in the purely masculine sphere, women are not at home and the desert of abstraction is in the hands of male competitors.

True, men make much of women. They divide them into two categories: one which they deem superhuman and which they 'adore'; the other a sub-human element which serves them for work or pleasure. In the Middle Ages Western man developed a cult for woman. But underneath this he reduced the working woman or the courtesan to the level of a tool. It was rare for him to love the real person.

The reason for the confusion of women today is easy to understand. It comes from the difficulty of realizing an entirely feminine vocation in a world which is dominated by the male element. I would like to make a serious study of this matter.

The death of a friend

Jean Anglès d'Auriac is dead. I can now look at him in his entirety. What an example he was of the philosophic life.

Born into a family of mathematicians in which, along with faith, the idea of rigorous intellectualism was handed on as a heritage, after having first been attracted, like his brothers, by mathematics, he decided to devote himself to philosophy and follow the lectures given by M. J. Chevalier.

Very early he conceived his duty to be that of consecrating himself to what he called *The Work*. This he did almost without teachers or precedents, entirely without thought for fame or for a career, urged on solely by a search for truth; he believed that truth alone would enable one to be and have *un bon esprit*. That is why the first of his books is called *The Search for Truth*, and the second *In Search of a Better Ordering of the Mind*. To attain to truth, which is the way to the ultimate good, he wanted, as a careful doctor would do, to find the most perfect diet for the mind. This makes one remember the thinkers of the seventeenth century whom he resembled. Like them, he held the problem of beatitude to be the first of all problems, and he shared their implacable integrity. 'I do not allow myself,' he wrote, 'any relaxation. Perhaps it would not be fatal to give way to some weakness. But it is fine to nourish a firm intention to conquer myself continually in the service of *l'ostinato rigore*.'

Or again, he says: 'The stake is not without nobility if, as I think, I am able in principle to prevent the birth or ensure the death in me of all unworthy opinions. I would like to decide always in favour of the better, and in the best possible way.' 'I must assent to truth in a way which is worthy of it and of myself.' How can one indicate the scope of *The Work* in a few formulas?

1. It was a research into the best conditions under which the human spirit in each one of us could be orientated, without illusion, without initial mistake, without falling away from the full truth, in order to be able to communicate this to others with all one's strength and to walk with them towards the good. And with him the good was not differentiated from the best.

2. It was an extremely cautious inquiry, going back to first essentials, based on the most incontestable position, submitting to the suspension of judgment anything that could be doubted, and discussing at length even its own legitimacy.

3. This inquiry was founded, in particular, on the idea that in the quest for truth only two positions were possible; radical affirmation on the one hand, and suspension of judgment on the other, this because opinion was a bastard status, doubt a provisional status, probability a practical *pis-aller*.

Did Anglès achieve his aim? One must admit that his work is often difficult to read. The ideal of excellence which caused him so many scruples, his mathematical mould, his wish to create an adequate vocabulary, his concern not to be influenced by anyone and to rely on himself alone, all this wove around his intuition a conceptual network—which was a formidable robe. Also, he died at the moment in which he had established his method and was about to make use of it. The things which we should so much like to know, these certitudes he established, we shall never know.

Yet having made these qualifications, the fact remains that among contemporary publications this *Work* strikes a unique note; it is at once old and timeless. The feeling for research, the love of truth before everything, the critical caution, the intellectual demands relative to morality, the Spinozist and the Kantian problems, the method of Husserl, all are to be found and not as derivations. His style is concentrated and his work vibrates with a greatness of spirit which is without equal.

To the judges of his thesis who had difficulty in understanding it, and who at last asked him the famous question, *Quid dicis de te ipso*, he answered with proud humility: 'Spinoza with freedom.'

Fully to appreciate the cost of such an effort, one must know that his health was vulnerable, and that the threat of a sudden end to his life hung long over his head. The expectation of death, which is the lot of every man, was for him no vague presentiment, but an idea carved in his flesh, an idea, clear, definite, serene. He was ready, for all his thought was shaped expressly to one end—to choose always the best. This is the deep meaning of *The Work*, and of its 580 pages, so abstract, so careful and so very tightly packed.

In order to pursue this end, in the midst of the threat to health, of his family responsibilities, of the duties of his position which he so scrupulously fulfilled, he gave up practically everything. Never any unnecessary reading, or travel or personal pleasure. Although he had a mind that was naturally very curious, he shut himself up in *The Work* like a Carthusian in his solitude. He never left his retreat except on two or three occasions in order to perform acts of courage for friends, seniors, or colleagues, acts which he alone could do. No one knew or could guess the secret of a life which was made up of privations and of reflection. Yet he was a man of the world, and even, in certain aspects, worldly; considerate, never speaking of himself, interesting himself in others courteously, with concern, with the manners of another century, with a subtle understanding of convention and manners, a discernment of people, and sometimes a rather excessive tolerance which made him resemble Marcel Proust.

In particular he was an artist in graphology. His aptitude for the study of handwriting brought him into contact with M. Le Senne, who had picked him out as early as École Normale days, and who presided at his *soutenance de thèse*. M. Le Senne admired him and was fond of him, and would like to have presided at the ceremony in which he was commemorated at the Congress. He had introduced him to the famous Belgian graphologist, Robert Maistriaux. The analyses of writing made by Anglès d'Auriac are models for reconstituting a character, one might almost say for prognosticating a future. As an intellectual or moral counsellor to friends or students, this character-reader, who was so alert to aptitudes (as well as exacting in ideals and indulgent to weakness), was unequalled. For this perspicacious man, who was so sparing of his strength, wasted his time on others with royal liberality, because above all else he was a 'good' man.

I remember that in his student's study, as also later in his study at Rennes, he kept a reproduction of the Louvre portrait of Descartes. No one could fail to see a likeness between Anglès d'Auriac and Descartes: the eyebrows, the black eyes, the smile, the independence, the lucidity, the withdrawal (the mixture of worldliness and austerity); the search for the best spiritual rhythm, the horror of doubt, even though doubt is a spur, the homage paid to the rational way, the secret sense of GOD, a word which d'Auriac wrote seldom, but always in capitals.

He said that he would not die before finishing *The Work*. And it was in the very week in which the first copies reached Rennes that he died—lucid to the last. He had long since assessed and accepted what he somewhere calls 'the changes which affect man's body in the event called death'. He left his friends the example of a man whose energies were devoted to co-ordinating his thought with his life, in the quest for what he called the *bona mens*.

Past prospects

After reading Madelin on the Hundred Days, I wonder, could it have succeeded? The *Morning Post*, then the organ of the Whigs, thought that it could and for these reasons: 'The very rapid success of the march on Paris shows popular consent. The Revolution cannot be wiped out in France. It must reappear: then why not now? Louis XVIII cannot be restored. The best thing would be a Napoleon who has learned wisdom. There must be a balance of power against the Cossacks. Napoleon can provide this. And with him the possible reversal of alliances: a Franco-British alliance.'

I like to look back on these 'futures' which have never happened, for we have too great a tendency to canonize what actually occurred. The Hundred Days typifies the phenomenon of transient success in which the provisional does not correspond to the basic situation; they were like a rally in the course of a grave illness. So were the *Chemin des Dames* in '18 and Von Runstedt's offensive in the Ardennes. It was possible at the actual moment to recognize this, but not with certainty. The argument of the *Morning Post* remains a possibility.

Portrait of a mother

28th MAY 1954

André Billy speaks of books written by sons about their mothers. And he quotes two of them, Albert Cohen's *Le Livre de ma mère* and mine. He says that Cohen's book is the work of a Jew who has evolved towards atheism, and mine that of a Catholic who has remained true to his mother's faith. He notes some traits in M. Cohen's mother which bear on the oriental tradition of woman's subjection to man. When M. Cohen was away from home on his birthday, his mother laid his place, and poured Samian wine into his glass . . . It was rather the reverse with us.

I realize that I am remembering my mother at the age which I myself am now. We can never imagine the dead growing old; for us they stay for ever at the age at which we lost them. A widow of the 1914 war said to me sadly: 'I cannot recall my husband's appearance and voice; he was twenty-seven when he died, the age my grandson is now.'

Those who have lost a mother too early in life understand this type of discomfort. And yet I think the levelling-up of age in death is a good thing in the case of a mother. I think the gap between a child and its parents is excessive in its early years, when to our parents we are just flesh and blood toys. Only gradually do we take on shape and coherence and the strange lag starts catching up on itself. Towards middle life the interval fills up, or at least seems to. This seems particularly true of the present day when there are no old faces or old women to be seen. Seen from behind we seem to belong to the same age group as our parents, and when we are with them we seem to belong to the same species. Just as, in spite of the dates inscribed on their tombstones, the dead always seem to us to be of the same—indefinite—age. This is how humanity's flow into the timeless is prepared.

The story of a son and his mother is one of a slow transformation from babyhood to the age when he can walk arm in arm with her and talk to her as a similar but slightly more mature person—as if to a mysterious image of himself, older and dissimilar, more weighted with years, yet lighter and purer than himself.

I think that such ties, formed without choice, are the firmest, because they lack the tension which a choice demands. It requires reflection to love one's father, because the bond between son and father is not a direct one. Thought enters into the love of the woman of one's choice, for one might have chosen otherwise! In the case of a mother, you do not will, you fall in with a sweet necessity.

Although one may be well informed about one's parents, one scarcely knows them and this is especially true as regards a son and his mother. The more I grope into my mother's past, the greater is my feeling that I know nothing about her. I cannot imagine her as a young woman, and still less as a girl. The pictures of her in girlhood look like some other, angelic being as if I were seeing the Virgin before the Incarnation. How strange it is that one is debarred from a return to one's source and that in this instance too one faces that law of knowledge which decrees that everything becomes obscure in the region of its beginnings! How unfathomable to children are the circumstances of their parents' marriage, of the union from which they spring.

I am left with the impression that my mother was one of those people who, in spite of great natural gifts, lacked favourable circumstances for developing them in their own way. I think that she should have gone to a university, as young women do today, and studied seriously. But on further reflection I believe that if Monsieur Pouget or my mother had had an academic background they would have lacked their most inestimable quality—a freedom from specialization, the kind of pure quality, the characteristics which made the one simply a man, the other simply a woman, just a woman, yet unique of her kind.

If Monsieur Pouget had been a theologian, an exegete, a qualified professor, a director of conscience, he would not have been the Monsieur Pouget whom I so greatly loved. My mother might have been a graduate, a teacher, a landscape or portrait painter, a prolific writer, or a woman of the world, recognized by the world, and playing a discreet role as queen of a few intellectuals—not, as she was, a perfectly simple woman busy bringing up two boys in the country.

But in either of these hypothetical cases science or art would have been science and art. And (which takes away all beauty just as a silly desire to please does from a face) then art or learning would have become self-conscious. They would not have been there like that underground stream which though invisible makes my meadow green. These ungerminating seeds, these talents unused, yet latent, these abilities whose possessors are unaware of them, all these are good.

Her eyes were half open under long lids. There was nothing *exalté* about her, only a great seriousness and calm, an inner attentiveness, and what she called a 'veil of light melancholy'. She said of melancholy that it was inseparable from any mind which travels far and from any feeling which goes deep. It is certain that she had to fight against this tendency to sadness, which I observe also in myself. One recognized it in the heightened flush on her temples, in her lined forehead, and her inward look. Her lips were long, wide, a little compressed; they expressed joy in life, a capacity to savour, her strong imagination. By strong, I mean self-contained, controlled, held in check by modesty, for education and training had taught her reserve. Her nose was aquiline, her forehead smooth and open. Her hair which was chestnut colour, like the depths of her eyes, was done up in a plain chignon after the fashion of the day. An intimidating face, because it was itself nervous as well as open, of a proud structure, yet gentle.

Her voice, which was almost unaccented, was not a singing voice, as women's voices so often are. It was even, quiet and pleasant, rather low-pitched and measured, without too much modulation.

Her hands were bony, long, and loose-jointed, formed less to caress than to beat time, agile but not supple. One noticed this at the piano. Her movements lacked grace. There was some stiffness and a hint of impatience in them. She went quickly from one thing to another, and what she decided to do she did quickly. She liked a kind of hurry in everything: the speed of the women running to the empty tomb. When she applied herself to anything (and she dwelt on the word *application*), she was slow; but I knew it was a self-imposed slowness. Left to herself she would rather have leapt to it. For instance, when she heard of a sudden bereavement, of some trouble . . . The bearing of a wild but gentle animal, such as a stag or a gazelle—terrified if one approached it— this describes her well. And also, what the Gospel says about the Blessed Virgin when she went in haste across wild country to visit Elizabeth: *per montana cum festinatione.* 'The voice of my beloved; behold he cometh leaping upon the mountains, skipping over the hills . . .'

I think also of these lines:

> She is so circumspect and right
> She has her soul to keep.

François Mauriac, with whom I have sometimes talked about our mothers and their likeness to each other, wrote to me that he was sorry mine had suffered at the hands of Monsieur Doumic. 'M. Doumic, with his pink *Revue*, forced a dry diet on your mother, and prevented her from getting to know the true splendour of Gide, Claudel, Péguy, Proust.' My mother did, however, read *Le Baiser au Lépreux*. It is true that she lived in that seemingly narrow period when the great creative impulse (Renan, Flaubert, Baudelaire) had died down, and the new wave had not yet appeared—or at least was not recognized in the provinces. Those who filled the stage and were acclaimed by Victor Giraud as 'the masters of the hour', those whom alone she read (for instance, France, Barrès, Bourget, Loti, Lemaître, Faguet), writers to whom we are now so unfair, were traditional and transitional people, in whom the spirit of our race paused and rested. Was I perhaps moulded overmuch to this classical taste? Have I perhaps suffered too from Monsieur Doumic?

Mentality

One day after I had sent him an article, he summoned me to the HQ of the *Revue*, and showed me proofs marked in ink in his careful hand. He asked me who had taught me the French language. He deplored the fact that I used a barbarous word to express *state of mind*. It was *mentality*. What did this mean? I had great difficulty in making him understand that, for me, mentality had a new, deep and irreplaceable meaning. The article appeared, but *mentality* vanished for ever.

The effect of 'mentality', I reflected!

My early education confined me to didacticism which was not my path. I am waiting for old age to bring me freedom to be myself at last. I am making for childhood. 'We are born old,' said the Abbé de Tourville; 'we must try to die young.'

Jesus and our time[1]

Mythological aspect. Historical aspect. Some problems to be faced:

Jesus and earlier times.

Jesus and subsequent times.

Let us return to him. Birth. Resurrection. Being.

The knowledge of this Being.

1st Chapter: Jesus the X of historical algebra. His presence in absence.

2nd Chapter: Jesus and the idea of myth.

3rd Chapter: Jesus and the idea of history.

That the solution is not a mingling of history and myth.

[1] This first sketch grew into the book on Jesus, published in 1956. (Note of 1959.)

A solution on which many seem to dwell. Is the bringing together of all these factors a possibility?

4th Chapter: The primitive event. Quote Proudhon here, G. Sorel. Something happened. *What?*

The Gospels. A figure emerges.

5th Chapter: Present the problem of divinity.

The subject for a book, or rather for a series of lectures to be made into a book later on is here. I envy the hegira of Sainte-Beuve to Lausanne, which enabled him to write Port-Royal. I like the Beuvian form, the orbit around a single inspiration.

A law of Manou decreed that a woman's name should be easy to pronounce, gentle, clear, pleasant and auspicious; that it should end with long vowels, and resemble the words of a blessing. I think that the name Marie-Louise answers to this.

I am considering a course of lectures at the École de Guerre on the 'Probable in War'. It would demonstrate what is likely and unlikely and show how caution makes us ward off the unlikely by anti-risk dispositions in time, space and number, these three dimensions. Observe these dispositions in nature and the human body and apply them to war. The reasonable gamble. Study from this point of view the campaign of Marengo with Vendryès.

What *Figaro* has published on the youth of Napoleon is very curious. Napoleon, aware of the one essential thing, taking no thought for the non-essential, such as writing out his exercises, drawing up plans: I would even say pronouncing correctly (not to mention spelling), reserving himself for his two domains, the *essence*, and the *dream*. But how did he conceal his negligence in a School where the rule was to fill up the excess of time of the barrack-room life with compulsory and stupid exercises? At bottom Napoleon only paid attention to what interested him. When in 1799 General du Teil set him problems which bored him, a sergeant did them for him, and Napoleon signed them. He said he could no more bring himself to draw lines than to write properly.

Can the past moment live again?

FRIBOURG, MAY 1954

Conversation with Monsieur de Plinval.

He believes that St Augustine staved off barbarism not so much by being an orator or writer as by being a thinker. His Africanism and his crudity of expression were not natural to him; all that developed later. In the *De Trinitate* Augustine reveals himself as a philosopher, and there he ranks high.

M. de Plinval spoke to me sympathetically about Pelagius whom he has studied, explored and explained. Ambrose, Augustine, Jerome and Pelagius—these he said to me were the Fathers of the West. Jerome who agitated against Origen wore Origen's plumage. Pelagius, said M. de Plinval, was a true writer. He had published and rehabilitated him. Pelagius was a practical man, far less heterodox than he has been made out to be. He has been misrepresented, as it so often happens, by his disciples, in particular by Julien d'Eclane.

Lecture at Fribourg on 'Fresh Beginnings in Facts and Thought'

I found my notes; they are the seeds as it were of a book about which I am always brooding. It might be called 'Recurrence'.

Recommencement and not commencement

The seasons and their return. The recurrences of feasts and their liturgy.

The renewal of our inner life. Anniversaries silently observed.

Reiterations and fresh starts in history. For instance, the return of a concept of Empire after the fall of the Roman Empire. The Napoleonic paradox of a 'second' Empire.

Renewals in philosophy. Neo-Platonism. Neo-Thomism. The idea of renaissance and of the Second Law (Deuteronomy). Can the Law be twice given?

The importance of this idea since Kierkegaard, perhaps since Descartes. Its importance in the concept of time and also in the interpretation of life, and in the depth of existence.

The importance of recurrence in the life and thought of the Church.

Let us start with an example, or rather an experience; that of an anniversary, of a renewal. Something has vanished for ever—the primal moment; something persists, the memory, the reiteration. But there are two kinds of reiteration, which correspond to two attitudes of consciousness, according to whether it recaptures or relives. This depends on whether it is according to the body or to the mind. Only the mind can relive. Of the strain of reliving. That one never relives in the same way. That repetition comes about by the action of the mind at differing levels of spiritual life and in phases.

The law of rhythms. The rhythms of bodily life and of the life of the mind.

On the eve of an event which could only occur once I was full of anxiety. I knew that it had not yet happened; that in a solemn moment it was about to do so, a sign of eternity, surreptitiously, passing into my being like a thief. I knew that tomorrow evening it would be a memory only, that its commemoration, that artificial renewal which I recognized would be accompanied by celebrations, would serve only to illustrate even more clearly the impossibility of reproducing what has only happened once.

I tried to analyse the celebration of an anniversary. A simple analysis (in depth) of some heartfelt anniversary suggests to us that at a certain altitude of the spirit (*altus* means high and deep at the same time), the recommencement, I mean the recurrence of what has happened only once, becomes possible. But think for a moment of all that this presupposes, and all that would result from it. Would this not provide us with a new way of sounding the mystery of existence? In a rather different fashion, a traditional way, but also by a continual renewing, as if this mystery were the recurrence of an Instant, which each time became more deeply significant.

This would enable us better to understand the *mysterium fidei*, the Catholic Mass in which the Instant of the Sacrifice on the Cross is repeated in a mysterious form.

This is why highly philosophical minds, those with the metaphysical vocation of plumbing existence to its depths, of brushing close to the creative act, *ontological* souls if one can so put it, have such a natural aptitude for contemplation. For if being is a vibration which repeats itself and in doing so is sublimated, if the Mass is an oblation which is renewed, if in such repetitions the seeds of eternity are already present in time—then . . .

Edith Stein. . .

The first teaching which emerges from such thoughts is that life is rhythm, and that the real way of adapting oneself to it, the musical art of life is not (as some aesthetes suggest) to cling to the very end of a fleeting irreparable moment, but to rediscover the rhythm of the depths. In fact, to exercise within oneself not merely a recollection of past and also fleeting events (as some reminiscent authors do) but to reawake and recreate a sharper memory of the rhythms of life: some of these rhythms which are almost visible on the surface, cosmic rhythms from which we cannot free ourselves, such as the renewal of the seasons. There are some which are individual to us, in so far as we belong to a nation or a civilization: such as anniversaries. Finally there are those which are completely private, such as the recurrences of fate of which I have spoken. There is a charm in what reoccurs, the charm of what is expected and which surprises without trespass.

But there is a second and deeper and more inward lesson. It is that nothing really begins over again, that all new beginnings have a positive or a negative value; that to start again is to decline or to increase.

VI

Plan of a book on Joan of Arc

JUNE 1954

If I consider the three spiritual disciplines known as philosophy, religion and one's country (in particular France), I see
that each of the three springs from the impetus of one
person.

Socrates, for that way of considering the whole which we
call philosophy; Jesus, for religion seen as love; Joan, for the
idea of nation as contemporary men conceive it—perhaps a
conception that will endure, perhaps one that will be valid
for only a certain time.

It is astonishing that it should be from the first challenge,
the unjust accusation, the trial and death of these three beings, that the three great and absolute dedications, those
to philosophy, religion and one's country, should have
arisen.

In the introduction to his Collège de France lectures,
Maurice Merleau-Ponty said very justly: 'To rediscover the
complete function of the philosopher we must remind ourselves that even philosophers, those we read and those we are,
have always accepted as their patron saint someone who did
not write or teach (at least from official platforms), someone
who addressed himself to the people he met in the street, and
who got into trouble with public opinion and with authority;
we must remember Socrates.'

From such a point of view Joan of Arc could be (as she was

for Bergson and Péguy) what Socrates was to Greece. I think, for instance, of what is called the moral problem—the choice between good and evil. Experience of life teaches us that in fact we rarely have to choose between good and evil. The choices which rend us are genuine choices, but they are between two forms of good: or between evil and the lesser evil, or between good and the better. And I see such rending choices present in the conscience of this young girl.

Trying to sum up the problems of conscience of Joan of Arc, I can distinguish these. The first is that of relationship to justice and force; that is the problem of peace or war. Should one use force? Or should one, on the contrary, make force give way to justice alone? Is there any objection of conscience to the use of force? Here is a basic problem presented by Joan on the threshold of modern times, and one which still disturbs us.

The second and still more important problem that Joan had to face is that of the letter and the spirit. Are there cases in which to apply the letter is to deny the spirit? Are there cases in which the letter should give way in order to reveal the spirit? This problem confronted Joan in the question of wearing men's clothes. It was forbidden in Deuteronomy and by ecclesiastical usage. Joan nevertheless always wore masculine attire and caused the letter to give way before a spirit greater than itself.

The third is still more serious perhaps than the first two— it is a modern problem, and is almost constantly present in our existing civilization; that of the relationship between vocation and institution.

We feel that we are summoned by a voice or by an inner law to achieve a good which is our own and to which we are committed. But this good, this order to be established, is sometimes criticized by the institution of which we are a living part. What should we do? Should the institution be made to yield to vocation? Should one betray vocation to submit oneself to authority? Difficult.

But a preliminary question presents itself, and whatever we may think it cannot vanish. In what sense did the person whom I call Joan of Arc exist? Is she not a creation of our minds? A myth created either by the political powers of the fifteenth century, or by historians and poets? When anyone with a critical sense studies Joan, he must face this question, and consider whether Joan existed, that is to say, whether our knowledge of her is a true knowledge which apprehends its object, or an illusory knowledge into which we merely project our own minds. During a course of lectures at the Faculty of Dijon, I gave much thought to this problem.

I kept continually in mind the two other terms of comparison: Socrates and Jesus. Let us ask ourselves, I said, this question: to what extent is Joan of Arc more known or less known (less knowable or more knowable) than Socrates or Jesus? Can we compare our historical knowledge of Socrates, of Jesus, of Joan of Arc? Who can tell us if the Apology of Socrates, the story of Phaedo, was not rewritten by Plato? Certainly it must be basically true. No doubt Socrates spoke ironically to his judges and drank the hemlock elegantly like fine wine. But as for the details which are humanly so important, the circumstances and above all the sayings—how can we be sure that Socrates uttered them just like that? And it is the 'just like that' which matters for an understanding, the *nuance* consists in exactitude to the last decimal point. It is the same with Jesus. One asks oneself whether this or that saying of his (for instance, in the Gospel which is furthest from the language of Jesus: that of St John) were the words spoken *just like that*; have they not been changed by the remote memory of the narrator? For this was a time when writing was rarely used and there was no shorthand and no tape-recorder. Imagine the interest which a trial of Jesus, conducted by magistrates (Roman or Jewish) hostile to Jesus, would have had if his words had been scrupulously reported and, above all, if such a trial had lasted six months. But to express such a wish is to posit an impossible condition. There was a time in which no one worried about basic exactitude (a demand which only emerged from seventeenth-century learning), in which no one possessed recording instruments and when printing had not been born. It was a time too in which tribunals were emanations of authority, concerned rather to condemn the accused than to provide him with the means of justifying himself; what possibility then could there be that the sayings of this insignificant peasant girl should have been preserved for us in a precise manner? We would like it more precise no doubt than that of our official Reports in which the words are checked against the shorthand script.

What makes the case of Joan so arresting is something that has never happened before and probably never will again: it is that the proceedings are accompanied by a portrait of the author by the author, not *legendary* nor even *literary*, and which has every mark of authenticity. This is due to the fact that Joan was examined by judges of great juridical learning and awareness; who being determined to destroy Joan in a 'Christian' manner took the greatest care to be accurate, going so far as to transliterate the sayings of the girl from Lorraine into Latin.

One must weigh the formality, the slowness, and the ordered perfection of this trial. Long ago at Montpellier, I had as colleague a historian, P. Tisset, who specialized in the laws of the Inquisition and with whom I often discussed the trial of Joan of Arc. He was lecturing at the Faculty of Law. Tisset told me that the trial was in accordance with the Inquisitorial Law; for instance, appeal to the Pope was not permissible in these Inquisition cases.

I can imagine the solemnity of the trial. In our day everything is public; with the advent of television nothing will be secret or invisible any more anywhere. But once everything becomes public then there will be neither echo nor illumination. And publicity whose only value lies in the burglary and rape of secrets will destroy itself. On the other hand, in a silent age, in a world in which space was greatly subdivided, the smallest incidents resounded through an attentive Christendom. How much the more then a political and religious drama which took place before the princes of this world . . . and the trial of this girl was the trial of the King of France. Two bodies awaited the verdict. The University of Paris (the most renowned of all for learning) and the Inquisition (the highest power in matters of faith).

Judges, timorous but not all corrupt, argued logically, juridically, and acted gently, sympathetically, one could say *holily* (if the word were not too shocking in the context), judges who explored in Joan's favour all the resources of the law; perhaps they even liked her, or at least did not want her to burn, but only to be cast into prison forever. Once the Latin text is broken, there appears moulded in this plaster cast, Joan's answer, which the judges said was fatal (*responsio mortifera*), and which they wanted to be preserved exactly and forever, in order that posterity might acquit them.

There is something at once comic and tragic in this. As a rule, the accused have an advocate who defends them, but who also distorts them. So far as they themselves are concerned they shut themselves up in silence, or if they speak it is from indignation or fear. Sometimes it happens that their answers are cut short. Or in ancient trials, such as in several 'Acts of the Martyrs', they are too concise, or so long that they seem invented or apocryphal to us, or sometimes it happens (as we still see today) that the accused accuse themselves.

There is nothing like this in the trial of Joan of Arc. No pause for retrospective invention or for legend-building.

These are Joan's words set down at the very moment, preserved, like the dead of Pompeii or Herculaneum, in lava, instantly congealed. One must say also that Joan could not really be known until the nineteenth century when the archives were thrown open to Michelet, and when J. Quicherat published his five volumes of documents. Before that there was no possible history of Joan of Arc, if by that one understands precise, solid knowledge. That is why one must excuse Chapelain, Bossuet, even Voltaire. Who knew Joan?

Her parents knew a child like others, and then the headstrong girl who left them. That was only one aspect of her being. Her comrades in arms knew the warrior maiden. That too was only one aspect of her being. The king knew her primarily as a counsellor. That also was only one aspect of her being. The judges knew the sibylline creature, and wondered if it was angelic or diabolic. Still another aspect of her being. The people believed that they had seen legend in action. To the people of France Joan appeared from 1429 onwards as she was for Péguy: the greatest saint after the Blessed Virgin; the apparition of an angel on earth. They saw the divine aspect of her being.

And besides all this what was known? People heard of the recanter, of the heretic, of the cursed maiden, of the king's sorcerer. The canonical letter concerning the first trial went all over the world and gave this impression of Joan; a new aspect of her being, a fresh revelation! Then came rehabilitation. French thought was riveted to the idea of a virgin, come to aid the throne. In the time of Voltaire this aspect had given rise to carping and cynicism. From the fifteenth to the eighteenth century Joan was, for want of sources, spoken of by hearsay in much the same way that we speak of St Martin, St Jacques, or Ste Geneviève. No one knew her. And no one did know her until the day when the authentic papers of the trial were able to be examined in the archives.

It is nothing new for certain people to be born twice; natural birth is not the birth to glory. For instance, is Pascal a seventeenth or a twentieth century author? I think that before his *Pensées* were published by Havet and Brunschvicg there was no true knowledge of Pascal. Aristotle lived in the fourth century before our era, but the great era of Aristotle was when the Arab manuscripts translated into Latin arrived in the West, that is in the thirteenth century. Stendhal lived at the beginning of the nineteenth century; the actual moment at which he influenced opinion as he had shrewdly foreseen was at the end of the century.

Our knowledge about Joan is recent knowledge. And since it takes about a hundred years for any work to be critically examined, I think that the knowledge of Joan is a contemporary fact. I even think that the *age* of Joan is beginning. One sees it in the number of books which appear every year about her. And yet I think I will add another one.

Bergson's testament

26th MAY 1954

I see from the paper that Bergson has named me among the faithful few charged to defend his memory should occasion arise. I wrote this to the editor of *Le Monde*:

'Dear Sir,—All those who were close to Bergson knew that he was careful never to appear carelessly dressed. His clothes, his talk, his writing, showed a certain fastidiousness. He did not like to let his thought be seen at work, but to reveal it in a state of perfection—in this he was more of a classicist than a modern.

'I remember that one day, when I was at the rue Vital, I

surprised him in the act of drafting a dedication in pencil. And I, who have such a liking for "sketches" and "blocking in" (as the painters say), asked him to let me have the text which was of no further use to him. He was too courteous to refuse me; but while he was speaking about something else he started improving on it.

'You know what Bergson always used to say with a curious modesty: that he had spent his life in studying three or four problems thoroughly, and that he hoped on these selected points to be able to show "presentable" results, which could be accepted by all thinkers. About everything else he spoke like everyone else. That is why he had a horror of interviewers, when they reared up to question him about votes for women or disarmament . . . Not that he had not got his opinions. But these were simply his feelings as a man, they were not the reasoned conclusions of a thinker.

'Bergson forbade the publication of his lectures and, with more reason, that of his letters. No one ever took such precautions against the curious. But when a lecture or a letter throws light on his philosophic thought, to forbid quotation would be to interpret his wishes in the manner of the scribes. Should one on one's own responsibility refrain from quoting something which Bergson told one, or some advice he gave? Would he have condemned Plato for making Socrates live again?

'I do not share the opinion of M. Jankélévitch. I regret, but I also admire the decision of this chaste genius. I could wish Sainte-Beuve's methods to be applied to philosophers too: explanation of a work by intimacy . . .'

The question of the publication of 'secrets' is a delicate one. It is understandable that, confronted with orgies of indiscretion, a man should wish to protect himself. But 'testaments' do not give much protection, for when a man has crossed the threshold of fame he belongs to everyone, even his carelessness and mistakes, in his rough sketches. It is an admission of ultimate vanity to be preoccupied with one's remains.

Liberation by the Russians

The anniversary of my liberation by the Russian army in '45. I pick up an old notebook. 'The next day was St George's Day—the saint on horseback—and at dawn we were awakened by the sound of riders, trotting and galloping, seeking contact with the Germans. When I saw them on the side of the road, I thought that I was back in the time of the Wars of the Empire and of the Cossacks. Napoleon's words came to my mind. "Europe will be mine or it will become the Cossacks'." '

'These sturdy lively horses were one with their riders, who seemed to have grown up on them. As a rule one man rode three horses, passing like an acrobat from one to the other. Sometimes one saw a vehicle drawn by three horses aligned —the middle horse merely trotting, the other two galloping beside him. The horse in the middle had a semicircular yoke, no doubt ornamental rather than useful; it gave the cavalcade a very Russian air to western eyes. I looked for snow and moujiks and furs. Every now and then a troop of riders passed with an officer, a standard or the crew of an anti-tank gun. All this refuted the theory about the uselessness of horses in modern warfare. I discovered that I was involved with Baranoff's cavalry. He was a Russian general who had become very famous for his defence of Moscow in 1941. This was a sort of lawless free-lance troop which had advanced beyond the lines into a no-man's-land. The corps was autonomous and able to defend itself against tanks. It could if need be outflank them and exploit the advantage of a free moving unit over mechanical vehicles ill supplied with petrol. It is possible that cavalry will remain the most mobile of units, and this suggests more generally that there is no advantage in an army losing a tradition, even though for the time being it appears useless. In any case, the galloping horses, the horses of deliverance, were fine to see.'

'So dost thou rush onwards, O Russia, brave troika, no one can overtake thee. Below thy flight the dust rises, the bridges shake—thou dost pass and all are left far behind . . . Why this giddy pace? What unseen strength informs thy supernatural steeds? . . . Russia, to what end is thy haste? Answer. There is no answer. Nothing but the sound of bells . . . She flies on, outstripping all things on earth, and peoples and empires scatter to let her pass.' (Gogol.)

I remember the passage which I have copied from *Nouvelles Orientales* by Eugène-Melchior de Voguë.

Love of speed is a passion with the Russians, and this although they attach no value to time as it passes and (as we were to be shown) they have a royal negligence about estimating delay. With them speed is not (as with the neo-Westerns) a necessity for making a fortune in business, it is a solitary inebriation, an approach to the indefinite. If one could race over the sea, no doubt a sailor would enjoy speed in the same way. I notice that a road—a highway planned in advance—irks them and that my Cossacks were more at ease on the open plain. 'Russia, to what end dost thou hasten? Answer me.'

Anniversary of the death of Maurice Blondel

I am one of those who did not come across Maurice Blondel through either his books or his teaching. It was only rather late in my life that I read him closely; I never heard him speak in public except in 1937, in a room at the Sorbonne, when foreign philosophers were questioning him about his doctrine.

This was quite a different matter from reading or being taught.

What reached me first, and at an early age, was a whisper, a sound of wings, a kind of secret emanation, whose meaning I did not quite understand, except that I believed it involved a Pascalian presentation of religion more adapted to the spirit of our age. Sometimes a book influences by its title alone; an author by the idea one gets of his personality. Such an influence concerns us all the more because it helps us, though we are still at the age of uncertainty, to come to terms with ourselves.

In my case, towards the end of the war, I became aware that somewhere in France, in a region unfamiliar to me (but which I knew was surrounded by pure light and shot through by the strident sound of cicadas), there was a 'thinking reed' of Christian thought, and even more improbably of Catholic thought—a teacher who like the scribe in the Gospel would draw from his treasure things old and new, *nova et vetera*, things all of which helped to narrow on certain fronts the abyss which separates many modern minds from the religion of St Augustine, Pascal and Newman.

It must be added that since my childhood, and up to my graduation, although I was brought up in the religion of my family, I had never had a teacher who was a believer. And how I revered my teachers!

To a growing intelligence this strange splintering of light is an enigma. How to reconcile the silence and the speech of our mothers with the authoritative voice, and the even more revealing silences, of one's teachers?

The name of Blondel, his name only, was a help to me in my confusion which nobody knew about. From the age of sixteen I knew that somewhere there was a book one could not get hold of called by a very simple name: *Action* (a word which from then onwards became full of meaning for me), a book which one would absorb with effort, with difficulty, in darkness and with an immense hope, as the Arabs did with Aristotle, by copying it out oneself, or getting it typed at a fabulous price, sacrificing many pleasures to pay for the typing. The students of Lyons did just this, and I have held one of their copies in my hands.

A strange fact which reveals a certain lack of curiosity or a certain reverence or reserve in me—I never had any wish to read this book called *Action*. I wanted rather to cherish its flavour, to receive its counsel by reconstructing it as I imagined it to be. Is it perhaps because of this uneasy reverence that today I prefer the admirable treatise called *Histoire et Dogme* (an essay on the 'philosophical lacunae in modern exegesis') to *Action*? I also prefer the *Lettre sur l'Apologétique*, and the little thesis on the *Vinculum*, which only yesterday helped me to measure the difference between Pascal and Leibnitz.

I did not desire to see Blondel in the sense that Paul says in the Epistle to the Galatians that he went to Jerusalem to *see* Peter (in Greek *historêsai*); that is to say, to question him while at the same time contemplating him. I have always feared seeing in the flesh those to whom I am bound in the spirit.

One day in 1924 when I was serving in my regiment my

captain sent for me and told me that I was about to have a great pleasure though not a military one: the new second-lieutenant attached to our battalion was called André Blondel. One day this good friend, who at the wheel was a poet of pure speed, drove me to his family estate near Alise-Sainte-Reine in Burgundy. Then I did see Blondel. I spent some hours with him. I told him of my ideas on Time. He told me as Monsieur de Saci would have done at Port-Royal that I was out of luck, as my new ideas had already been voiced in St Augustine. At that solemn moment (like the moment of the Annunciation) I conceived the title and the subject matter of my thesis on *Eternity and Time*.

Since that calm, sweet and serious moment, I was both helped and hindered in reading Blondel (and those of you who have seen an author after having loved him unseen will forgive me this confidence). Between the pages I could detect like a watermark the face, the expression, the gestures, of Blondel, in particular those of his long enveloping hands, and like a muted accompaniment in the wings, I heard his voice, fervent, inflexible, insistent.

When I did not follow very well, I shut the book in order to invoke the man. Or I said to myself that one should preserve a perfect work, silent and still, for posthumous consideration; that it would be better to go to Aix-en-Provence and ring the bell in the rue Roux-Alphéran. There I could listen to and contemplate a man who was extraordinarily like the old type of metaphysician, like Aristotle or Leibnitz, dwelling in Universal Being, yet always a lover of the individual; recreating the idea of the Whole in every particle of being; always taut, yet free; busied unceasingly in reaching beyond himself to Transcendence, yet always attentive to detail.

He well knew, having experienced it in himself, and also from having heard it from his friend Victor Delbos, that a philosopher's work cannot be detached from his character, from his appearance and even from the expression of his face. That face, that gesture, the ring and the tone of that voice, are strangely alive and eloquent in my mind. More so, no doubt, than if I had seen him every week or if I had been his disciple in the town of Aix. For the human mind is so made that it thrives on and is better satisfied with the marginal or fortuitous things that happen to it.

Maurice Blondel, like many Christian philosophers since Origen and Augustine, meditated by choice on the Fourth Gospel. He loved to draw inspiration from the threefold sublimity which is the guide to all teaching and all judgment: 'I am the Way, the Truth, and the Life.' *Ego sum via et veritas et vita.*

It could even be argued that his deepest preoccupation was to realize this triple accord—impossible in human terms —of a doctrine which should be at once life, truth and way, and by which the spirit might at once 'live, move and have its being'. *Vivimus, movemur et sumus.*

To some people Maurice Blondel's influence is mainly that of a mystic, of a master of the spiritual life; one such no doubt was Monseigneur Mulla, whose meeting with Blondel led him from the Crescent to the Cross. To others Maurice Blondel influences chiefly through the secret and subtle architecture of his metaphysics, and through his *truth*. Such a one is his disciple, Jacques Paliard.

And indeed the *life* and the *truth* of Blondel's thought are very present to me. But I must say that it is in terms of the 'way' and of the method of Blondel's ideas which stirred me as a young man and which still influence me. And in this I believe I represent a number of his unknown friends who, without being specialists in ontology and theology, without perhaps being endowed with the capacity to choose in these difficult spheres, are grateful to one who has taught them that action, thought and prayer are at bottom one and the same thing.

Piety is a gift which is not evenly distributed by the Spirit which enters the hearts of men. And at a first glance it does not appear that philosophers would derive any advantage from possessing this gift of Spirit, since their first reaction to it is usually one of protest.

Perhaps the most remarkable thing about Blondel was that this gift of piety which often renders the soul too mellifluous, causing it to mistake its emotions for thought; this gift which we see in Fénelon, dissolving thought itself; which in Joubert made thought too dazzling, preventing him from identifying his true ties; this gift whose spirit is delicate—like every gift from on high—in Maurice Blondel's case, alone among the men of his time, transformed itself into the most measured, exact and progressive instrument and became his mind's best friend.

This was noticeable in his statements, in his private conversations, and noticeable also in his last words. With him the spoken word always shaped itself naturally into a wide, flowing, ascending synthesis. And the gestures with which he accompanied his speech seemed to describe a dome or a cupola. This movement recalled the flight of a dove which having flapped its wings a few times takes to the air, circles round, and then comes to rest; but when he fell silent, the listener, remembering that flight, realized that it had come under a very private architectural law. I observed something of the sort with Bergson. He did not let a conversation take shape by chance. He seemed to be reading inwardly a slow phrase which he uttered with some difficulty. Maurice Blondel had essentially the melodious gift common to his period; and he used this oratorical gift, not like Jaurès to stir up, but on the contrary *to bring all things into one*, to indicate the solidarity of essences and the relationship between lines of thought.

One must admit that the character of our language has to be strained to achieve this and it is permissible to feel that

Maurice Blondel's style suffered from a certain supercharging. His metaphors which are rather allegories than parables provide no rest for the mind, which cannot relax in them from its inner tension. From this stylistic point of view one might place him *du côté de 'chez Proust'*, in the camp of those who have enriched their phrases, not by stretching them into rhetorical emptiness, but by making every particle of speech into a *monad*, which is a reflection of the universe. In Proust too I find in an aesthetic form this gift of piety; I find it in his demand for discipline and marshalling, in his determination not to write anything which is not a symbol of the whole work, the reflection of the entire past conceived as a living tradition, a tiny mirror of the whole.

Blondel's piety had yet a last characteristic, a quality which brought him close to the unbelieving philosophers who were made akin to him by having that particular inner gift of which I have said that it can also grow in earth to which every definite faith is alien, as with Marcus Aurelius, Spinoza and Xavier Léon.

In Spinoza, and even in Leibnitz of whom he has drawn the most sympathetic portrait (sympathetic because they were made akin by the fact that Leibnitz too saw creation as an ever-expanding genesis—'a march towards inexhaustible perfections'), Blondel discovered a piety which gives 'access to transcendence'. In fact it was Spinoza to whom he had recourse when he wanted to open an alien mind to that Christian aspect of the spiritual life which is piety.

The faceless voice

I have had a belated experience which has taught me something which I thought I knew: what the *word* is. Not long ago,
one peaceful morning the Sphinx questioned me before a
microphone, trying to penetrate right to 'the division of soul,
spirit, joints and marrow'. I had to forget that I was speaking
in front of another man, and to feel that I was alone, face to
face with truth. There were times when the effort I was
making to give the best reply to a question was so painful
that I stopped, seeking the least unsuitable word, as a painter
hesitates between the cobalt and the ultramarine on his
palette. Everything was set, mark you, to make me think that
I was alone; that if I hesitated or quavered no one would
notice it; and that what I said was of no consequence.

Facing me behind the microphone the kindly smile of the
Sphinx was comforting. He seemed to say to me, the liar:
'No one is listening to you.' But I knew quite well that this
was untrue; that indiscreet, bored, unknown people, that
foreigners, enemies, were about to penetrate my secret,
and that I would speak to thousands. I repeated to myself
Joubert's wise advice: 'Speak low, so that the deaf may
hear.' Whereas a visible audience always makes me rather
nervous, this one gave me confidence. Why? No doubt because the radio realizes the wish of every mind, which is to
be able to communicate with other minds (and an invisible
multitude is in fact only a single entity) without the unpleas-
ing intervention of the body.

The body is either clothed, adorned, arranged and artificial, or it is something which careless nature has daubed
with too long a nose, a skull like a rock, and endowed with

clumsy gestures. I dread television which violates faces, and compels us to ape ourselves.

The radio which conveys the voice alone—that voice which is a pure mirror of the self—multiplies unknown contacts, shy encounters, conversations without echoes, between two people who remain hidden. No indiscreet gaze meets another. The speaker is relieved of the embarrassment of owning a body; the listener of the vexation of bestirring himself to go out on a wet evening, to take his seat in public where he will be conscious of neighbouring eyes gazing at him. The disturbance of clapping or booing is eliminated; and for the speaker the fear of not being applauded to exactly the right extent. The almost sensual contact at which a speaker always to some extent aims does not exist here. So much the better. For I think this is vulgar. Such tricks are unbearable when seen again in cold blood, and that is why I find it intolerable to read an orator's speech unless he is a poet also.

In the empty studio I enjoyed the silence wrapped around the spoken word and I remembered something said by Saint-Exupéry: 'The spirit's sphere, the space in which it can spread its wings, is silence.' How silent light is! And how desirable it would be that the spoken word, travelling from sender to receiver through the great trembling void, should be surrounded by silence. How desirable too that he who listens should not see the face of him who speaks, and that this one individual and the countless listeners should be unaware of each other; or rather that they should know each other only in the homeland of the spirit.

When speaking into a microphone one feels far distant in space from one's listeners; and one is much further removed from them in time, since a voice may be recorded many months before transmission. This dual displacement of space and time adds to the mystery of the spoken word. It gives one the impression of being a stranger in the world, as though one had already been transported to a kind of 'beyond', from where one speaks to those still alive solely through the voice, which conveys intimacy better than the features, because the voice, which is more of the body than the face, is a better medium for the soul. If a dead man had to choose between these two ways of making himself known to his dear ones, I wager he would prefer the voice because of its gentle and individual inflexions.

The parallel between St Augustine and Newman

He, non-infallible teacher, has formed the intellect of Christian Europe.　　　　　　　　　　　Newman on St Augustine

SEPTEMBER 1954

One may question what help Newman got from the thought and the example of St Augustine. He refers to him several times in his works and knew him thoroughly. Yet you cannot say he took him as his model. Why? Because Newman, who was more English than Latin, clung closer to the Greek fathers.

He thought he saw a resemblance between the Anglican Church (isolated from Rome, but strong in tradition and doctrine and capable of self-renewal by the initiative of an outstanding man) and the Church of Alexandria in which St Athanasius prefigured him. This analogy was to fall to pieces in his hands. And as a mirror for the Church of England, he came to substitute for the Church of Alexandria (in union with Rome) the Donatist Church (separated from Rome), which in fact was what St Augustine fought against.

This change of analogy was the springboard for his conversion from Anglicanism to the Church of Rome. But neither in

Alexandria nor even in Africa did he find St Augustine. Alexandria was filled with the figures of Clement, Origen, and above all Athanasius. It is true that the story of the Donatist controversy was known to Newman through reading the anti-Donatist writings of St Augustine. Yet in these writings, St Augustine does not appear in his inner and pre-Newman aspect. It is the leader of the Church who is here revealed, fighting for the Church's rights, and seeking to confound its subtle opponents. If Newman (as I think) began to study St Augustine from this angle, he did not meet the Augustine who was of his species. On the contrary, St Augustine here reveals himself as more African than Latin and in the ways best fitted to alienate Newman's anxious, tender and sensitive mind. This was the hard, dogmatic, harsh, repressed, violent side of Augustine, which he displayed in a pugnacious irony. Newman's leaning towards Athanasius, Basil and Chrysostom was a choice made by the heart. And just as a classical mind, meeting Hugo or Shakespeare, reveres them as the greatest among the aliens, so Newman honoured Augustine, without following in his train, never thinking that one day he would be called *Augustinus redivivus*.

It is true that Newman like every Latin Christian and, above all, like every faithful follower of a Reformed Church moved in an Augustinian atmosphere. He said that St Augustine had produced a 'second edition' of Christianity. And he well knew what he owed to him in relation to the doctrines of Grace and even of Predestination. We must remember that Newman believed that at about the age of sixteen he had an inward feeling of being predestined, a feeling which never completely faded away, although it lost its first Calvinistic colouring.

Newman might have devoted himself to the theology of Grace. He treated it with brilliance in his lectures on Justification, in which he contrasted St Augustine and Luther. But the bent of his mind was not in that direction.

This is the place to define more clearly the difference between these two minds.

One of the aspects of St Augustine's primitive nature was violence: violence of mind, body and speech—something wild and ardent and at times morose. It was this which alarmed Monica, and made her postpone his entry into the catechumenate. This violence sublimated itself, and the rage of the flesh turned to fervour. It endowed his speech with that hidden fire, that phosphorescence of the Word, which transformed Latin rhetoric into a kind of untranslatable poetic prose. The violence of certitude changed into a perhaps excessive taste for the battle of ideas. He was certainly basically right in unmasking Pelagius, and in crushing Julien d'Éclane, but one might suspect that he delighted in polemics and, like those who are too much in the right, that he felt no pity for the wounds he inflicted; and that, as for himself, he hardly felt the attacks made upon him, because they provided him with an opening for a fine counter-attack.

Newman's nature, too, seems to have included a certain hardness, something untamed and morose. There are those who point to that egotism which often accompanies genius (just as the genius of the military leader compels him to a necessary forgetfulness of the dead). But Newman was sensitive, even more than susceptible, retiring into himself like a sensitive plant—like the snapdragons which he loved at Trinity. When sensibility is very deep-rooted it tires quickly. Newman's way was that of the artist, who ceases work when the spirit ceases to blow upon him, whereas St Augustine went on beyond his inspiration through sheer momentum, like every orator.

Nevertheless, these two minds do resemble each other, for Newman when indignant turns orator, and St Augustine, when he wishes to base his doctrine on experience, turns autobiographer as would a contemporary.

Up to now we are only in the ante-room of our subject. A man's message is more important than the man himself. And every message is related to the needs of the time.

The resemblance between St Augustine and Newman is that at a distance of fifteen centuries from each other they both understood the relationship of Christianity with 'duration' and with personal life; more precisely, they understood the relation between the inner duration of the life of the soul to universal history.

It is enough to mention the two books, the *Confessions* and the *City of God* on the one hand, and the *Apologia* and the *Development* on the other, or if one wants to give them titles, the *De Duratione Interna*, and the *De Duratione Universi*. One might say that the treatise *De Gratia*, and the treatise *De Ecclesia* were written by Newman and Augustine in a fashion which is personal and inimitable.

Newman, like St Augustine, experienced conversion, but his is a different experience. He was saved from all the suffering which the body's resistance adds in terms of pathos to conversion, whereas St Augustine did not enjoy the sweet deepenings which accompany a continuing passage from faulty to full light, the factor which gave Newman a particularly acute sense of the development of the Church. In other words, Newman did not have to make a total turn about—a *metastrophe* in the Platonic sense. And if he went *ex umbris et imaginibus ad veritatem*, this was not through any uprooting of the will, but by the workings of the mind on historical data.

There is more anguish in Augustine—and his experience is alas! more universal; whereas Newman's entirely intellectual experience can only be understood by those few minds which have studied ecclesiastical history. That is why, on the level of inner experience, Newman the righteous man is outstripped by Augustine the sinner. What St Augustine gave to Newman was an example of the lonely dialogue between

Creator and creature and the thought that one must think and act as though there were no one in the world except God and oneself. Newman did not extract from this idea a system (like Descartes or Leibnitz) or a mystical way of life (like St Teresa of Avila), but it influenced him (like Augustine) to turn from soliloquy to autobiography. For both of them this uninterrupted conversation of the soul with God alone did not take place in a desert and was not cut by occasional ecstasies (as with Plotinus), it consisted in an endless reflection on existence: on meetings, on temptations, on beginnings, on defeats, on faults even.

Hence, in Augustine and Newman, the methods of Plato and Plotinus were shaped anew, thanks to the contribution of the prophetic or apostolic experience which gave such emphasis to historical contingency and to 'the divine event'.

It might have been a temptation to a fourth-century Christian mind, fed on Platonism and Aristotelianism, to devalue the historical aspect of Christianity by making the history of the world into an image of eternal realities.

What still tempts a Christian spirit of the nineteenth century or the twentieth century, brought up on Positivism or post-Kantian idealism, is to devalue again the contingent aspect of Christian history by seeing it as a dialectic process devoid of any true inner tensions.

Here Plato, there Hegel, confronts Christ and his first interpreters, not so much to abolish as to weaken his message by diminishing the share which temporal existence has in this message.

From this point of view Augustine's work is like Newman's in the sense that the experience of intimacy with creativeness, which derived from their personal history, urged both the one and the other to reflect on history and to discover in it the presence of the same intimacy—the Catholic Church playing in the universal history of humanity the role which awareness of self does in the life of the individual.

From that point of view also, the two Works (belonging to two notable epochs, hinges on which history turns) are in opposition to the main Adversary, that is a philosophy at once imperialist and logico-materialist, in which thinking and suffering humanity is tempted to seek a solution of its problems. But for the fall of Rome a materialist stoicism centred on the Roman Empire (in appearance a temporal Eternity) could have provided a philosophy of Power, capable of making war on Christianity and driving it into the catacombs. The ideas of St Augustine were far more strongly opposed to this than he himself realized. And the *City of God*, that striding *Summa*, became the charter of the Christian Middle Ages, into which in the time of St Thomas even Aristotle was absorbed.

In our day, man, thinking and suffering in masses, is tempted by a philosophy in which the Idea is not distinguished from the Matter or the Fact, and which seems to find realization in an organized proletariat, a proletariat which thanks to the power of Russia already constitutes a vast empire. It is clear that Newman, the solitary of Edgbaston, did not foresee this problem of the masses, although he perceived the problem of intellectual incredulity. He was absorbed in specifically Christian problems, not in this case that of authentic Grace, but of the true Catholic Church. But in both cases experience and doctrine went far further than their point of first application. Newman, as Przywara has recognized, by adding yeast to the philosophies of Kierkegaard and Hegel (the allegiance of contemporary intellectuals is evenly divided between these two) provided them with an original solution. Like Kierkegaard he had experience of the inner Christian time-scale, not in the form of the instant which separates and which is able to possess the Infinite, but in the form of a duration able to receive the eternal according to its own mode. In this he was linked to the Augustinian tradition, which the Reformers ignored or disrupted. Above all he provided an answer to Hegel (such as Plato might have done had he read Aristotle) by showing that the true 'becoming' of history (which he did not contest and which actually brought about his conversion to the Roman Church, a parting from Anglican immobility) was not a god *se-faisant*, an immanent dialectic, but that this 'becoming', on a privileged axis, was directed by an Idea that was divine—that History, in that sense at least, had meaning.

Here Newman, like Augustine, offers to the days to come a tool of the spirit with which to found a new City of God, to prepare, like Augustine, a new Middle Age.

The art of the hiatus in Jacques Chardonne

NOVEMBER 1954

Jacques Chardonne, that enchanting letter-writer and unknown as such, sent me his *Letters to Roger Nimier*. I fear that some day he will reclaim the letters he has written to me, in blue ink on any paper to hand, in which all the down strokes seem unconcernedly to have happened of themselves.

Hazy ideas, evocations, ellipses, confidences taken back as soon as given. Random advice to a young writer. Abridged films in which one sees by silences (as if in La Fontaine written by La Rochefoucauld) processions of sensitive loving lives so happy and so unhappy at the same time. Retrospective pictures of what Europe might have been without victories or wars, had men been wise. Judgments of contemporary authors—sometimes as in the case of Barrès severe. Long pauses between ideas, between pages, paragraphs and words. A wonderful grasp of spaces, gaps, hesitations, respites. The story of a friendship of mind and tastes (rather than of affection) between a slightly disillusioned but still youthful old man, and a young writer, grown old already. This is the strange book called *Letters to Roger Nimier*, which proves that Jacques Chardonne does not adopt a manner in his novels; that he is straightforward when he writes for the public and always fastidious when he lets himself go.

VII

Thoughts on the work of a pioneer:
Père Teilhard de Chardin

Reading the tributes which *La Table Ronde* has published in praise of Père Teilhard, I tried to pin down finally, for myself only, his features, his intellectual physiognomy, and his place in the history of Ideas.

On the evening of one Easter Day, Père Teilhard who was visiting friends collapsed and died almost an hour later without regaining consciousness. How fitting that it should have been Easter evening! He who meditated on 'recapitulation', he who across the History of Species looked to the time when God should be all in all—it was right that he should have died on Easter night!

On his last visit I was struck by his air of detachment from everything; he was more alert, forthright, more eager than ever and rather uninhibited. A long skull, rather like a well-chiselled flint; steely eyes, looking straight into yours; long, supple hands, as well fitted to hold the skull of Sinan-thrope as the smallest of its teeth. He had an indefinable something that was Anglo-Saxon, something too of the explorer, the eternal traveller which supplemented without contradicting the underlying Jesuit mould. And all this was shot through radiated by an immense vitality.

I often used to read his writings and tried to place him in the scheme of things, and it was not easy . . .

One must distinguish between pioneers and masters; they are two vocations which are rarely yoked. Pioneers advance in the undergrowth; they are the vanguard, they tear their hands on thorns. They grope. One must allow them freedom to go astray. When the pioneers have done their work, the masters arrive and they build practicable roads and bridges over which people will pass. As Péguy said, they put up signposts.

'With a keen eye, a ready hand, and a confident step, he goes forward not knowing how, by instinct rather than by rule. He leaves no trace and he cannot be a model for anyone else. One is fascinated and bewildered.'

Newman said this, possibly about himself.

One wonders whether Newman was not by a rare chance himself both master and pioneer. But Père Teilhard was undoubtedly a pioneer. It was his vocation, his illumination, his purgatory.

It was in England where the Jesuits, banished from France, had taken refuge, that his character was shaped by the philosophy and theological teaching of the Company of Jesus. My two Jesuit uncles were his companions. The Jesuits of those days were routine-bound. He was disheartened. His cast of mind and his inner experience inclined him to science and mysticism (a little like Pierre Termier), not towards that half-way house furnished with concepts which is with us in the West, the much worked-over domain of theological philosophy.

And this sets me to thinking about the development of thought in this little outpost of Asia since the time of Socrates and Plato.

What can I say? Except that in Europe man's thought (both in Greece and Judea, and well before Christianity) did not adapt itself to a cosmic order of knowledge combining the science of external things with knowledge of salvation. For want of a better term let us call this combination a *Gnosis*. Gnosis did not appear in Plato who only studied the Cosmos belatedly, in *Timaeus*, the last of his dialogues, which does not moreover link science to the spiritual life, already dealt with separately in the *Symposium* and the *Phaedo*. One might say that there are slight traces of Gnosis in St Paul, for instance when he tells us in the Epistle to the Romans that all creation groans, waiting for the revelation of the sons of God. (I am not even certain that St Paul means the *physical* creation; did he perhaps think only of souls?) What is certain is that Western theology has not followed this path, and came quickly to distrust it—no doubt because of systems described as gnostic which imperilled the Faith by a bastard mingling of the Gospel with philosophical conceptions about the origin of the world.

One might say that Western theology after Gnosis was agnostic, anti-gnostic; that it eliminated from its field hypotheses of a scientific type; that it distrusted the cosmos and knowledge of the cosmos as such; that it followed the way of Socrates and left the cosmos to the 'physicians', concerning itself only with things of the moral order for fear lest the demoniac might intervene in things of the physical world. Theology developed in a very *pure* atmosphere (in the sense that one speaks of a *pure* gas), a little rarefied with respect to science. One may wonder whether that was a disadvantage. I think it an advantage. The way in which knowledge of the cosmos changes, in which 'natural philosophies' succeed each other, shows how transitory is the picture of the cosmos which we think of as scientific. In our time, when we see the face of world systems change so speedily, one can recognize how dangerous it would be for the Faith to ally itself to one or other of these systems. It was a great mistake to seem to link forever the Incarnation of the Son of God to the concept of an immobile earth. And one would be equally wrong in seeking to detect an inevitable link between the Christian religion and a vaguely defined evolution.

This is not to imply that Gnoses are useless. They are the

stuff of philosophies, also sometimes of theologies, the mixed soil from which springs the even-petalled flower.

What a lengthy détour to place Père Teilhard and to understand his isolation! He certainly belonged to that race of men who need to *touch*, to *believe*, rather than to *think* in the conceptual intervals which stretch between feeling and faith. He told me about the origin of his mystical vocation and how, at the age of six (if I remember aright), when touching a piece of wrought iron (a ploughshare in fact), suddenly he sensed hardness, certitude, life, consistence, reality, the created, which is in *matter*. But at the same time a devout mother told him about the Sacred Heart of Jesus. Matter and the Sacred Heart, these two extreme poles of contemplation were thus revealed to him as a child. Henceforward for him, matter was never condemned or suspect, or held in fetters or considered incapable of leading to the Spirit. The Heart of Jesus, its mystical capacity for synthesis, the heart which the witness, in the Gospel of John, saw pierced by a spear on the Cross, he conceived of as the prime mover around which all things must finally unite. And between this Matter and this Heart appeared the epic poem of life, its upsurge, its evolution. In the eyes of Teilhard this was not, as it was for Bergson, a dispersion into segments around a single source, but a reunification of species and of humanity in the vision of a *point Omega*—an ultimate. That is why for his geometrical mind, evolution was related to Christ. He awakened, he aroused (he also annoyed by lack of precision in his language, e.g. his excessive use of capital letters). He offered to philosophers and to theologians a flow of lava, which was like the volcanoes of his native Auvergne. He saw these as a child (like the young Pascal, also an Auvergnat), he contemplated shapes which had hardened, as if all stone had first been fire and all cessation motion.

While we await a critique from his friends and his opponents (united in the search for truth), I would like people to remember what during the thirty years I knew him always seemed beyond question in Père Teilhard: his vocation (so compelling from his early years) to conjoin to Catholic thought and prayer certain aspects of modern feeling which are generally monopolized by atheism; and what is more are fodder for attacks against the Christian conception of the world.

Like M. Pouget (but in a way which was more poetic, more detached, vaster, less Hebraic, less peasant-like, and to my way of thinking less reliable), he was imbued with the profound feeling that nature was in travail, that creation was continuing and progressive. He loved the cosmos as it came from the hands of Jehovah, but a cosmos in which, if I dare say so, the Son and the Holy Ghost work even to the present day to complete, as St John said, the Father's work.

I remember how, about 1920, he freed the young men of the École Normale from false limitations, telling them that the pursuit of knowledge was a priestly work in which the mind took hold of what was actual, to assume, sublimate and offer it. He showed us that it was a tragic misunderstanding to believe that the earth's attraction led away from God, and he told us that Christians must enlarge the rather restricted picture they had of Christ, and bring Jesus into a world-dimension which had been so much expanded in space and time. Among the scattered works of Père Teilhard, it is the laboratory notes, made only for himself or for some friends and confidants, that we must above all preserve (along with those bearing on his speciality) the texts of his religious meditations. Here is the source. Here too is the message.

It is no ordinary piety which takes for springboard what the normal ascetic regards as a hindrance; which glorifies creation in what seems to be its most opaque aspect: matter, earth; or in the most alive and disturbing: life, genesis; or in the most ancient: the preparations of prehistory. His is a piety which is not scared of all this, but on the contrary uses it for food and shelter. There is something of St Francis of Assisi in such piety, but a Francis who would have sensed his brotherhood with the cosmogeny through the medium of scientific research.

I am impressed to see how many of those souls, numerous in our day, who love the world too much to love anything else, could assimilate Père Teilhard's kind of piety. The Christian faith is unbearable to them because it seems to them to disdain research and hard work, and the plenitude of today's pace and today's time. Claudel's mysticism also tends to recharge the universe with its original creative force. But Claudel is too much of a poet to become food for scientists.

Père Teilhard had a charismatic ability to give back to religious minds a sense of the cosmos and to lead them to a reading of the Bible which had become stale to them. The love of the earth, of suffering and of time which Marxist mysticism rediscovered and immediately corrupted with its *gangue*, moves in Père Teilhard towards union, joy, and eternity. And the rod of the Cross appears not as a torture invented to cause suffering, but as a law of unification, simplification and sublimation.

I rediscovered in him certain tones which recalled Père Gratry, who enchanted my youth.

From this point of view Teilhard's thought enters into the history of mysticism. Technique and mysticism, and not philosophy or theology, were his true spheres. One does not add to his stature by ignoring his contours. It is the contours which define a face.

I do not want to speak of the accusation of pantheism which has been brought against him. I was surprised to read in the papers that certain free thinkers were astonished that he had not left the Church and the Company of Jesus! He, who thought only of unity, belonged essentially to the Church. All his work is a story of the unification of all

249

creatures in Christ. He emphasized continuity, evolution, life force, progress. I do the opposite. I am aware of discontinuity, emergence and change. But such aspects were not alien to Teilhard's work, although he does not stress them.

A stranger in the Company of Jesus? Teilhard de Chardin, who proved that obedience is not an empty word! In some ways he was like the first Jesuits, the conquistadors who are so hard to place, who dreamed of bringing faith to continents. He was like St Francis Xavier with his Indies, his Japan and his China, upsetting traditions, but not pausing long enough to get organized. He too was more of a stimulator than an organizer. The continents which Teilhard de Chardin planned to annex to a Christian vision of the world were those of unimaginable duration, of mass statistics, of macro-evolution, of the human horde.

He had a keen sense of the immense periods of waiting in infinite spaces of time (for him they were not frightening but calming), of the times which preceded Israel and Jesus, as of those trials of the human prototypes before Adam . . . He dragged us from our time scale, which is so limited. He tried to see God's work on God's scale. Hence his optimism. Perhaps pessimism is linked to a small scale and to short sight.

Last conversation on the plurality of worlds

21st JUNE 1954

We were talking about the plurality of worlds. He thought this was not only likely, but probable. I had just read in the *Civilta*, the review of the Jesuit Fathers in Rome, a study by a Thomist theologian in which he emphasized that plurality of worlds is not incompatible with the redemptive Incarnation. Père Teilhard thought it fitting that the Grace of Christ might be offered in an equivalent form wherever there were free and potentially supernatural creatures. 'Although one cannot,' I said to him, 'make laws for the Omnipotent Will.'

'But,' he answered, 'as I think Sertillanges said, there must be proportion in the work of Wisdom. And the more we enlarge the world and the possibilities of the biosphere, the more it seems disproportionate (and therefore unworthy of God) that in the immense universe so much energy, matter, and synthesis should be expended upon humanity as it is.' Then he smiled, preparing to tell me something important and amusing, which he was enjoying secretly in advance. 'Here is a true story which I read somewhere the other day. Just listen to this. An American airman, a Catholic and a theologian in his spare time, met a flying saucer in the sky. He had read the article in *Civilta* of which you spoke. It was not impossible to imagine a human species which knew neither original sin nor the redemption. The saucer drew near. The aviator-theologian said to himself: "Should I fire? If the saucer contains Martians who have not known original sin, the bullets will ricochet, since these beings, not having sinned like ourselves in Adam, are not mortal." You see,' he said, showing his fine large white teeth, 'that the questions we are asking ourselves, like all supreme questions, have very practical consequences.'

He was in a mood for anecdotes. And he went on: 'A young *Jociste* asked me: "Father, when I am repairing an aeroplane engine, am I constructing Christ?" Don't you think that this boy expressed very clearly the unavowed question of our day —that which the Communist mystique seems to answer? Well, my work is intended to face up to that.'

What was most comprehensible to him was the universal Christ, born before all creation, he of whom St Paul spoke in the Epistle to the Colossians. But he was well aware that this Christ could only be made real by a real historical Incarnation, by the entering of the Word into a lineage, into a *sinus*, into a *phylum* (this is the birth . . . *natus ex Maria Virgine*).

And then by the Incarnate Word emerging beyond the frontiers of death and space-time (*resurrexit tertia die*: that is the Resurrection).

He picked up a card which he had beside him (an invitation from the Explorers' Club to a lecture at the Musée Guimet). On it he drew spirals, whirls, converging lines, and notably two circles. One in solid line represented the supernatural; the other, which was dotted, represented nature, and had two separate centres joined by a sort of bridge or wide arc. I wrote down two words which he gave me as his keys: *VALORISER, AMORISER.* I have preserved these diagrams as a relic, a last trace of the mystical seismographer. In my notes I find what he said to me. Especially this: 'that Christ since his resurrection is the place of the convergence of the whole, having been freed from the limits of the historical Incarnation . . .'

'Humanity, to the extent that it understands its increasing convergence, can only move towards him. And if by chance there are other forms of humanity (which seemed to him very probable on account of the millions of galaxies and because it is the law of life to go to the extreme), we cannot imagine their biological form nor even whether they had had an Incarnation or its equivalent. But we could be certain that such human species in their genesis are ascending towards "point Omega" where they will be reunited to ours in the Risen Christ.'

'Being?' he said. 'Being? I wonder whether there is not a concept deeper than *esse*; I mean *unire*, *uniri*, to be united?' And I noticed, playing on the word, that for him there were no *essences*, only *escences* (florescence, senescence, adolescence).

My first meeting with the Tharauds

In a small book which filial piety led me to write some time ago, I told how my mother taught me to read. I am not now speaking of the alphabet, for I cannot remember that she ever taught me my letters. I mean a more impenetrable alphabet, that of characters, natures, analogies and relationships, such as those between minds and countrysides. It was in the recollection of this 'reading' that I rediscovered the brothers Tharaud, whom I had so greatly longed to meet in the flesh, though I had never had the chance of doing so.

When I was thirteen I discovered the world of novels. My second-form teacher, who was not very prudent, lent me all kinds of books, provided they were well written. This disturbed my mother. And she wrote to a wise priest, a friend who was then at the front (where he was killed a few days later), to ask his advice about how to direct my reading. Long ago I published his answer, which was rich in wisdom and foresight. I give here the last part of it.

'You cannot control your sons' reading for long—I mean what they read on their teacher's advice. Would it not be better to read with them, to choose passages in a book, after having explained the plot to them, and particularly to choose these so that they may profit from the plot and situations, or at any rate understand them without moral loss? Difficult, yes, but what noble work for a mother, and how proud her sons will be of her when they are twenty!'

My mother took this difficult advice[1]. But as she could not

[1] My mother derived this method also from the correspondence of Vigny with his adopted daughter, who lived at Trégnac in Lozère. Vigny did not want his children to go to a boarding school. He wanted them to hear the talk of the family circle every evening—the family circle,

do everything, she got one of her friends, Madame Danis, to help her. I read *Madame Bovary* with Madame Danis. Possibly my mother was too shy to read it with me and therefore chose an intermediary. This was not the case with *La Maîtresse Servante*. She read several passages aloud to me. I think the Tharauds' language pleased her more than Flaubert's. For she was sympathetic to the gentle modulation of lament which runs through the plot of *La Maîtresse Servante*. One must remember that this book is about Limousin, and that Creuse touches Limousin. What we discovered together was far more than a painting (in fact there is not much description in *La Maîtresse*): we found an atmosphere—the attentive peace of the countryside which is everywhere present.

I noticed how often the word *moist* came into *La Maîtresse Servante*, the word which Baudelaire likes so much and used so well. With us either it has just rained, or is about to rain, and nature often seems to have been disappointed in love and found quick consolation . . .

Fromentin was another friend. Later on I came to know Jacques Chardonne. And from then onwards these three formed a definite group for me. Writers from the Charente, but related to Limousin and Marche by an affinity of temperament hard to define.

What struck us in *La Maîtresse* was what Halévy called 'the end of the notables'. *La Maîtresse Servante* describes the fall of the squireens of our countrysides. And in these days in which this humble aristocracy is, so to speak, dying a second time, abandoning its turrets, and selling up its houses and lands, this novel is topical. The resigned lament of a dying class is symbolized by the narrator's mother, a

---

'the port from which they must set out and to which they should always return'. It was Vigny who recommended the *Sources* by P. Gratry, the book which my mother gave me, and in which one must delve for that 'second education which,' said Vigny, 'one gives oneself.'

rural land-owner, like many whom my mother and I could name.

Behind this unchanging historical drama (for one perennially hears the plaints of some aristocracy) we listened in *La Maîtresse* to the liturgy of the land and its work. Although it is not a religious book (any more than it is really a love story), one shares in it the natural religion of the land and of the dead, which is omnipresent in our countryside of the Centre.

The face of the young imprisoned woman always attracted my mother who herself loved the country so much, but never had time to enjoy it or go for walks, because she was chained to her duties. It is strange too that this book about the past (for everyone of whom the author speaks is dead) is wrapped in sadness, regret and remorse towards the dead: the three women who suffered because of him. I should like to quote the pages which long ago shook my emotions profoundly and which still vibrate in my memory. The reader must forgive me. No doubt he will understand why these pages which I have retained from the far away past mysteriously herald the future. In this one I see my godmother once again:

'When she had said her say, I gave her my arm to walk, as we were used to do, the hundred yards down the avenue from the front door to the road. She took it with a kind of tired resignation, and I felt more touched by this gesture of abandonment than I had been by all her fits of temper. How much I would like to walk with her again! She was sometimes so light, sometimes when sorrow weighed her down so heavy, on my arm. How much I would like to be able to leave this room where I am writing, to go down to the little drawing-room, to pause in the avenue while she snipped off (with hands which always wore black gloves and carried secateurs) some withered geraniums or a petal-less rose. She told me that she had once been pretty. There was nothing left of this now, except the nobility of a figure unbowed by age. The habit of commanding or rather of being obeyed gave a kind of energy to each of the thousand wrinkles with which her face was criss-crossed.

'But deafness, and no doubt also the sorrows which I had caused her for many years had, at the end of her life, imprinted a desolation on her features and in her eyes, which I cannot recall without a feeling of bitterness and of irremediable grief.'

This piece too: 'Water retained on the earth's surface by the granite sub-soil made channels everywhere, and often one found in the midst of a sparkling area a small square reservoir which in our part of the world we call a " serf "—perhaps to show that a spring is imprisoned there. Mariette often reminded me of these imprisoned springs. They are there, constant, flowing, always ready for our domestic needs, and in them one sees the sky.'

Then there is this farewell: 'Adieu, sir, I am leaving you. Forgive me for having tired you for so long by my futile regrets. How much affection has been heaped on my head! What sap, what abundance of love there is everywhere in life! I think that if each one of us looked around him he would be astounded that so many people have valued him so highly.'

I cannot believe that the Tharauds ever wrote anything better than this book. To my way of thinking they never did so well.

It is disheartening to publish a masterpiece in one's youth, and after that to see one's whole career as nothing more than a vain attempt to regain that first inspiration. Having once put forth one's power, why start again? One has proved to oneself that one is possessed of power—that's enough. Why do it again? It is better to remember. Thus I see a sort of desperation in these brothers, an appetite for life and for a career which launched them, indolence and all, into the great world as observers.

La Maîtresse Servante is contemplation, not observation. A stern contemplation whose note I do not find elsewhere. The Lorraine note, to which one might relate it, as heard for instance in *La Colline Inspirée*, is far more romantic than the Tharauds' language, which is always direct and has nothing elaborate, hazy or oriental about it.

I, who am not of the west, try to compare the prose of Jacques Chardonne, of Loti, and of the Tharauds. I do not think I am mistaken in finding a marine element in it. And no need to establish a positive connection between subjects; this shows itself already in *Dominique*, which I consider to be a novel, through which sea breezes blow even though we hardly see the sea.

For me, the Tharauds are primarily landsmen, liking the sea for adventure only. That is why I annex them, via Limousin, to the France of the Centre.

P.S. La Tragédie de Ravaillac, which a friend of the Tharaud brothers recently advised me to read, strikes, it is true, quite a different note from *La Maîtresse Servante*. *La Maîtresse* is a melancholy mystery and like our Centre countryside gentle and without mysticism or violence. While *La Tragédie* in which I think I see the influence of *La Colline Inspirée* (*La Maîtresse* reminds one more of *Colette Baudoche*) is quite the contrary, for it is a drama of fatality. No one will ever change my feeling that the Tharauds were forcing themselves a bit when they aspired to tragedy and that their true vocation was that of evoking mysteries on a human scale. I would happily apply to them Lamennais's fine saying quoted in *George Sand* by André Maurois: 'Life is a sad mystery to which faith holds the secret.'

A sculptor visits me

Today, 7th October 1954, Chauvenet, the sculptor, came to see me at 11 o'clock and showed me the drawings he had made of Monsieur Pouget. He means to make a medallion of Pouget, not in order to put it in his showcase but simply to have a record of beauty: the beauty of Monsieur Pouget's countenance which has impressed him so much. First he took two photographs of him, which, he said, gave him a great deal of trouble. In one of these Monsieur Pouget's face appeared much more refined, sculpturesque, and aristocratic than it was in reality. It is strange how death *aristocratizes* features, inevitably refining them by diminishing the flesh, and emphasizing the bone structure. Perhaps we also project on to them some image of meditation, since the face of the dead seems to us to be already contemplative. Anyhow the reason matters little. The face on the medallion was quite different from the one I knew.

I had already noticed as I kept watch in the death chamber that by the early decomposition of his features death had done away with any excess of flesh. It had, I said to myself, made the edges and the architecture of his forehead more prehistoric. It had perhaps hollowed out his eye sockets, sharpened his nose, and relaxed his mouth. It had given the lines of his face a sort of bitterness, but a noble bitterness.

Chauvenet interpreted Monsieur Pouget's features in an individual way which was new to me. He had come to ask me whether I recognized Monsieur Pouget in his medallion. I would say the Chauvenet profiles showed Monsieur Pouget in a new light; they were rather his inner thought, his inner self, since fundamentally this inner self (hidden by the peasant shell) had many shades, subtleties and delicate indentations like the petals of certain flowers.

Chauvenet's two medallions revealed this. For a medallion reduces bulk, bulk which is the mark of matter. A profile is always fine and Monsieur Pouget is shown as belonging to the Jesuit type, ascetic and emaciated, a learned Jesuit, such as the Company had so often produced.

This thought plunges me into reflections about faces. It seems to me that a face can be viewed from many changing angles; that it is sufficient to look at a human face in sunlight, and to move slowly around it, to see in this one face many different faces, which up till then have seemed quite unrelated.

I think it was Novalis who said that every one of us is an Idea, and that this Idea is legion. Well, in the same way it is enough to think about any face, especially that of a child or an old man (I do not know that it is so striking in middle age), to see how it can differ from itself, if one changes one's angle of view by a millimetre.

A man who seems sad has spurts and flashes of gaiety, and one who seems cheerful reveals melancholy in some tiny curve. Another who seems frank has a withdrawn look, a contraction of the features or a dark look which shows up hidden hypocrisy; someone who seems shut in lights up in a minute. And so on . . .

It was moving to see the patience, the concentration and the will to precision which Chauvenet put into the re-creation in an art form of the face of a man whom he had not known; he wanted to be sure of the likeness, and he asked me continually: 'Is that right?' And this even though he was not trying to make an exact reproduction of the face, since he was transposing it into a medallion. It is the essence of art to ask someone who knows 'Is this right?' and then not to worry any more about it, but to make one's own reconstruction.

I showed Chauvenet various nineteenth-century drawings, so that he should tell me which deserved to be considered as

models. He picked out particularly a charcoal drawing of
Corot's, made out of 'nothing'—which contrasted with his
usually too academic style, his anecdotal style, Chauvenet
called it. Then he chose a drawing by Rodin of a dancer,
which revealed how Rodin worked. In his preliminary sketch
(probably a gouache or a water colour) he caught the forms
in motion, then went back to Indian ink for the outlines. But,
when making these outlines, he did not draw them tight
round the patches of colour; between the shading and the
outline he left a sort of void. This space gives a feeling of
movement which makes the motionless sketch in the flat
colour quiver.

Chauvenet also showed me what was least bad in my own
output, notably my 'little Cambronne' to which he granted
absolution; and my 'Pilate' which he did not absolutely
despise. He said this type of broad sketch was the right thing
for me. He even thought that if I went on working on my
sketches, not in the least forcing them and leaving them unfinished, I should at least please myself. For the art of the unfinished is one thing, and of the finished, another. Our epoch,
sated with achievement, likes the headlong. Here is a chance
for the amateur.

Bergson's house

Saint-Cergue
Saturday, 4th DECEMBER 1954

Arrived about nine o'clock in the morning at the little Swiss
village which was still asleep. The houses are strewn on the
ground like toys. They do not look rooted and dug in like
those of the Centre, no doubt because of the absence of age,
history, and (to tell the truth) of wear and tear and the
ingrained dirt which in our countryside makes a house a

natural object that has taken on the muddy consistency, the patina of the land. Wear and tear, patina, the lack of artificial cleaning; no room for anything like that in a Puritan theory of life! Here there is no shabbiness. No noise even. Bergson must have enjoyed this pure silence, Bergson, whom I always met in undated surroundings, which at the command of a fairy might have been transported from one continent to another, from one century to another, as Bergson said of great intuitions.

I think that in Switzerland virtues and vices must be very secret. I visited two churches, one Protestant, one Catholic, both equally clean and neat. This peaceful juxtaposition of two beliefs demands an obstinate fidelity, dumb and unexplained, from both. I saw that long ago at Jerusalem. But cities of juxtaposition are necessarily silent cities too.

> *Étranger qui viendras, lorsque je serai morte,*
> *Contempler mon lac genevois.*

These lines of Anna de Noailles run through my mind.

A sea of cloud over the lake. Geneva is under cloud, like the drowned city of Ys. I think of the Genevese as of fish, of another species. This sea of cloud is like a firmament, a solid surface on which one could slide, skate or walk.

I ask people about Bergson. The librarian said: 'I was born in 1917. I always heard Bergson spoken of at Saint-Cergue. What struck me when I saw him was the blue of his eyes. Hindus came and prostrated themselves before his house. He told me: "Neither my wife nor my daughter really knows how to make coffee. I believe that I alone have the secret." '

The inn-keeper said: 'I've known him since 1904. He stayed at my hotel then. The place pleased him so much that he told me he wanted to own a house here and to live in it until his death. It was I who sold him the plot of land where he built L'Échappée. This word had a double meaning: escape *towards* the lake, and escape *from* Paris.'

The mayor said: 'Bergson was very sensitive. He could hardly bear men's malice or indiscretion, or criticism—or publicity. But it was he who in 1917 interpreted France to the Americans, which made it possible for America to come into the war. He saved us then.'

Someone else said: 'He knew exactly how to arrange his life.' Another: 'I knew *who* he was. One day as a child I went to the hairdresser. I said: "You cut the hair of a remarkable man. Will you keep some for me next time?" "Alas," said the hairdresser, "he is bald, and worse still he comes very often." '

All that made me remember how Bergson entered my life in 1922. I went with Jean Moreau-Reibel and Charles-Henri Puech to invite him to a dance at the École, just when his rheumatism had chained him to his house. I saw him several times after that. I remembered what he said in his slow, relaxed speech, which, like his handwriting, was a little too perfect and mannered for my liking, but easy to fix in one's mind. I wrote down, sharp and burning, the first pieces of advice he gave me:

'When you write a book later on, do not think too much about time, plan, or composition. All that will come. Make certain of your subject and your goal. Chevalier said that I wrote *Évolution Créatrice* at a breakneck speed. That is true, but I had written it many times previously. It is impossible to write a single line without having an idea of the whole. But once you have this idea of the whole in your work, then everything comes together. The chapters break up of themselves, so do the paragraphs and even the sentences in a paragraph. The *whole* is present everywhere. And it is better to write quickly, so as to preserve the spring, the movement . . .'

'Rise above being academic. In our day people tend to regard the history of philosophy as though it were the history of furniture or of costume. I do not approve of this. For if what you want to write is pure history, true history, then that of the historians is more interesting. I do not believe in a history of Ideas. I am sure that this idea came to us from Germany. There cannot be any true genealogy of ideas. But in every great philosophy there is something inward to be grasped. And that is why our work has value. It is a matter of finding the inner life and the truth, of walking straight forward without considering what people are thinking of one, or about fashionable theories. If my books are of any interest, it is because they bring the mind back to *things*, and cause it to abandon preconceived notions and go on its own way. If there is joy in life, that is where it lies, and what would philosophy be worth without that joy?'

Visited L'Échappée, that 'convenient, clean and beautiful house'. Simple comfortable furniture. No family relics. It is not a home, not a house, not a habitation, just a huge luminous timeless place. The view seen through L'Échappée is of Mont Blanc and the lake, those two opposite stillnesses. Two 'sources' perhaps? The view is cosmic, world-wide. Not the kind in which I like to find inspiration—almost the contrary. There are no trees with falling leaves, no local history is written on the place, there are no far away steeples, just the *nature of things*—nature alone. This brought to my mind that Bergson in his early days published a version of Lucretius.

He drew inspiration from the peace, the whiteness, the purity, the unchanging spectacle. Thanks to comfort, altitude, luminosity—the Swiss cotton-wool—he was able to be alone with himself in the wilderness, to listen only to the whisper within. Mont Blanc and its range gave him the idea of the inaccessible; it was the high source. The lake symbolized the low source; *l'elan vital* losing its drive. There, already, was to be found the opposition of quality and quantity, the soul of the doctrine, and of the conflict between the two directions. Between the horizontal which calms our faculties, which materializes them, and the upward leap towards the rare, the pure, the certain, the tough, the difficult, the unique, inaccessible, virginal whiteness.

I saw this landscape through *the escape* and gave it these possible interpretations. My eyes, disconcerted at first, got used to it. The colours were symphonies of blue and dark green, with, in the Mont Blanc range, that brilliance which is more white than white and which has never inspired me; now and then in the lake there were spangles of light—and all this bathed in the excessive peace of Switzerland and the silence of silence. But when I looked closely at these blues, what variations there were. The cobalt of the lake is shot through with a current of pure ultramarine! And the glaciers too have an evanescent blueness. The range of blues is as varied as in Cézanne's backgrounds.

In the hotel visitors' book Bergson wrote this thought (to my mind rather pessimistic) about love and its maturity: 'One cannot come to your lovely country, without having a feeling which I would compare to love, if it did not become warmer as it gets older.' Bergson knew Switzerland when he was a child. At four years old he came to Gingins, a village between Nyon and Geneva. The house he lived in is still there.

Staying at Geneva

Geneva is not that mixture of wealth and poverty which is I think one of the charms of Rome. Everything is soft and easy-going. The sea has turned into a lake; the Reformation is again a Church, and even noises happen within a silence. As the coarse grass of pleasure (the frivolous transitory kind) springs up so quickly around the Roman Church, so here one imagines serious delights. The banks stand up, eyeless, like fortresses. The cafés have no terraces. There is no sign of women or of money. There is a likeness between Geneva and

Lyons in this—just as, from another angle, there is a like-ness between Nice and Naples. The Reformation Wall always impresses me with its men of stone. It strikes right down to my heart's depths and they are so like my teachers who were there primarily to say No.

A mixture of a harsh spirituality which is diluted by a Swiss gentleness. Switzerland is a country without visible stresses (although its inhabitants do sometimes commit suicide); it has not known the wars; it looks at things objectively, it is neither amused nor bored, it does not seem to understand passionate love, it accepted Calvin as it now accepts an atomic laboratory.

I had a talk with a pastor, a hard man, who reminded me of a friend of mine who is an integrist. But the latter's stern-ness does not extend to doctrine; it stays centred round the level of bones and nerves.

When severity of temperament is not controlled by an authority sterner still, it mounts up to the thinking and ruling parts. The pastor told me how he had often in his life re-volted against God and experienced a head-on conflict with the Almighty, like that of Jacob and the angel. I cannot find any trace of such an experience in myself, even the slightest, which could make this intelligible to me, unless one attributes a religious value to the revolt which is in all wrong-doing. But rebellion against God is fundamentally foolish. This view shows that I am not at home in the depths of the true Protestant experience.

The rebellious individual ... Can he still exist in the being who is redeemed, liberated, but yet a slave? Is there still a valid spirituality in the Book of Job which I find so splendid intellectually? I also complain, but gently, to divine love that it should present itself through the medium of so many enigmas.

Studious childhood

In this October month, which is when the schools go back, I watch a perennial spectacle near the lycée which bears the charming name of Montaigne. A mother takes her child to school, but not quite the whole way. She stops and sends him off like a ship, like a farewell kiss. Glad to be alone, he goes off bravely to school looking around to smile at his mother. It is a picture of man's perpetual journey between home and business. Or better still of the journey from the kingdom of love to that of the law.

Alain was right in saying that a child, in his solemn little heart of hearts, prefers school with its time-table and its impassive masters, to the family table at which one slithers, without knowing why, from tenderness to scolding. Anyway, once the child has crossed the threshold, and the door of the majestic lycée frames him like some lordling, he feels himself a chosen man, he perceives that soon, at long last, he will *know*.

When I see the doors of duty close and the mother turn back, I begin to contemplate the child. Sometimes I think that he does not know he is a child. Humiliated by the grown-ups, he dreams of growing up in his turn so as to have his revenge upon them. Childhood, as one recognizes when one reads Proust, is a retrospective illusion. It only exists in the memory (and memory is akin to regret) of the mature man as he pores over the past, relishing it and believing that he wants to return to it. In reality we do not want to become children again. In middle life we would like to don that robe of freshness and surprise, that grace of ecstatic attention which is childhood's charm, but which a child does not appreciate.

The child going into school is solemn; his eyes avid of reading, his still untarnished admiration which will fasten upon someone even more sedate than he is, the man whom he calls 'teacher', this man whom he will set up against his father. For where there is conflict between teacher and father, it is the teacher who will be in the right.

The child venerates the world of symbols: letters, numbers, multi-coloured maps with their keys, rulers, spelling that is Greek to him, strange grammar, rhyme. He does not realize, poor little fellow, how much past convention plays in the rules. We make him believe that not saying 'the gooses' is a natural law of the same nature as the moon's orbit or the falling of a stone. Later the child, having assimilated all this, will need to unlearn it, so as to become an inventor or a poet, indeed to find himself. The burden which science adds and which school boils down into digestible tablets is the tradition of the past, while the child is the future in embryo. When I see him enter this academy, I think, in the end it is he who is going to win. In the heart of this child-population lurks the genius of the species, which will renew the joy of the earth and of the school as well.

In the meantime we teach them how to work, and they teach us the art of not working, which is their privilege. We give them rules and they give us back imagination and innocence. We weigh them down with our solemnities, and they suggest to us the significance of joy beyond all anxiety. We show that everything is more difficult than they think; they take their revenge on our lined foreheads by teaching us that everything is basically easier than we imagined.

Bergson, Bréhier, Brunschvicg

Centenary of St Augustine on whom, about 1926, I began my thesis. I recall that very first start of my work, when, having decided on my plan and on the research I would undertake, I shyly presented my project to the *maîtres* of Paris.

First to Bergson, that was on the 11th January 1927.

M. Bergson said he hardly knew St Augustine. The resemblances, which have sometimes been noted between his images and Augustine's, were not due to any direct influence. Both in their form of thought were musical and bright, proceeding by motifs and affinities, having a feeling for totality in motion, understanding, as musicians do, the mind's power to expand or contract a given span of time.

Bergson encouraged me to study Plotinus. He had devoted to him his first course of Sorbonne lectures, and was greatly inspired by him, notably in the slightly gnostic part of *Évolution Créatrice* in which he traces the origins of place seen as an inversion and a reimmersion of consciousness. The relationship which he postulated between the body and the soul was close to that of Plotinus. Perhaps he had absorbed Plotinism through Ravaisson's works: possibly in the affinity between Ravaisson and Schelling. Both have here and there the idea of a genesis of 'Nature' by a diminution, a kenosis of the spirit.

Bergson recalled his memories of the College. He quoted to me in good, well-articulated Greek the formulas which he kept always in mind, notably one which he thought was of capital importance. *Praxis astheneia theorias*: action is a weak-

ening of contemplation. Here Bergson summed up what he
thought was the mistake of Hellenism. To re-establish Plotinus's prestige, he told me that he had come across a wonderful passage on the theory of consciousness. Plotinus was, according to him, the only Greek who had faced the problem
of consciousness. I received this saying as though it came to
me from a water-diviner.

Bergson also cautiously advanced the theory that St
Augustine was probably the originator of the Christian and
modern conception of time. He did not say of 'my' conception, but he boldly linked these two opposing words, *Christian*
and *modern*. At that time *Les Deux Sources* was secretly
taking shape. He was never averse to giving his listeners a
surprise.

This was the time of a quarrel about Christian philosophy.
Bréhier had unintentionally involved him in this. He had
simply stated, as though it were a generally accepted fact,
that in the herbal of doctrines which he was composing, with
the patience of a Linnaeus, he had never found a plant
labelled Christian philosophy, but only the plant *Apologetics*
or the plant *Theology*.

I often visited Émile Bréhier on Sunday mornings in his
house in the rue de l'Yvette. And I regret that I never expressed my esteem and gratitude adequately; he was so reserved in his friendships, a little *farouche*. He listened to us in-
tently, very upright and unyielding like a castle in chess. Yet
at times his inner fire shone out. Our Sunday talks centred
on the problem of knowing whether Christianity was original,
whether faith had not interposed ideas which reason could
not absorb.

There is, he said, a way of thinking in terms of myth which
admits the reality of Time and sees the Creation, the Fall,
the Incarnation, the Day of Judgment, as so many events.
And there is a rational way which only admits a non-
temporal scheme. Did Bréhier imply that the former way

of thinking was inferior? I thought so before reading his last work in which he sets down his admiration for Père Laberthonnière, who in a short syllabus demoted 'Greek idealism' in favour of 'Jewish realism' to which we owe the discovery of the concept of time. I think that my teacher strove earnestly for a reconciliation, and the moving tones of this upright man as he used the words, 'My beloved Stoics', clearly showed his bent.

His difficulty was to understand how a Christian thinker could also be an authentic philosopher. Philosophy demands a free mind, unbiased at the start, which operates in terms of active doubt. The Christian, on the other hand, knows the solution to the problems. No doubt he uses his reason, but he does not take risks. M. Bréhier submitted that there was no Christian philosophy any more than there were Christian physics. When he had to sum up Blondel's work for his *History*, he described it as apologetics which made Blondel indignant.

I have often expressed M. Bréhier's view that the paths of the Christian and the non-Christian are different. The Christian does not seek a solution; he believes he has it. His position is that of a geometrician who accepts a theorem and seeks to demonstrate it. The uncommitted are like this same geometrician when he finds himself faced with a problem which must be solved: genius is necessary to solve a problem, but talent suffices to discover a proof of what one already knows to be true. From the logical point of view both paths are equally reasonable. Christianity has put forward theorems but does not demonstrate them. It presupposes a philosophy. It implies the transcendence of God, the reality of time, the existence of the individual event. But whenever it is proved that such ideas are fruitful, conformable to experience and attainable by the use of reason alone, has not a work of philosophy been performed?

The philosopher of whom I was thinking and whose

thought I opposed was Léon Brunschvicg; it was he who insisted (along with his living antithesis, Jacques Chevalier) that I should leave the Faculty of Literature. I had a complex relationship with L. Brunschvicg of which gratitude and reserve formed a part. Some years later while at the Sorbonne, Jean-Paul Sartre was to conceive an equal degree of dissatisfaction with LB's idealism; this led him very far. It marked the end of a reign.

I could speak freely with Brunschvicg, for his unfettered mind (as one said in those days) was at ease everywhere and with everyone. He stood at the centre of all thought. He reconstituted its origins; luminous when it could be made to lead towards his own thought, shadowy and decadent when diverging from it. I did not criticize this dichotomy between light and shade; secretly we all make the same sort of distinctions.

He found a way of appropriating to his own theory of conscience *Les Deux Sources* which had just appeared, and which was indirectly opposed to him, since it rehabilitated, as he sadly remarked, 'the God of Genesis with his six days'. I never knew anyone who was more adept at teaching his method by never talking about it; he simply taught history. The moment of treason was when a philosopher recognized a nature distinct from the mind, a creation and above all a 'personal' immortality, an 'individual' providence. All through history there had been two strains: the impure who join spirit to flesh, and the pure, the disciples of Spinoza and Fichte. The grace of passing from impurity to purity came through the science of mathematics which proved reason's creative power, and this was the true salvation. I remember the day on which Brunschvicg, whose face, so intelligent but devoid of expression, recalled the Sphinx, courteously asked me to tell him which, of Spinoza and Pascal, was the Jew and which the Christian. I saw that in his view Pascal was the Jew, because he worshipped figures, believed himself to be immortal and prayed, whereas Spinoza, who worshipped 'in the spirit and in truth', was the true disciple of Jesus.

All Brunschvicg's thought led to an apotheosis of true conversion. It was a matter of leaving the cave and its shadows; but not in the way we conceive such deliverance. For him conversion consisted in repudiating the flesh, rationalist or Christian, and ascending to the spirit. In my case, if I were to acknowledge a 'first conversion' (analogous to what Brunschvicg suggested) designed to purify the childish mind, it would be that of seeing in absolute idealism a fallacious resort to extremes, which appears to me as a spirit worshipping itself, arrogating to itself the right to create 'natures'—in fact, mistaking its work for Being.

To my mind, conversion in its loftiest form consists precisely in renouncing so subtle a temptation, and in submitting mind to being by accepting a premiss. What Brunschvicg termed spirit, I see as a disguised form of flesh which must be renounced in its turn in order to attain to a third state. And even from such a point of view I reinstate the primitive flesh. For beneath its images, its naïve realism, its often legendary history, it has the merit of not severing the relationship between mind and essence.

What astonished me was his conception of spiritual life. There was no authentic spiritual life except in immanence, that is to say, in the atheism of the pure. To live 'spiritually' was to be aware of one's freedom, reason, eternity, and one's creative and generous powers. To the extent that I have tried all through my life to live an inner life, I have had the opposite experience: that of dependence on a source of our being, of the impossibility of creating, and I have experienced time as separation.

I remember with what piety Brunschvicg quoted St Augustine's words to me: *O si viderent internum aeternum.* This *internum aeternum* was for him the eternal inwardness, which he grasped in himself in the act of thought. For me it was the intimate and creative eternity, which it is not given to us to contemplate, but which is the soul of time.

It is just this experience of the life of the soul in time, with its beginning, its developments, its ages, its rhythms, its *akmé*, its biological decay, and its spiritual sublimation (and, at the end, death), it is just this which seems to me to prove that *time* is something created—and not by us. For one cannot see why the spirit should will itself to be dispersed, tried, progressive, subject to decay and so quickly cut off . . .

Although he did not form part of my jury, M. Brunschvicg was kind enough to sit behind the row of the Five, like a judge of judges. I saw him between my judges, as the Shulamite of the Song of Songs looked at the Bridegroom through the trellis.

The start of man

24th OCTOBER 1954

Étienne Borne asked me to speak on the origins of man at the *Semaine des Intellectuels* which he organizes. He said that the subject suited me. When an idea which is already in you is suggested by a friendly voice from outside, it is a sign. I need a stimulus. What simmers inside me needs a fillip to bring it out, which I cannot provide myself. So in response to Étienne Borne's request, I put my ideas in order.

For over thirty years I have been thinking about these problems of origin and I recognize that they still attract me. Why did I do exegesis, why did I study so closely the relationship between the Gospel and the Church, in those days when the Abbé Loisy received me with friendly irony in the rue des Écoles? Why did I follow the teaching of Vialleton at Montpellier? And why do I with passionate curiosity question anyone who has in any way been concerned with the story of origins, as I did for instance Père Teilhard, when he was here for the last time in July?

I recalled the method which consists in unfolding primary concepts and discovering two ideas contained in a single term: different in bearing and interpretation. I decided not to speak of *commencement*, but of *origin* and *emergence*, calling *origin* the moment of true creation (although nocturnal and imperceptible), and emergence the moment of appearance.[1]

I would say that every creature in time comes into being twice; first in an instant which is his authentic origin, when what is to characterize him is, as it were, inseminated into his depths together with the things that will give him life and make him go forward; and then at a second moment when what he has been only potentially and often inactively manifests itself to the outside world.

In the first moment of origin an individual cannot be brought under observation. Darwin himself said: 'The mystery of all beginnings is insoluble by us.' All origins are beyond investigation. Nocturnal, one might say nuptial. At the second instant when the individual appears, in which he is 'born', he is already formed. We are born with a prehistory, old already, like the religion of Jesus, which was already so ancient when it was founded, when he came 'not to destroy but to fulfil'.

For these reasons, I reflected that it was difficult to gain experience in this matter, vital though it is. If I could be present at a beginning, I should no doubt not see anything: for there the individual is infinitesimal. He has not yet appeared—*nondum*. And when I witness an *emergence*, then it is too late for the student of beginnings. The individual is already complete—*jam*. Between the *not yet* and the

[1] This idea was the theme of my book *L'Église et l'Évangile* (1959).

274

already I furtively insert the transition from nothing to being.

In the problem of human origins, seeking what is common ground, without entering into controversial questions, such as polygenism, I ponder on the findings of anthropologists about this long transition, spread over thousands, perhaps millions, of years, during which the *nappe humaine*, as Teilhard de Chardin called it, from pithecanthropes and sinanthropes up to the *homo sapiens* of the neolithic age, the start of civilized humanity, began and was unfolded.

It seems to me that in the development of this *nappe humaine* we can see an illustration of the distinction between *origin* and *emergence*.

If you think of the diagrams of evolution you will observe that they are shaped like a flower. First you see a stalk with various whorls diverging, and small marginal leaves. (The sinanthrope and the neanderthal for instance are two such whorls terminating in an *impasse*.) But the upward movement of the stalk continues to a point where a sort of fan or bud emerges: Teilhard's point Alpha. But what interests me in this is not Teilhard's theory, it is the distinction between two beginnings. The prehistorian and the anthropologist, whoever they may be, agree on two moments as crucial to the man-forming impulses.

The first occurring perhaps in the lower Quaternary or in the Tertiary period (the *préhominiens*) is the origin, since man's characteristics were then inseminated into an animal form. Here starts the impulse which will never come to a standstill, though it will take diverse forms and make lengthy pauses.

The second beginning, which in my language represents emergence, is the moment when *homo sapiens* appears; the creature capable of art and religion, who makes society, who is able to conquer space and to develop continuously in time;

he is our ancestor, we directly descend from him. He is the first New Man—the *néanthrope*.

The immensity of the time scale astounds me. In Herbert Wendt's fine book, *À la recherche d'Adam*, I read that taking past time from the beginning as a twenty-four hour journey, we must wait until 23.30 hours for the emergence of the Peking man, 23.50 for neanderthal man, and until five minutes to midnight for the emergence of *homo sapiens*.

I reflect on the significance of the extraordinary slowness of things. What happened in the interval while the animal becoming man let the power of reason sleep within him? Why has no one sought the meaning of this period of pre-history, in which we observe not an acceleration, but a slowing down, which is much more curious?

2nd NOVEMBER 1953

I have sought out several spheres in which to test the validity of my distinction. I thought: Let us consider a human action, one of the great choices of moral life. And since wrong is always more brightly coloured, let us take the story of a sin. When does one sin? When does the decisive act occur? It is certainly not at an identifiable moment which the canonists call consummation, and which classical novelists rightly ignore, as Molière scamped his marriages. The primary act, the one which commits you, is the first consent, accepted as genuine; the looks exchanged, which will be binding later on; the 'no' which should have been said, but was not; silence at a casual moment when one should have spoken just a single word, but preferred to keep quiet. That, to my mind, is the origin; the point of true failure or of true courage.

Reflecting on this, I thought if it is so, if the story of free-dom can be divided into these two instants, how difficult it is to grasp the instant in which we are free! For in the origins of origin one has no clear awareness of the act and of its consequences; one does not realize that one is being made prisoner by a glance or that silence is forging a bond. And in the final moment which is that of emergence and consummation, all initiative has become impossible. You are imprisoned in a mesh, and the act of sin seems to unfold within you, without your being able to do anything about it. I see that here I have joined in the experience of the Masters of the Soul who have always preached great vigilance about one's own unnoticed beginnings and also great sympathy for the sins of others.

The death of Colette

10th DECEMBER 1954

What I thought saddest about Colette's death was not the affair of the funeral. It was that no one knew what her thoughts were about the after-world. Her silence has needed to be interpreted. And I think that she was surprised by the rally before death. By the rally I mean the moment of false hope which, I have often noticed in the very gravely ill, comes just before everything falls quickly into ruin. The people around the patient are reassured and declare that he is cured. He gets a grip on life once more, and at the moment when he is about to plunge into the undiscovered country, he thinks about the pleasant meal which a doctor will allow him to have, about the little walk in the garden which will be permitted, and about the comforts of convalescence.

It is good that a slight betterment of life goes along with and heralds death. One more moment of respite—one more of happiness! Truly, even after slow and long illnesses, all death is sudden. We are cut off in the middle of a sentence, between two breaths, and before the symphony is ended. Struck down in full flight. The text is seized from us, because the time is up, before we have rewritten the fine ending. That too is good. One must plant, sow and go on building up to our last breath. One must not be taken unawares, but it is right that we should be interrupted. A full stop.

That is why I wish that Christians would work with others to make death less sombre. I hate these black trappings, 'the empty skull, the eternal grin', the letters with large black edgings. I am amazed that believers still put up with the conventional phrases about grief and cruel loss, unaccompanied by any compensatory hope.

The post-war philosophers have spoken a great deal about nothingness: Heidegger in Germany, Sartre in France. They have returned with amazing and sombre strength, more sincere than ever before, to the eternal theme of the Greeks, Jews and Christians. We are born to die, we are in the situation of those condemned to death. There is nothing to be done about it. It is a universal condition which makes pleasure and even freedom absurd. I like to read such despairing analyses. For it seems to me that at the heart of the remarkable absurdity of death—never better analysed than today—there springs the thought that it is not possible, that it is not thinkable.

I am certain of it. What is difficult in thinking of the beyond, so inevitable and coming nearer and nearer, is the impossibility of imagining life without a body. The body, said Valéry, is 'the sole object which protects me from the dead'. The ironic corpse seems to protest against hope. One must also admit that it does not seem to be part of man's nature to be curious about what happens after death. The more he knows about other things, the less he wants to know about this. If Lazarus came back, he would be asked to sit in a corner and keep silence. What a strange lack of curiosity!

When I watch a funeral go by (something which is getting rarer and rarer and is hardly ever to be seen in Paris), I think of the prostrate victor who has become the last of men and I say to myself that he knows more about the one essential thing than all the geniuses combined.

The crisis of love in middle life

11th FEBRUARY 1955

When in January Pierre Sipriot interviewed me on the subject of human love for the National network, he had to conform to the conditions of his broadcast: 'To speak in prose and be aware of it.' (To my mind a curious instruction, for I feel that to speak in good 'prose' one should do so unconsciously.)

Sipriot had to find an author whose work fitted in with my ideas on the development of love. He made the happy choice of Fromentin's *Dominique*—Fromentin is among my minor prophets of the admirable nineteenth century. I like to run through his trilogy. *Un Été, Dominique, Maîtres d'Autrefois*: a painting, a novel, another painting but raised this time to the condition of thought.

What claims our attention in *Dominique*, coming through the banal intrigue of a hopeless love, is the action of a man who is conscious of the graph of his existence. Before his love story is introduced (in this book, love is a parenthesis between two friendships), we are shown the hero of *Dominique* in a lonely room, setting down dates and figures. These figures are repeated with modifications which 'affect the sense without changing the principle'. Geometry of this kind helped Dominique in his attempt to grasp the identity of his inner being, irrespective of circumstance and change.

Such is the meaning of this most unusual novel. Here is a

279

romantic who has experienced passion and its crises, as indeed he had to, but who overcomes it to arrive at peace. If I had time to define words, I should say that Dominique represents the victory of *destinée* over *destin*. One's fortune is the reflection of fate; it comes about through our co-operation with a mystery of order cutting across events which seem fortuitous, but which lead us eventually to where we really ought to be.

There is also in *Dominique*, more than in any other novel of the nineteenth century, an astonishing awareness of the links between love and time. As a rule, the human mind studies love at the moment of its uprush or of its havoc-making activity and only seldom considers its silent growth through deepening tenderness, through all-enfolding peace, and through its renewal at every stage of life.

I am at present preparing a new edition of my book on *Human Love*. I have been thinking about the law of love's increase in the midst of crises overcome, about the quiet ascension which makes human love into a work of art, and which takes time, chance, and affection for its raw material.

Love has its crises. The first, which brings it to birth, is not the only one. Last winter the Abbé Caffarel, who has edited the *Anneau d'Or* for so many years, came to discuss a very serious question with me, to which he wanted to draw the attention of married people: the crisis of middle life. 'Middle age which is the line that divides our days,' as he put it.

He had collected different opinions about this headland in the life of married couples. I told him about Michelet's ideas. And he quoted to me these verses by Péguy:

Le fruit qui était sûr
voulait tomber,
Le fruit qui était mûr
voulait rester.

Cœur tu n'as pas plié
Dans la bourrasque
O cœur vas-tu sombrer
Dans la bonasse.

Vain rajeunissement,
Tant de vieillesse.
Mais vain vieillissement,
Tant de jeunesse.

This is the age we call that of the noonday devil, the age when David turns towards Bathsheba, the age of masculine passions (Juliette reigning over Hugo, Marie Duval over the stoical Vigny); the age of violent, self-willed aberrations like devastations which are often stronger in proportion as the man had been calm and fulfilled.

Not seldom, too, does a woman feel at this time a second period of sensuality coming to life in her, something that is new to her; it is as if she had to drain a cup which is going to be taken from her. She develops a sudden affection for some third person who is often in her home, a sort of ambiguous maternity.

The children are no longer there to be brooded over. The family is no longer an almost enclosed nest, but more like an hotel, with meals always ready, a room where one has the right to air one's moods, a place to leave or to come back to as a refuge, a centre for ceremonies, an institution.

In short, the couple are strongly tempted to effect under the guise of past love a friendly disassociation, and live two separate lives until death.

The man acquires a routine, he goes to the pub more frequently. He busies himself with committees, meetings, research. The woman no longer entertains as she did in the past, but now she has a profession, based on charities sometimes, or clubs, and she always has an excuse for going out. They meet at meal times and at bed-time.

That married life should become, as it does for many, a juxtaposition, is almost inevitable if one gives way to boredom, if one forgets the vulnerability of love, if one is unaware of the laws of its phases, of the rhythm of its development. Conjugal love is not so much the cause of marriage as its result over a period. But if marriage, in the midst of the wear and tear of time, is to increase and to sublimate love, then there must be great wariness, thought and care. The danger of middle age is that the union brought about by a first attraction and maintained by habit and duty, may become an association of one-time lovers, an honourable retirement.

I have written in my book about the difficulties of this transition, which is linked with biology, and the interplay of human psychology. But I do not want to end on a gloomy note. I am convinced that nature is good, and that at the side of the disease she has placed the remedy.

Middle age is the age of habit. And there are habits of the affections; feelings, even, may be habits. Passions are inflamed and inflaming. The feelings woven into our being are those of love possessed and matured, of gratitude, of pity when necessary, of indulgence, always. By then the difference between the masculine and the feminine ways of feeling becomes narrower. According to physiology, the woman after the menopause becomes masculine at any rate in body. And inversely by one of those compensations of which a life lived with one other person offers many examples, the male nature softens. Perhaps through the influence of life with a woman, or because the duties of fatherhood are less exacting—for instance, vis-à-vis his grown-up daughters, now at the age when he first met their mother, whom he rediscovers in them. The toughest man, without becoming effeminate, becomes gentler. As an example, one can reread the letters of Napoleon to Marie-Louise written during the battle for France.

I think too it is a foolish idea to put beauty in the singular, as though only one kind existed, the kind we associate with the bloom of a young face. Women too fall for this fallacy: they start as a spring flower and end up as a polychrome statue. And art caters for this change in our days as it always has done. I believe that beauty is an action of body and soul which cannot be divided. It is not unrelated to the life that has been lived; it concentrates in it those great unchangeable spheres, the expression and the smile. Middle age is that time in which the expression, its luminosity, its radiance, spring not from nature, but from inner experience, from trials accepted, from true love, from repose in love. And this is growing beauty, independent of care and make-up, with goodness as its partner.

> *The years, so far from doing her wrong*
> *Anointed her with gracious balm.*[1]

The oblatory phase of love is beginning. And like every final phase of an evolution, it brings out what was latent from the start.

Youthful love may seem to have been based on mutual desire. Love was like an animal instinct adopted by the spirit. Founding a family was a sort of social rite. But by now the biological and sociological substratum fades away. One sees the architecture more clearly; the essential becomes visible; we are nearer to the truth. This shows up more clearly in the love of a woman for her husband.

Besides, nowadays old age no longer exists as a physical condition, or even as a social status. It has ceased to be the aristocracy which is open to all, the honoured estate of the poor. The 'old lady' has vanished. Her hair is whatever colour she chooses. Penicillin prolongs everything. And such prolongation of life is not a bad thing for love, which needs the partnership of appearances.

[1] Coventry Patmore: 'The Angel in the House.'

To grow old in love, said Hugo, is to become identified. But I have no faith in this word identity, which is as false as equality or unity: such mathematics do not suit man. I prefer Patmore's verses about human dissimilitude:

The nuptial contrasts are the poles
On which the heavenly spheres revolve.

Are the stars and nebulae inhabited by thinking creatures?

Whatever they may be, I think the U.F.O. (unidentified flying objects, as the English call them), which appear in the heavens, have the virtue of reviving an age-long problem: that of other worlds. Everything that disturbs my assurance, widens my vision, suggests out of the way hypotheses and shakes me up, everything that awakens me (as Kant said) from dogmatic sleep or urges me to make a new leap—all such things do me good.

In recent weeks I have used the excuse of these mobile objects to enlarge my knowledge of the human race, by asking various people what they thought about the probability of other forms of life. I quickly found that one can identify four types of answer, dependent on whether an atheist or a believer is being questioned.

There are atheists who make it a rule to assume nothing which is outside their experience. These are atheists of positivist origin who are cautious in the extreme. Experience, only experience. The rest is silence—silence even in the inner mind, which tackles only questions capable of solution, since all others are meaningless. For such people, creatures of another world can have no existence or interest until one can obtain a fragment of their substance and examine it in a laboratory.

There are other atheists who, like Lucretius or Spinoza, love nature with a kind of adoration, but who could not be devoted to it unless they could endow it with life, that is to say, a capacity to bring forth new and unimaginable forms. Their conception of divinity is to suggest such metamorphoses. We thinking bipeds are one of nature's caprices; why should she stop short at us? Why should she not progress further towards some kind of superman? And why in one of the innumerable planets or galaxies should she not have produced Other-Men whose form we cannot know?

I observed a similar division amongst believers. Some rest in the old idea of our unique solitude under the vault of heaven, and are perhaps not anxious to add more difficulties to the conception of the Incarnation of the Word; they think that one earth, dwelt in and visited by God is enough, and that everything else is a backcloth, installed for man's honour and glory.

When last year I was working on my book about M. Pouget and thinking about the plurality of worlds, I found myself rather isolated amidst these unexplored problems; it was then that a friend put in front of me a private note of Claudel's saying he had lost his faith because of the supposition of the plurality of worlds. I chanced writing to him. He answered me on the 25th March 1953: 'Sir, it is true that the idea of the plurality of inhabited worlds horrifies me, and I do not see what place it can have in the Christian scheme. The fall of the angels, the creation of the world, original sin and the Redemption, form a whole held together by organic links which exclude any element of imagination. I know only Jesus, as St Paul said, and him crucified. The rest is a dream without substance or significance.'

Then I remembered what Bergson said to me long ago on the same theme. The previous week I had been at Saint-Cergue, at that villa which he had built in 1914 on a unique site; one sees through a V of pines Mont Blanc and the lake, both motionless. I was looking at what Bergson saw when he wrote *Évolution Créatrice*. And I remembered that for Bergson, the singleness of our planetary system appeared, in 1906, as something unlikely. According to the law of probabilities, it seemed to him likely that the extraordinary adventure which we call life, the basis of thought, might in principle have reproduced itself elsewhere, given the immense number of the galaxies. What would he have said nowadays when the known number has increased so prodigiously?

On this planet called Earth the vital spark met with difficult conditions, ponderous matter which weighed down the spirit, as Solomon says in the Book of Wisdom. The last words which Bergson printed in his last book are *rebellious planets*. Who knows? May there not have been planets more docile in which matter was more transparent; in which the Fall never happened, at least in which the Fall was less heavy; in which life was arranged not around the carbon of the sun, but on the basis of some different solar gas, or in other forms unimaginable by us?

Catholic theologians are silent on these possibilities. Did St Thomas admit that there could be other Incarnations of the Word? Revelation, at bottom, teaches us only what is necessary for salvation; it confines our curiosity to this earth. But if in the angelic world there are so many different species, why in the world of creatures, made of mind and matter, should one not find different categories? As to the Incarnation, one may suppose two hypotheses: either that one sole and unique Incarnation (that of the Word in Nazareth) and his death under Pontius Pilate should have saved and redeemed all other worlds; or that the Word itself may be offered to all creations or to privileged creations in ways which it is impossible to imagine.

Different minds have different and almost irreconcilable

286

modes of feeling. I would like to try and define my own, without placing any other value on it than that it is mine. I have asked myself what would happen inside me if I learned for a certainty that there are thinking beings other than those on earth. Would I feel a kind of horror, or a friendly curiosity? Would I be like the Greek (Aristippus I think) who landing on the sandy beach of an unknown island and seeing traces of inscriptions, said to his friends: 'So we are at home here?'

It is very hard to say, for friendship with another being requires some physical resemblance—a like animality so to speak. Faced with a being of completely unimaginable form, but which behaved as a thinking creature, it might be that one's body would tremble, and one's thoughts take flight . . .

The Christian in me would immediately wonder whether such creatures know God, and what their place is in creation. If they do know God, how do they link up with the plan of the Incarnation and the Redemption? I would wonder too whether the background from which they emerge has anything corresponding to the Fall of Adam, whether they have been given divine grace or if they are only 'reasoning' beings.

And I should think (as I have read these past months in certain papers) that this meeting of Christian planetary man with a creature of reason was the greatest historical event since the 'hominization' of life on earth.

If I were omnipotent, how would I have chosen between the theories of Claudel or Bergson, both of which are feasible?

I admit that this marvellous starry sky (which I see so seldom except for a few clear nights in August) is inexplicable to me because of its emptiness. This milky profusion, this slow rotation, might give me a spectator's false pride. Can it be that I am the sole 'thinking reed' amidst these galaxies?

Are there not in space other forms unimaginable, yet pleasant to speculate upon; may there not be thought and love?

It seems to me that, had I been the creator of worlds, I would have created them with the gesture of a sower. I would have scattered galaxies—those pale islands—knowing that in most directions there would be setbacks, sterilities, failures; that life, the most speculative gamble, can succeed (and in particular maintain itself) only once. But what would that matter to me, provided that somewhere, perhaps at one point only, the improbable should be born out of the improbable and survive, and that there, amid a different species, some poor creature might come groping towards me; provided in fact that in this infinity of dispersed matter,

> *Gouffre mystérieux d'où sort une fumée*
> *D'hommes, d'êtres et de soleils,*

I might hear now and then a cry.

These lines are from Hugo's *Plein Ciel*. It was André Bellessort, my teacher, who introduced me to them long ago at Louis-le-Grand.

Elbows on his desk in front of forty bewildered students, he trotted out Hugo, as he said in his private lingo. His eyebrows, seemed alive. His neck was swollen like a bull's. He read us these verses which he said were among the finest of the French language:

> *La brume redoutable emplit au loin les airs.*
> *Ainsi qu'au crépuscule on voit, le long des mers,*
> *La pêcheur, vague comme un rêve,*
> *Traînant, dernier effort d'un long jour de sueurs,*
> *Sa nasse où les poissons font de pâles lueurs,*
> *Aller et venir sur la grève.*

La Nuit tire du fond des gouffres inconnus
Son filet, où luit Mars, où rayonne Vénus,
Et, pendant que les heures sonnent,
Ce filet grandit, monte, emplit le ciel des soirs,
Et dans ses mailles d'ombre et dans ses réseaux noirs
Les constellations frissonnent.

This poetry was too modern to be enjoyed at the end of the last century. A poet's sensibility is not confined by the present.

Henri de Montherlant at Port-Royal

On the copy of *Port-Royal* which he sent me, Montherlant had written these words: 'The only question about this work is: does it or does it not help Christianity?'

I imagine that by Christianity he means Catholicism, otherwise the burning question could not have conveyed its full meaning.

For an adequate answer one needs to distinguish two points of view, dependent on whether one is dealing with the Port-Royal of history, or the *Port-Royal* of Henri de Montherlant.

The history of Port-Royal, from start to finish, is that of the idea of purity in the Church. One first sees nuns, then laymen (no sacerdotal element in this instance) earnestly seeking to reform the Church, repudiating the world, ardently, and going back to first principles. But little by little one observes them coming to love purity for itself, delighting in it as their private property, isolating themselves, and even bringing the Church into question.

What do the purists see facing them? Authority, less pure no doubt, but laden with the weight of humanity, drawing up a swarming net of wriggling fishes of all kinds, disallowing a division between the pure and the impure, before the consummation of the Day of Judgment.

This conception of the idea of the 'pure' among men is ever present in States as in Churches. When the part of ourselves which is ardent and proud listens to this story (especially during adolescence) how warmly it responds and takes the side of the purists! How it delights in protests! It is otherwise when one has become mature, when one has recognized responsibilities, the inevitable intermixtures, and the pride of the purists and the solitaries; then one begins to feel more indulgence.

From the dramatic point of view the subject is unrivalled. Sophocles realized this in *Antigone*. What men praised in Joan of Arc was the protest of the spirit, the appeal to an unwritten law, which is inscribed in the heart only. Together with that of fate, this conflict of law and faith is the finest theme for a writer of tragedies.

Why then, one may ask oneself, has Port-Royal had to wait until 1954 to find its author? France, which has no theatrical vocation for tragedy, was no doubt too Catholic to recognize itself in this revolt against authority, too subtle to appreciate these logical virgins who reasoned to distraction about insoluble questions. Claudel and Péguy looked elsewhere, and wisely.

French tragedy, generally speaking, derives from Spain. And I may say that when I opened *Port-Royal*, I wondered whether Montherlant was not about to offer us a Spanish monastery.

This subject must have had an almost invincible attraction for him. There was a profound sympathy between him and it. Aridity, zeal in aridity, love and at the same time self-contempt, a lapidary style, overbearing argument, something rebellious even when assenting, something harsh even in tenderness. And if I dare say so, more affinity with pride than with greatness of soul, in so far as one can judge them in a stage production. But Corneille's Chimène had pride, and Claudel's Violaine greatness of soul.

It seems to me that there Montherlant has overreached himself in the best sense and pressed pride to rise to greatness. He has shown the souls of the Nuns in a state of doubt about what they ought to do and in conflict with themselves. Montherlant has narrowed down the distance (minute and yet infinite) which in my view for ever separates Port-Royal from the kingdom of the Saints, and, for instance, Jacqueline Pascal from Sœur Thérèse de l'Enfant Jésus or Edith Stein. He clearly saw that the essence of tragedy (whether in a true or legendary story) is to lead you back to your own soul. And here we have the conflict between that part of the self which believes it is right, and the anxious part which doubts its decision, or merely acquiesces in it.

I am not a Port-Royalist. I mistrust people who, as Joubert said, prefer the rule to goodness and who have the certainty and the sorrow of being right. How can one ever know? There are those who profess to be purer than others and reap implacable consequences. Where are the proofs? There are those who are 'sad, tender, able to endure all woe'. But it is harder to live than to die. At Port-Royal we are in Jerusalem, and I love Galilee. As for knowing whom all this helps and whom it burdens on the level at which Montherlant has introduced the debate, the question has no meaning.

Search for my interior unity

This evening I am trying laboriously to rediscover an interior unity in my thought and work . . . I am well beyond middle life. It is time to sum up. I would like to take my bearings, to see my point of convergence if I can.

I do not know if the scheme which Père Teilhard gave me last year is correct as regards the evolution of living beings, and if, after diverging, the axes of life come together (I see no trace of such movement in the world of species). But this scheme seems to me adequate enough to describe the curve of the graph of human time. In the first stage of life the fan opens—at least I opened it, replying to several calls, blazing several trails; I was rather scared by the necessity of choice, and wishing to preserve in what I had chosen the shadow, the warmth, the reflection of what I was compelled not to choose.

Today I would like to discover, if I can, this centre of myself towards which I grope, the unity which I see as ahead of me, though in fact it is an inner centre. The future, as we imagine it, is the projection of that which remains unconscious in the intimacy of ourselves.

JC said to me: 'You will have to live a long time in order to become integrated, many-sided as you are. For years I thought it could not be the same person who wrote *Césarine*, the *Portrait of Monsieur Pouget*, the *Problem of Jesus*, and *Temporal Existence*. In this lies your strength and your weakness. You have no real readers. Each of them has read only one book of one kind. And were he to compare that book with the works of those who have spent their lives writing on one particular subject, he would find you wanting. Few have known the whole range, few have recognized that a harmony unites all that you have written, and still fewer are those to whom your unity has been revealed.' Every man seeks the thing which he uniquely has to say, seeks the secret of his self which he cannot see because he carries it on his back. We can never know ourselves, since life in this world forces us to look forward, whereas to know ourselves we should be able also to see our back view.

Where does the diversity of my interests and styles come from? From never wishing to shut myself up in one way of thinking or of living—in a part, in a system, or in a party. Literature which at the outset attracted me by its human and universal character, soon seemed imperfect, limited and, to tell the truth, useless. The questions asked by professors of literature (and I sat under some very famous and contrasted ones, Lanson and Bellessort for instance) seemed to me to by-pass the question most vital to man: the search for truth. Problems of truth are no doubt present in tragedy and in novels, particularly the modern novel. But in these instances the problems are only implied and are dealt with by insinuation and allusion, by passion or feeling. They are never presented openly in the light of day. Philosophy, whose function is to expose problems to the light, often covers them up because (since Kant and still more since Husserl) it has become more and more a technique of preliminary questions. Poetry goes ahead, it is prophetic. Philosophy tends more and more backwards. It looks for the presupposition of the presupposition. And this leads it to put the real problems in parentheses, those which grip one by the throat: who am I? Does God exist, and what is God?

I have always had an affection for literature which is still the least enclosed and broadest discipline for the whole man, and, in spite of all the conventions of language, the least ridden by convention. In it one can talk of prose and poetry, of problems of grammar and of metre, and of the history of

Ideas. The (clandestine) world of love, on which there is silence everywhere else, even in moral science, is there, although almost always in aberrant forms. If I decided in my youth to devote myself to philosophy, this was because I thought it was more explicit, more able to satisfy that supreme faculty: the power of knowing the whole and communicating with the whole, the power I call *thought*. I love this word—*pensée*—which is the name of my little house, of Pascal's disorderly fragments, and also of an alert little flower![1] Such was the storm which determined the way I was to lean. Towards philosophy in the first place.

In this I took as centre for my research the problem of time; the time of ripening and maturing but also the problem of time centring round an intemporal point, a *justification* of time. For I have always felt that human time which uproots, estranges and seemingly annihilates one is at first sight *unjustifiable*: why are we submitted to this trial, why were we not made immortal all at once? This is my problem which I have difficulty in acknowledging. This is what, through me, Job gently and silently asks God to explain. But I have never separated philosophical from religious research. And I think that I have been led towards understanding this relationship in a fashion that is rather new.

Too often philosophers have failed to study religion as a *datum*. They decide in advance that the religious fact is part either of nature or of history, that it has no absolute value, only a human value: the value of a symbol for translating by an art which is fuller and also more magical than art, the desire for an 'eternal intimacy' which is at the heart of man. Alain (in his book *Les Dieux*), when he described the birth of the gods issuing from man, seems to me to have been a good pupil of Hegel. This is what one finds in another way in the aesthetics of Malraux and his imaginary museum.

But is it right to solve a problem at the very moment one

[1] The French word for pansy is also *pensée*.

presents it, to insert the solution surreptitiously into the original statement? What I have tried to do is to study the religious data, in particular the Judaeo-Christian data: the great stream in time which runs, can one say, without gap or discontinuity (although with long pauses) from Abraham to the present Pope, with Christ nailed at its centre as a seed of eternity, consummating the past and founding the future. To study this with freedom, without prejudice or presupposition, seeking to clarify the postulates, the ideas and concepts which such a datum embraces, and which it requires in order to be fully understood.

I am absolutely convinced that this work is necessary! No one could understand the existence of Catholicism without defining and repeating the intermediary ideas, which are essential, if a contemporary mind is genuinely to assimilate Christian truth. The investigations made by Gabriel Marcel belong to this kind of research. I am thinking of his studies on hope, on the creative vow, on commitment, on problems, and on mystery. When I was twenty Jacques Chevalier did me a great service by guiding me towards my two masters: Père Pouget to whom he introduced me, and Newman whom my mother had already revealed to me. Following in Newman's wake, I have tried to define ideas which are more particularly implicit in Christianity considered as history and also the idea of development, without which the history of Judaism and that of Christianity are unintelligible.

An entire branch of my studies must be seen in this context. In particular one book of mine which I consider important, and which I ought to republish (for it went unrecognized) is that on Renan and Newman. It has always seemed to me that the intersection of Renan and Newman is filled with eternal significance. Let me recall it. On the 6th October 1845, Ernest Renan, aged twenty, left the Seminary of St Sulpice. His meditations had led him to think (in spite of his good teachers) that the Christian faith, and particularly the Christian conception of the Bible, was out of harmony with *le Devenir*, the idea of *becoming*. Two days later on the 8th October 1845, in the village of Littlemore (which, strangely enough, means what it says) John Henry Newman, at the age of forty-five, abjured Anglicanism and was received into the Church of Rome because Catholicism seemed to him to be the development of early Christianity. On the face of it, the same idea of vital change had led Renan away from Catholicism and Newman into it. In reality here were two different conceptions of change, one endless evolution, a sort of immanent deity; the other a change which was directed, a change which started from a created germ, and which, like a life, moves towards a plenitude.

It is the links between these philosophical ideas and the facts which fascinate me. I studied them from different aspects, and in various ways. All links interest me. The secret link between man and man which in time, as in God, is the sign, the rhythm, the mystery, of life and of love.

Then between these two branches of philosophy and of religion, in order to incarnate thought (if I may put it that way) in being and in history, I wrote some biographies, but of a particular kind. I should find it very difficult to write the life of someone who was unknown to me, who was not intimately connected with me: I have been asked to do this, but I could not do it. My least unsuccessful effort in this sphere is certainly *Monsieur Pouget*. This was the portrait of an idea (of a method, a critique, an anguish), the explanation of the life of a peasant who was earthy, evangelical, questioning. In the same spirit I also wrote a small book on my mother which has remained virtually unknown and is unobtainable.

My essays on comparison will be introduced here. From my grandfather Ancelot (a relative of that Ancelot who was linked with so many of the romantics) I acquired a little book which I have religiously preserved. It is a comparison between Pascal and Leibnitz, written for the Académie of

Clermont-Ferrand to which my grandfather belonged. In it he says that to make a carefully established comparison not only provides an exercise, but that the 'meditation it entails can strike from it, besides the direct light arising from the examination of each separate subject, the reflected light given out by the two subjects in confrontation.' I love to compare. Without this two-in-one act it seems to me that an object is not brought into relief. When one is trying to discern the link between ideas, and that between individuals, whether they complement or oppose each other (and opposition too is likeness), then it is well to compare these double stars.

I compared St Augustine to Plotinus so as to get a better grasp of what difference Christianity had made. Next I compared Pascal to Leibnitz in order to establish the difference between these two geniuses, the one a Catholic tinged with Jansenism, the other a Protestant tinged with Catholicism. Later I compared Renan to Newman, to establish the difference between their two interpretations of history. I have made other attempts of this kind in my lectures.[1] If life and time permit I have several others in mind to do. These are my dialogues of the dead.

Finally another branch always in bud for me comprises books on all sorts of methods and wisdom, essays on the art of thought and of life. I have always distrusted abstractions, projects, perfect beings, pure ideas. The idea must be incarnated in everyday life, in particular in the application of one's thought to the difficulties of technique. Nietzsche rightly said: 'The most precious truths are those which one discovers at the end; but these most precious truths are methods.'

Some time ago General de la Ch. read my books on *Nouvel*

[1] As with Bergson and Ravaisson—Bergson and Spinoza—St Thomas and Spinoza. I have others in mind as well, for instance: Newman and Kierkegaard—Bergson and Husserl. (Note of 1959.)

Art de Penser and *Travail Intellectuel*. He asked me to lecture during this year to the students at the École de Guerre on these subjects. This was of great value to me. I recognized my *poiétique* (as Valéry used to say) and saw that at their summit thought and action are neighbours.

My old friend Jacques André, a man of action *par excellence*, has asked me to collaborate with him in a book which would be a breviary and in which all these experiences would be summarized. He would like to print it first in a limited edition.[1] I dream also about a book on spirituality. All these branches spring from the trunk. And this Journal which I have always kept is like a slender thread on which my 'seeds' are strung. It is an essay in variety and inner unity; or as my fellow-prisoner Patrice de la Tour du Pin would say, it is a *wandering contemplation*. There is a connection between variety and unity, because what is new, having drawn one outwards for a moment, brings one back by an inner way towards a deeper unity.

In memory of Joubert

I enjoyed the Joubert Exhibition at the Bibliothèque Nationale. It offered us relics. Sometimes a single word on a scrap of paper. Small patches of light framed in determined handwriting with decisive down-strokes reminding me a little of Bergson's in his last years.

Looking at these manuscripts and souvenirs in 1955 roused further thoughts. One could not but sketch out mentally the chapter of a book on *La Sagesse dans les temps des Troubles* which Joubert would have promoted. So withdrawn, so careful to avoid getting involved, he yet survived all that

[1] This is what Blaizot did for *Invitation à la Pensée et à la Vie*. (Note of 1959.)

period of war and revolution. He used to say: *Excelle et tu vivras*. And that came true with him.

In the Directoire period Joubert, the fact of him, was an irony. Never was any mind less suited to such an epoch; yet in that epoch he had to live. Like many people of that day, he was born to magnificence. It seems that when he was young, his mother was worried about him, because she thought he was too generous-minded. He answered that he certainly did not wish that any man's mind should take precedence of his. This in spite of the fact that his physical make-up unfitted him for life and its stresses. He felt himself exiled in two ways: by his lack of vitality and by his feeling that he was superior to many other men.

At the Nationale one can read a letter to his indolent fiancée, Victoire Moreau (of the 3rd September 1792): 'Were I there I would help you, I could at least turn the pages. And it would relieve you to that extent.' Joubert himself always wanted someone to turn his pages. His lazy temperament ('I am hard to please and am unbearably tired') tended to make him feel contempt for the means of expression, or induced him to lofty extravagances in the style of Novalis or Nietzsche. But Joubert held his own. Times such as those he lived in are more helpful than one might imagine to this sort of wisdom. Favourable to those who can dominate, since things return to a consistency of damp clay, as after the Flood, such troubled times suit subtle minds which would tend to exhaust themselves in more civilized surroundings. In such periods they isolate and perfect themselves through solitude. Joubert had not very much to complain about. And he, who had thought deeply about fate, who knew that when a mind appears, another emerges to complement it, realized that the relationship of our being to its environment is controlled by laws unknown to us, but quite definite.

Joubert had the merit of choosing his friends or rather

(since one hardly chooses in such matters) of making the best of the opportunities which came his way—this in spite of an extraordinary awareness of their shortcomings. But just as he could believe in himself in spite of his humility, he could see what was lacking in others without ceasing to love them. For instance, he has left us pictures of Pauline de Beaumont and of Chateaubriand, which are very true and of the kind that a merciful but clear-sighted judge might have given us.

'Tenderness is passion in repose.' The transition from passion to tenderness was with him a slow ripening, or, as we should say today, a sublimation. So was the transition from the outlook of the eighteenth century to Christian Platonism —it took place no doubt in about 1804, and thanks to Malebranche. Or again, transition from the strict taste of that century to what one might call 'Valéryan' art. In every field he exalted, refined, achieved; redeeming time, bringing into it the operation of eternity, which he described as a form of progress in which the good is improved by the better.

At the Nationale I read his essay on modesty. Astonished that it came from a schoolboy's pen . . . 'I will first define it in a loose indefinite way; then by degrees I will give it a precise and new significance.'

Joubert had a radical distrust of nakedness. By naked one must understand what has not been worked over by the mind or presented beneath a veil. One might argue that modesty is never better demonstrated than in someone who has been deprived of clothes, who is frightened of being looked at. I would suggest that some statues of Aphrodite express modesty, and that nothing is less modest than some fashions which appeal to the senses by concealment. But I do not know if Joubert would have agreed with this view. In his opinion modesty was attained only by covering up: the body was a seed, which should start by being hidden, buried. Joubert did not say 'until the resurrection of the body', but no one more than he has left in writing sayings, words and formulas

300

which reveal what a glorified body might be. His mind's work was to prepare in time, and starting with language, the glorification of all things.

His individual virtue was good nature. 'Good nature,' he said in a page which is on view (dated July 1790—what a time for good nature!), 'consists in not refusing one's interest to anything that claims attention, or one's attention to any innocent thing. It is childhood, enlarged, preserved, strengthened, and developed; to the average man, it serves as happiness and is a great source of pleasure and relaxation to the busy or the great man.'

Superficially this is quite contrary to Joubert, since in his writings he aimed solely at quintessence and allowed no loosening of style or idling. But if you look more closely, there is no real difference. His natural *bonhomie* which made him an ideal companion was not a slackening after times of effort. He brought to it the same application as he did to his writing and his thought. He was unfitted for sustained discourse. One of the charms of his *Pensées* is that they have the informality of talking; or perhaps I should say they are like a conversation between angelic spirits, who have no problems of expression to overcome; and in fact this is what our conversation should be like if we were pure beings. This made Joubert delight so much in Madame de Sévigné and he recommended Pauline de Beaumont to read Voltaire's letters; he found in these authors (who are so typically French and exist nowhere else) examples of good nature. A type of good nature which La Fontaine could not keep up for long; which Pascal, too harsh, did not attain in his *Provinciales* (admittedly its content was too inflammable!) and which was perverted in Voltaire by the eighteenth-century mind. For one might almost say of good nature as of innocence that it escapes one at the moment one starts looking for it or becomes self-conscious about it. Joubert, said André Beaunier, was delightful in his half-humorous way of presenting truths under the guise of indulgence. As for instance when he wrote about Fontanes: 'His only fault is a certain suppleness of opinion, which is very agreeable in him and which his friends would be very sorry to see corrected . . .'

Joubert was Chateaubriand's only genuine friend; in him he had an admirer who could never become his rival. With Joubert Chateaubriand could afford to be completely himself. He who only lived for the good opinion of others (what is so falsely called renown) found himself face to face with a man who analysed him from all angles, who sized him up, smiled, and went on liking him in spite of everything. Joubert vis-à-vis Chateaubriand filled the difficult and essential role of counsellor, as Sainte-Beuve with the young Hugo, or Caulaincourt with Napoleon. It is an unusual function. A sterile office since one has little reason to suppose that one's advice will be taken. In the case of Chateaubriand, Joubert's advice counted for little. Time's revenge is strange. Today no one reads Chateaubriand (I mean from choice) except for the *Mémoires*, but we return to Joubert. In his lifetime Chateaubriand had a status, but status fades away; Joubert on the other hand had only an influence. Chateaubriand was inseparable from the events of his life; his talent was for the perpetual transfiguration of events, and of himself, of what he saw, felt or did. This histrionic capacity, which, according to Newman, exists in all men of letters, he used not only for rhetoric and reminiscence, but to drape his life in purple with many well contrived folds. He was removed as far as it is possible from the truth. Talent and his pride in his talent continually led him away from his centre. With Joubert it was the opposite. Spectacles, events, readings, were filtered as they passed through his mind; their dregs were deposited and only the pure sap remained.

Joubert had no imagination, he had only taste. In this he belonged to the previous century which lacked the Celtic element that Chateaubriand introduced and which resembled a new form of yeast. In their friendships with women (Joubert had many: Mme de Gontaut, Mme de Duras, Mme de Levis, and particularly Mme de Beaumont and Mme de Vintimille), Chateaubriand and Joubert could but part company. The one sought to captivate, Joubert, on the contrary, to protect.

I did not see in the Bibliothèque Nationale the original letter of 24th September 1804, in which Joubert wrote: 'Tell Madame de Beaumont, I beg of you, that since I have been immoderate in my effusions to her I shall need to take great precautions with myself whenever I talk to her about anything.' Reserved natures do occasionally become effusive to excess, for their moderation is not a sign of inadequacy, but of constant self-control. The stillness and wisdom of Joubert were quietened ecstasies.

As one looks at these show-cases, the names of many authors of 1954 come to one's mind and one wonders: 'Who in a hundred and fifty years' time will live?' I copied some *Pensées* of Joubert's, till then unknown to me. This one from *La Mettrié*: 'Death and love are consummated in the same way, by expiration.' And this note: 'Kant (Immanuel). He has written a great deal.' And, between two asterisks drawn by Joubert in a rather cryptic way: *SURGIR*, on a little scrap of paper.

Modesty: Joubert does not use this word in a sexual sense, but in a sense which includes sex as a particular category. Joubert places himself in the position of nature as it creates seeds. These seeds which are dormant, solitary, secure, should be, he says, brought slowly to maturity. The seeds which hold the purest essences must avoid any premature contact. Nature provides them with protective coverings, wrappings, pauses and slowings down. Modesty mounts guard over the mind, which would move too swiftly and experience pleasure too soon if left to itself. In the form of reticence, measure, moderation, modesty protects the moral being from the vertigo of contemplating itself and of indulging as Narcissus did in an excessive delight in itself. It enables the things of the senses to be fitly enjoyed or rather fitly employed and, as Joubert says: 'It provides us with something incorruptible which makes it possible for us to love unceasingly.'

Here we are at the antipodes of the present fashion, in which nothing is veiled, nothing kept for the future, or slowly accumulated or reserved for intimacy—a time in which everything is instantly and roughly thrust forward, without growth or flowering or ripening. A period in which we have lost that sense which it takes so long to acquire and which pagans can teach us (I have Virgil in mind), the sense of mystery and initiation (which are so essential in anything to do with the sexual side of love), the sense of trust, of private life, of intimate writing—the horror of making a premature appearance, the sense of silence which surrounds words.

See what rules for a healthy life, what a technique of happiness he deduced from this: 'In the infinite multitude of things that may happen to us, not one of these sad or happy events but can draw us from a high and noble thought . . . It matters little that the soul should be pleased by the events, provided that its reaction to them makes it content with itself.'

From this angle I place Joubert alongside Novalis or Nietzsche. Novalis said that the secret of all this is to elevate all events to the status of mystery, all citizens to a state of nobility. Nietzsche asked the well-known question: 'Is ennoblement possible?' *Ist Veredlung möglich?*

Joubert has rightly been compared to Mallarmé. He too sought the formidable essence, the condensation of time into a moment, the drop of clear density: the word. In my opinion Joubert succeeded better with his throw of the dice. 'My memory preserves only the essence of what I read, of what I see, and even of what I think.' I want to record a few more sayings of his which I like: 'God made the world. And what if he had not made it and created only souls? It is not the author of all things, it is the creator of spirits towards whom we turn, and whom we adore above all things.' (Alain, too, was fond of this thought, which holds the truth of idealism.)

'We live in a sick age. God sees it. Our minds are wounded. He will forgive us if we surrender absolutely to him what remains to us of sanity.' (Mauriac I think might write that tomorrow.)

'It is not perhaps unimportant to give this piece of advice to writers: never write anything that does not give you real pleasure.'

Prayer

'O God,' cried Silvio Pellico, as he came back from his long imprisonment, and walked up the path to his house, 'grant that my mother should not be dead.' How well I understand this feeling. All one-time prisoners understand it.

I am at the moment in a state of waiting with uncertainty for an event which has already been decided and it occurs to me that this is the usual state of the soul, since it is always awaiting what for the Eternal already is. I say these prayers:

Deus cui omne cor patet, et omnis voluntas loquitur, da ut, quae spero, jam in Te possideam.

Deus qui mihi aeternaliter donasti ea quae mihi incerta sunt, fac ut libertas mea tuae voluntati semper inhaereat.

Deus cujus scienta in me mirabilis est et qui in utero matris formasti me, fac ut sim quod spero, quoniam futura mea semper manent in te.

Claudel's grave

Claudel is dead. I recall the final moment of our only meeting, one of those last minutes of a conversation when one is already standing and one tries to find a last sentence, and then the essential thing comes stealing in (like the light which returns after sunset). He was inquiring into his destiny, and he asked himself the question which those who have many vocations must ask at the end: 'Have I achieved a unity?' 'That beauty and ordered splendour of which I have sung so often—what has happened to it in myself? Have I been faithful to my religious and my poetical vocations?' And finally, in silence, the supreme question; not for Claudel who cared hardly at all for reputation, the question: 'Who do they say that I am?' but: 'Who am I?'

He was like a stele with the inscription *Oui*, like the Tower of David with its suspended shields, like the Ark of the Covenant, like the Golden House; an anachronism or rather an Annunciation. A black stone with no beauty of its own, yet venerated in a holy place. His eyes were very gentle. ('Thy eyes are doves,' said the Bride of the Song of Songs.)

The strange difference between a man and his work seemed to me in his case to have been carried to its limit, and seeing him I could not fail to think about it.

A human being lives and spreads himself on several levels; that I know. But has one given sufficient thought to the life of this same spirit on its innermost level—an existence that is impenetrable, solitary, reflective or subject to passing ecstasies, which can be noble and generous in its conceptions or secretly a prey to anxiety—as distinct from the same life simultaneously living on the banal level of everyday existence with its tedious compromises, its animal reflexes? I have always asked myself how one can think at the same time of the eternal life and the evening meal.

'One dresses, one eats twice a day. I go out and there I am back again, to sleep,' says Ly in *La Ville*.

To my way of thinking this twining of infinite longing and frivolity, or more simply of the great and the small (observable at this very moment of writing in which I have to give equal consideration to the idea and the pen-stroke), this insertion, this amalgam, this tissue, is the daily mystery, simple as the bread which nourishes, but impenetrable. I wonder if we do not all carry within us (as Dostoevsky suggests in the immortal figure of Prince Mishkin) the image of a God-man, existing in two forms although indivisible, and only truly himself in the higher part. I wonder if some hint of this duplication in unity does not exist in us all, but especially in poets and visionaries.

But one did not get the impression that there were two parts in Claudel the man. To record my true impression: I believe that at the heart of this contented life and of this industrious temperament which loved mathematics and office hours and which was of the land and now and then uncouth, there was a second and quite distinct life of poetry and inarticulate prayer. He told me that he wrote only after praying, without erasures, and that he knew exactly when he had to stop. When he was in Guernsey Hugo wrote standing upright, and let the sheets fall for a servant to pick up. He, too, hardly ever reread his text. Faced by such centaur-like structures, I question how in their consciences the link between the man of inspiration and the common man is formed. Did they live in a kind of lucid distraction, or in a state of passivity like that of mystics? Or were their heads filled with wild schemes, like those of inventors? How did they pass from such heights to ordinary calculation? One could not apply this problem to Valéry, who categorically denied inspiration and wished to be only a technician.

I do not think that those who were nearest to Claudel would have anything to tell me about this riddle. Nor even that he himself, if asked, would have provided the answer. He was the problem; to me this surly patriarch, pierced every morning by the Seraph's dart, was himself the question.

I would like to add something more. He had a higher life as a poet, and a banal human life like everybody else, able if he thought fit to chat with M. de Norpois to his heart's content. But one did not often observe in him that middle state in which I work: the life of dialogue, of methodical reflection, of concept or of narration.

Lacking this middle level he looked to me like some natural object, for instance, a tree whose trunk is a gnarled pretext for passing from one stage of foliage to another.

Claudel will not leave us drafts or erasures, stories or secrets of technique. His letters are miniature treatises inspired by a strong desire to convince and to save. We shall never know any more about him. He did not confuse his tracks. There was nothing underhand, no secrets, no foot-prints. One would like to say of him what Hegel said of the Alps: *He is.*

P. L. Couchoud went to see a sculptor at Brangues, near Vienne, who is engraving on a tombstone the inscription Claudel chose: 'Here lies the husk and the seeds of Paul Claudel.' What a fine definition of renewal! One part of the plant, the husk, decays; another part, secret and seminal, the bud, breaks out.

I remember that apropos of my book on the Resurrection which he had read closely, looking, he said, for 'thoughts about the unexplored regions of the afterworld', we spoke of St Paul's thought: *One sows a body animated by the soul. There arises a body animated by the Pneuma.* This inscription is like a reply.

Tonight I reflect that this applies to all our actions, to all our lives. When one rereads one's draft or looks back upon one's past (yesterday, a year, a whole lifetime), one would like to make the impossible division, to put on one side what was ill-expressed, ill-lived, ill-loved—yes, to leave it to perish and decay. To keep what attained to peace, beauty, the eternal . . . 'What is virginal, living, beautiful'. To take this in one's hands as though it were bread, as though it were a treasure, as though it were our body, show it to one's friends behind closed doors, give it out in a beloved countryside by the shore of a lake, break it as the day fades.

This is indeed what we should try to do on every day of our life after sleep and tiredness, those winters of the soul.

Awake, my soul. Forget what is base and unworthy of remembrance. Forgive and be forgiven. Another dawn is breaking.

Index